Boy Crazy

Adolescence is the best of times. It is also the worst of times – a time many would rather forget. Challenging the resulting widespread amnesia regarding the developmental and clinical repercussions of adolescence, Janet Sayers advances an intriguing account of the revolution it effects in our adult psychology. In particular she highlights the fantasies bequeathed us by adolescence – notably those of divided selves and loves, and of 'boy crazy' grandiosity and romance.

Illustrated throughout with fascinating examples from a groundbreaking study of school and university students' pre-teen and teenage memories and dreams, *Boy Crazy* weaves these together with telling vignettes from fiction, film, and therapy. Using these examples controversially to argue that men and women often pursue radically different paths in response to the sexual 'awakening' of adolescence – while also often being alike in seeking to escape its conflicts through male-centred idealisation of themselves or others as heroes or gods – *Boy Crazy* provides an important introduction to recent findings and theories in developmental and clinical psychology, particularly its Freudian, Jungian, and feminist variants.

Boy Crazy is readily accessible to specialists and non-specialists alike and presents an exciting insight into the otherwise little-researched fantasies of adolescence and their impact in shaping our adult lives and loves.

Janet Sayers qualified in clinical psychology at London's Tavistock Clinic. She is now Professor of Psychoanalytic Psychology at the University of Kent in Canterbury and also works part-time as a BAP-trained therapist both privately and for the NHS. Her previous books include *Mothering Psychoanalysis* and *Freudian Tales*.

Boy Crazy
Remembering adolescence, therapies and dreams

Janet Sayers

London and New York

First published 1998
by Routledge
11 New Fetter Lane, London EC4P 4EE

Simultaneously published in the USA and Canada
by Routledge
29 West 35th Street, New York, NY 10001

© 1998 Janet Sayers

Typeset in Times by Routledge
Printed and bound in Great Britain by Creative Print and Design
(Wales), Ebbw Vale

British Library Cataloguing in Publication Data
A catalogue record for this book is available from the British Library

Library of Congress Cataloguing in Publication Data
Sayers, Janet.
Boy Crazy: analysing adolescence, memories, and dreams / Janet
Sayers. p.cm.
Includes bibliographical references (p.   ) and index.
1. Adolescent psychology. 2. Adolescent analysis. I.Title.
BF724.S325 1998
155.5–dc21   98–10662 CIP

ISBN 0–415–19084–3 (hbk)
ISBN 0–415–19085–1 (pbk)

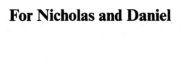

For Nicholas and Daniel

Contents

Acknowledgements

My thanks first and foremost to the women and men, who must remain anonymous and for whom I have changed all identifying details, who have written and talked to me about their teenage memories and dreams. My thanks also to my colleagues at the University of Kent for giving me the time and facilities for my research; to the Rockefeller Foundation for providing me with such wonderful company and surroundings at the Villa Serbelloni, Bellagio, to write up my findings; to audiences in England and America for their enthusiastic reception of the ideas discussed in this book; to my family, friends, fellow-teachers, therapists, patients, and students who have taught me so much about the revolution wrought in our psychology by adolescence. Last, but by no means least, my thanks to those who have kindly read and commented on various versions and drafts – Houri Alavi, Nic Bayley, Hannah Dyson, Mary Evans, Stephen Frosh, Frank Furedi, Kate Hawes, Jeremy Holmes, Alex King, Pat Macpherson, Bernie Paris, Glen Roberts, Nicholas and Daniel Sayers, Ann Scott, June Thomason, Jane Ussher and James Williams. They might not agree with what I have written, but the help and encouragement of all of the above have been invaluable – for which, again, my heartfelt thanks.

Some of the dream and therapy examples that appear in this book are taken from my chapter 'Women's and men's stories', in Glenn Roberts and Jeremy Holmes (eds) (forthcoming) *Narrative in Psychiatry and Psychotherapy*. Reprinted by permission of Oxford University Press.

Extracts taken from the book *Cat's Eye* by Margaret Atwood published by Bloomsbury Publishing Plc in 1990. Reprinted with permission of the author.

Part I
Introduction

1 Remembering adolescence

Some years ago I was invited to talk about adolescence with a distinguished feminist academic, Carol Gilligan, at a conference in Cambridge. I was delighted to be asked, not least because I was personally very involved in adolescence at the time. My sons were teenagers and this had led me to musing about my own teens. I therefore readily accepted the invitation.

When I came to think about what I would say I found the phrase 'boy crazy' occurring to me. Perhaps I was thinking of my own teenage boy craziness. Perhaps the phrase occurred to me because of research I was then doing into men's and women's fantasies about men and masculinity. Whatever the reason, I was appalled to find that in the subjects I know best – feminism and psychoanalysis – there was almost nothing written about adolescence. What then could I talk about? What could I say?

Most of all I was appalled because I knew from my own experience, and from that of my relatives, friends, students, and those I work with as a therapist, that adolescence is often crucial to making us what we are as adults. I learnt much the same from scattered references to adolescence in Freud's writings. I therefore decided, after the conference was over, to pursue the subject further.

Since Freud's followers had written next to nothing about adolescence, I decided to put what little they had written together with other relevant findings and theories. True to my Freudian roots, I also collected memories and dreams. This book is the result. At the end of this chapter I will introduce what I found. This included discovering that the phrase 'boy crazy', with which I began, was not fortuitous. It turned out to encapsulate particularly well what is often most central to the transformation brought about in men, as well as women, by adolescence. Before explaining this transformation further, however, and before saying something by way of introduction to Freud and to today's widespread forgetting of adolescence that my book seeks to redress, I will begin with those who, by contrast, do remember the transformation wrought by adolescence and by their teens in their subsequent adult lives and loves.

Remembered teens

Examples abound. Again and again, in their autobiographies, writers dwell on pre-teen and teenage incidents making them what they are as adults. So too do media celebrities. An example is the British pop star, Jarvis Cocker. He tells a reporter of his teenage metamorphosis from an ugly duckling into a nascent star. He describes himself, aged 12, as a Lederhosen-clad 'swotty, speccy, beanpole *and* the only boy in class to have long hair cripplingly shy and utterly introspective . . . with intensive guitar practice supplementing daydreaming in the school dinner queue'.[1]

He goes on to describe the transformation of his life when, aged 17, he and his band, Arabiscus Pulp, won themselves a John Peel recording session. 'And that,' says Cocker, 'was it.'

In another article, Sarah, the Duchess of York, attributes the origin of her notorious status as binge-spending, self-bribing, estranged, and betrayed wife of Prince Andrew to her mother bribing, betraying, and abandoning her in her early teens. An interviewer writes:

> When she [Sarah] was 14, her mother announced that she was leaving to live with the Argentinian polo player, Hector Barantes . . . Mum was literally here one day and gone the next. She offered a feeble bribe as 'consolation': a new bedroom, which she would especially decorate herself before departure. 'So you don't mind?' Mum asked me. 'No, no. It's perfect. That's great.' The teenager was doing her best to say what she hoped the adult wanted to hear. This incident, she believes, sowed the seeds of much subsequent sad, 'trying-to-please' behaviour. . . . A year later, her mother and the polo devotee were married. 'And that,' Sarah recalls, 'was that.'[2]

Others remember the formative impact of adolescence in their novels. It is a major theme in perhaps the longest ever autobiographical novel, Proust's *Remembrance of Things Past*. In it Proust's narrator dwells at length on the forces impelling the obliteration of his dreams and memories of childhood by the sexual awakening of his teens. He also muses on the unconscious and involuntary memories of adolescence awakened by his adult sensations of taste, sight, sound, touch, and smell.[3]

Similarly, novelists today often relate their adult to their adolescent selves. They make adolescence a central theme in their work, like Jenny Diski in her novel, *The Dream Mistress*. It is based, Diski says, on the transformation wrought in her by her father deserting her and her mother when she was 11, and by her mother's ensuing depression. A journalist reports:

> Diski's mother refused to work or to sign up for social security. They stopped paying the bills and the rent; soon the bailiffs came and took everything except a bed and a chair. . . . Eventually, Diski and her mother

would be thrown out. . . . In the weeks before that abrupt and final humiliation, however, there was a quieter, more corrosive humbling to be
endured. 'We had to walk around with no shoes on,' says Diski, 'So the
people underneath wouldn't know they'd taken the carpets.'[4]

The scene, we are told, has left its mark. Diski, now middle-aged, continues to
recreate the emptiness of the flat of her pre-teens both in her fiction and in her
life. She still lives in a flat she keeps bare of carpets in memory of the bare,
uncarpeted home where she lived with her mother when she was 11.

Memories of the formative impact of their pre-teen and teenage years on
their adult lives are not, of course, confined to novelists and media celebrities.
Ordinary, uncelebrated women and men similarly remember their adolescent
years making them, for better or worse, the grownups they are today. Kate, a
retired social worker, tells me it was her teens that launched her into the two
driving forces of her life – sex and politics. She remembers a specific incident
impelling the passions firing her adult years. Like the incidents described by
the Duchess of York and by Jenny Diski, the teenage incident Kate remembers involves her mother. She says:

> One day my mother made me a dress which was so pretty, with a full skirt,
> in a light boil, and a big sash round the waist, and she allowed me to go
> and buy my own hat to go with it, and I felt so different in this dress. And
> I found I had a power – I had sexual power. That's when I discovered it.
> Because boys looked at me, and turned their heads. And I thought, 'Oh,
> this is great. This is an area where I shine.'

Women and men replying to a 1993 Mass Observation survey asking them to
describe their experiences of growing up also often dwelt on transforming
incidents from their teens.[5] Often, like Kate, they remembered incidents
involving sex. A journalist wrote of the adult reverberations of his 'tearful and
anxious mother' confessing to him, on his seventeenth birthday, that he was
illegitimate. A business executive remembered train-spotting. He wrote of
'dirty old men . . . sitting next to me in cinemas or in single compartments on
trains and fumbling, etc.'. He remembered not telling his parents. He remembered his 'amazement' on discovering, when he was 13, that 'my father did
know what "rude F" and "rude C" were and that he could enjoy a dirty joke'.

Others writing for this same Mass Observation survey remembered the
crippling effect on them as adolescents of their parents' sexual inhibitions and
repressions. A woman teacher wrote of feeling left in 'a moral vacuum' as a
teenager by the 'terrific sense of embarrassment about sex in our family. We
never talked about it'. Another teacher recalled finding himself divided for the
first time in his teens from his parents by both their and his sexual prudery and
inhibition about talking about his then increasing sexual attraction to men,
not women. He blamed his resulting adolescent alienation from his parents for
his continuing tendency not to talk with others about his feelings, whether or

not they involved sex. Others recalled the fateful effect on their subsequent lives not of keeping their feelings from their parents but of their parents accusing them, for the first time when they were teenagers, of keeping from them, deceiving them, and lying to them about what they felt and did.

Both women and men seeking psychiatric help often link their ills to their teens. Surveying all first referrals to a consultant psychiatrist through the early 1990s, I found that many dated the first onset of their symptoms to their pre-teen and teenage years. Forty-year-old Gail, for instance, linked her recurring anxiety and panic attacks, for which she now sought help, to her pre-teen unhappiness when her father, to whom she had been a 'daddy's girl', left her and her mother for another woman. Gail was 12. Although her father still lives in a nearby town, Gail grieved, she has never seen him since.

Others in my survey – men as well as women – attributed their problems not to losing and being distanced from those to whom they were attached in their pre-teen and teenage years, but, quite the reverse, to their fathers and others becoming too close to them, and abusing them in their teens. Harry, in his mid-thirties, linked his nervousness and heavy-drinking, beginning in his late teens, to being repeatedly sexually abused – between the age of 13 and 14 – by an elder in his church. Others tell similar tales. Stories of sexual abuse in adolescence are legion. Both women and men often tell tales of their nascent puberty prompting those they knew well into sexually abusing them, just as the novelist Nabokov depicts it prompting his fictional character, Humbert Humbert, into sexually abusing his 10-year-old stepdaughter, Lolita. But this is often forgotten.

Forgetting adolescence

Despite outrage about the film of *Lolita*, and despite the current furore about sexual abuse, its frequent beginnings in adolescence, and the adolescent onset of the ill-effects of earlier abuse, are often forgotten. So too are other effects of adolescence in shaping the psychology of both sexes, for good and ill. Instead, psychologists and psychiatrists explain the adults they study and treat in terms of their immediate life experiences. Women and men often explain themselves similarly – in terms of what is currently happening to them. They explain themselves in terms of their immediate well-being and woes. They explain themselves in terms of their biology, with women often attributing their troubles to the vagaries of their reproductive systems. Or, likening themselves to other members of their families, both women and men explain themselves in terms of their genes. Alternatively, influenced by recent developments in psychology, they explain themselves in terms of their early attachment to, and separation from, those to whom they were closest as children.[6]

In the process they forget adolescence. Why? Is it because adolescence, as hinted in some of the above-quoted memories, is a nightmare we would rather forget? Certainly therapists – including Freudian therapist, Paul van

Heeswyk, in his enchanting 1997 book, *Analysing Adolescence*[7] – often begin
their observations about young people with the words of the shepherd in
Shakespeare's *A Winter's Tale*:

> I would there were no age between ten and three and twenty, or that youth
> would sleep out the rest; for there is nothing in the between but getting
> wenches with child, wronging the ancientry, stealing, fighting.[8]

Others compare the advances and reverses of adolescence to those of the
French Revolution:

> It was the best of times, it was the worst of times, it was the age of
> wisdom, it was the age of foolishness, it was the epoch of belief, it was the
> epoch of incredulity, it was the season of Light, it was the season of
> Darkness, it was the spring of hope, it was the winter of despair, we had
> everything before us, we had nothing before us, we were all going direct to
> Heaven, we were all going direct the other way.[9]

They also refer to the opening line of L. P. Hartley's 1953 novel about adolescence, *The Go-Between*, as does a journalist, reporting a recent study of
disorders in young people,[10] who notes: 'We may celebrate youth in the
abstract but in practice we often behave as if it is a foreign country rather than
the place we all came from'.[11]

Another journalist, reviewing *Kids* – a film about underage sex, AIDS, and
drugs – writes, 'it makes you confront things you'd do anything to avoid either
as relatively uninvolved spectators or as anxious parents'.[12]

Those I interviewed for this book often told me they wanted to avoid and
forget their teens. A man in his late seventies complained, 'God help me, my
teens have clung to me all my life.' A woman in her eighties, recalling her love
for a man killed in the Spanish Civil War, emphasised, when I asked whether
she was a teenager when she met him, 'Oh no. My teenage years were the worst
in my life. I met him in my twenties. That's when everything that was best
began happening.' Her teens, she added, were best consigned to oblivion.

Younger people, whom I asked to record their memories of adolescence,
also often indicated that they wanted to forget. One man dismissed his teens
with the quip, 'Sex, drugs, and rock 'n' roll'. Others – men more often than
women – wrote nothing. Or they wrote that they had forgotten. A 21-year-old,
apologising for his lack of response, wrote 'Sorry, it's being [sic] too long – I
can't remember anything'. A 19-year-old excused her meagre reply in terms of
forgetfulness making her memories of the past too unreliable. 'Often,' she
solemnly declared, 'my memories may not clearly be true but interspersed by
dreams – and affected by photographs.'

A few younger teenagers (more often boys than girls), asked to write down
their dreams, claimed they had not only forgotten them but never had any to
remember.[13] More often older teenagers (again more boys than girls), as

though heaving a sigh of relief that the disturbing dreams of their early teens were over, wrote that they were now free of them. A 17-year-old, after recalling a recurring childhood nightmare of being made to sing in church as he had been made to sing in choir school till his voice broke, wrote: 'I very rarely have nightmares any more, most of my dreams, I think, are about normal situations which happen through my own eyes. I find I remember my dreams a lot less than I used to.'

Adults similarly claim not to remember. They too want to forget. The psychoanalyst André Green speaks to the disquiet of many adults about remembering their teens when, summing up his contribution to a conference about adolescent psychosis and madness, he concluded, 'We outgrow adolescence with the idea of having lived through an exalting moment that we will never forget, but, in reality, sometimes when we look back we realize we had a narrow escape.'[14]

Perhaps it is precisely the feeling of psychoanalysts, as well as of psychologists and psychiatrists, that they themselves had 'a narrow escape' and want to forget their own adolescence, that contributes to their forgetting the impact of adolescence in shaping the psychology of those they study and treat.[15] Perhaps the resistance of psychoanalysts to remembering their own adolescence also contributes to their current neglect of sex, including adolescent sexuality, in favour of attending instead to the early childhood determinants of the psychology of both women and men.[16]

Yet psychology is above all an adolescent subject in the sense that it is in adolescence that we first become acutely self-conscious and psychologically-minded. Little surprise then that many young people read and talk about psychology. It seems to hold out the promise of addressing their deepest longings and fears, not least their dreams and nightmares, since their earliest teens, of love and sex. Hence, arguably, the willingness with which many young people helped me with my research for this book. Hence, too, the large numbers of young people opting to study psychology at school and university; and the beginning of academic and applied psychology, as we now know it, with studies of adolescence.[17]

The foundations of modern psychology were laid at the end of the nineteenth century. Adolescence then became a major topic of research not only by psychologists but also by other scientists, writers, and artists. Some argue that *fin de siècle* interest in adolescence was due to it constituting a metaphor of the transition from the old century to the new.[18] The preoccupation of turn-of-the-century writers with recording their teenage reminiscences might also have been due to increasing social pressure on people at the time to produce and confess themselves in terms of their sexuality.[19] This included pressure to recount themselves in terms of their adolescent sexual development. Still others argue that concern with adolescence at the beginning of this century was due to panic about growing urban and working class delinquency.[20] Meanwhile the attention of middle-class men to their own adolescence might have been due to youth signifying their transition from childhood in the country to adult life in town.[21] This brings me to Freud, for he too wrote of his teens as signalling his transition from the country to the town.

Freud

In an essay alerting his readers to the frequent screening of teenage memories by early childhood, Freud described his urban nostalgia for the rural life of his infancy. He recalled the following incident:

> Three children are playing in the grass. One of them is myself (between the age of two and three); the two others are my boy cousin, who is a year older than me, and his sister, who is almost exactly the same age as I am. We are picking the yellow flowers. . . . The little girl has the best bunch; and, as though by mutual agreement, we – the two boys – fall on her and snatch away her flowers. She runs up the meadow in tears and as a consolation the peasant-woman gives her a big piece of black bread. Hardly have we seen this than we throw the flowers away, hurry to the cottage and ask to be given some bread too. And we are in fact given some . . . the bread tastes quite delicious.[22]

Letting his mind wander in association to this memory, Freud says that he found himself recalling later memories from his teens that were much more formative of his subsequent life than the early experience of infancy provoking them. Free associating to his memory of himself, aged 2 or 3, he remembered himself, aged 17, first falling in love. It was his 'first calf-love', he wrote. Its object was the 15-year-old daughter of a family he had known as a child, with whom he and his family were then staying. Hardly had he fallen in love with her, however, than she went away to school. Her leaving made his teenage longing for her all the more intense. If only his family had never moved to Vienna, Freud yearned, he might have grown up as strong as the young men with whom she had grown up in the country. Perhaps he would then have been as successful as they doubtless were in winning her love. This led him to think of marriage, the wedding night, of defloration – thoughts, Freud wrote, that 'cannot venture into the light of day'.[23] Hence, he said, his remembering not the inadmissible sexual thoughts of his 17-year-old guilty self but the innocent childhood scene of the little girl with the flowers, of himself and his cousin snatching them, of her crying, and of their all being comforted by the motherly peasant-woman giving them delicious bread.

Whereas Freud found it easier to remember his childhood than his teenage self it was the reverse with his patients. They often dwelt first and foremost on their teens in telling him about their problems. Often, like today's psychiatric patients, they attributed their ills to more or less traumatic or trivial experiences from their teens. They dwelt on incidents, wrote Freud, such as, an attempted rape . . . the involuntary witnessing of sexual acts between parents . . . a boy of her [the patient's] acquaintance stroking her hand tenderly and, at another time, pressing his knee against her dress as they sat side by side at table . . . hearing a riddle which suggested an obscene answer.[24]

Freud argued, in 1896, that the ill-making effect of such incidents was due to their reviving memories in his patients of being sexually abused when they were 3 or 4 by a nursemaid, governess, tutor, adult relation, or by an older sibling who had been similarly abused. Freud claimed that it was the patient's sexual arousal, following puberty, in remembering these abusive incidents that caused these incidents – by 'deferred action'[25] – to be so anxiety-making that they could not be remembered in words but only in the disguise afforded by the patient's neurotic, often bodily, symptoms.

In 1897, however, Freud rejected his 1896 thesis that his patients' ills were due to their having suffered childhood sexual abuse – or 'seduction' as he put it. Instead, he argued that their ills – their neurotic symptoms – were due to adolescent and recent events recalling not their having been sexually abused as children but fantasies about sex which they entertained in seeking to fulfil their own sexual wishes as children. Freud's patients, however, often told a different story. They continued to date the first onset of their symptoms not to childhood but to their teens.

An example was an 18-year-old patient whom Freud called Dora. She attributed her symptoms – including a nervous cough, and anorexic disgust at food – to her father's friend, whom Freud called Herr K, sexually propositioning her when she was 13, and again when she was 15.[26] Freud attributed Dora's symptoms to Herr K's attempted seduction reviving her childhood sexual wishes and desires involving her father. Dora's sexual wish for him was represented, Freud argued, by a recurring childhood dream in which she imagined her father saving her as a child from a burning house just as, aged 18, she wanted her father to save her from Herr K, and from therapy with Freud. She told Freud that she had just had this dream again. In it, she said,

A house was on fire. My father was standing beside my bed and woke me up. I dressed quickly. Mother wanted to stop and save her jewel-case; but Father said: 'I refuse to let myself and my two children be burnt for the sake of your jewel-case.' We hurried downstairs, and as soon as I was outside I woke up.[27]

Dora went on to tell Freud of another dream which she had just had. It transpired that it had been evoked by thoughts of a man who was then courting her and had sent her a picture postcard reminiscent of the urban scene with which she began this second dream. It also transpired that this dream was evoked by her having decided to quit therapy with Freud after her next two sessions with him. When she told him her dream, her therapy with him only had two and a half hours to run, this time period figuring as follows in her dream:

> I was walking about in a town which I did not know. I saw streets and squares which were strange to me. Then I came into a house where I lived, went to my room, and found a letter from Mother lying there. She wrote saying that as I had left home without my parents' knowledge she had not wished to write to me to say that Father was ill. 'Now he is dead and if you like you can come.' . . . I then went to the station and asked about a hundred times: 'Where is the station?' . . . I then saw a thick wood before me which I went into and there I asked a man whom I met. He said to me: 'Two and a half hours more.'[28]

Dora recounted this dream when she was 18, after beginning therapy emphasising the origin of her symptoms in her father's friend attempting to seduce her in her early teens. Freud's other patients similarly often emphasised the teenage origin of their symptoms. A young man, now known in psychoanalysis as the Wolf Man, visiting Vienna in the early years of this century from his family's estates in Russia, consulted Freud for treatment of symptoms that he said had first begun when he was 17. It was then, he said, that he contracted gonorrhoea and became impotent and a failure both in sex and work.[29] His impotence and failure, it seemed, were due to his equating being potent and successful with submitting to what his father wanted, just as he claimed to remember seeing his mother, when he was 18 months old, submitting to his father in sex, his father penetrating her from behind so the boy could see she had no penis. He was reminded of the occasion by a dream he remembered having when he was 4 years old, in which:

> it was night . . . I was lying in my bed. . . . Suddenly the window opened of its own accord, and I was terrified to see that some white wolves were sitting on the big walnut tree in front of the window. There were six or seven of them. The wolves were quite white, and looked more like foxes or sheep-dogs, for they had big tails like foxes and they had their ears pricked like dogs. . . . In great terror, evidently of being eaten up by the wolves, I screamed.[30]

He equated the scream-making wolves – with their big tails and erect ears – with his father and other male figures. They both excited and terrified him. He too wanted to be the man penetrating the woman from behind as he remembered seeing his father penetrating his mother when he was a toddler. It was with this idea that he excited himself in his teens. Freud reports that, from puberty onwards, the Wolf Man 'had felt large and conspicuous buttocks as the most powerful attraction in a woman; to copulate except from behind gave him scarcely any enjoyment'.[31]

Mindful of such examples, Freud likened the triggering by adolescent sexuality of his patients' childhood preoccupations with their parents' coupling to the Greek myth of Oedipus who, on discovering that as a young man he had murdered his father and married his mother, atones for his sin by having himself blinded. Freud argued that, like Oedipus, both women and men, when they are young, want to marry one parent and murder the other. He claimed that they, too, often atone for this sin by imagining being punished: not with loss of their sight but with loss of manhood – with not having a penis (in the case of women) or with threatened loss of their penis (in the case of men).

Freud illustrated his theories about the adolescent repercussions of the castration complex which he claimed both sexes suffer in early childhood, in terms of Sophocles' play, *Oedipus Rex*, and in terms of Shakespeare's tragedy, *Hamlet*. He also illustrated his theories with examples from nineteenth-century and turn-of-the-century dramas and fictions. These included Jensen's now little-known novella *Gradiva*, Ibsen's tragedy *Rosmersholm*, Hoffman's fable *The Sand Man*, and Dostoevsky's novel *The Brothers Karamazov*.[32]

But what of adolescence today? Does it too involve the Oedipal and castration complex plots that Freud claimed these fictions and dramas illustrate? Is adolescence still beset by the same memories and dreams that beset Freud's patients at the beginning of this century? This brings me to the findings and theories which I mentioned at the beginning of this chapter.

Memories and dreams

In the following pages I will draw, as Freud did, on novels, plays, and other published fictions and reminiscences of adolescence. I will also draw on memories and dreams told me by women and men I see in therapy. Unlike Freud, however, who drew in his theories almost entirely on examples from his work as a therapist, I will mainly draw on non-therapy examples. Many come from fellow teachers, students, friends and acquaintances telling me about their teens. Other examples come from asking undergraduate and graduate volunteers to write down their teenage memories and dreams anonymously after lectures. Still other examples come from arranging for 11- to 17-year-olds attending two parallel, single-sex, state secondary schools to write down, again anonymously, their best remembered recurring childhood and recent dreams, together with a note of their age and who they lived with.[33] The data on which I will draw is thus confined to the 'manifest content' of what my respondents and others have chosen to write and say about their own and other people's teens. Their observations, however, are revealing. They indicate two rather different paths often taken by women and men through adolescence.

In recounting these paths I will begin, in Chapter 2, with men's memories and dreams of early separation and detachment from expressing or knowing about their emotional closeness with others. I will then explain, in Chapter 3, how this contributes to men often experiencing themselves in their teens as divided within themselves. They are thus often akin to Jarvis Cocker (with whom I began) recalling being self-divided in his teens, between his 12-year-old and 17-year-old, introvert and extravert self. They are also often akin to Proust's narrator (with whom I also began) remembering being divided in his teens between his past and present self. In Chapter 4 I will then go on to argue that men's experience of being self-divided in their teens contributes to their being more at risk than women of schizoid and suicidal splitting.

Next, in Chapters 5 and 6, I will turn to women's memories and dreams of adolescence as involving not so much self-division as division and conflict in their attachment to their friends and families – particularly to their mothers, as illustrated by the examples of the Duchess of York and Jenny Diski (with whom I also began). I will then explain, in Chapter 7, ways in which teenage divisions in their relations with others contribute to women being more at risk than men of depression and eating disorders from their teens onwards.

More often, however, as I will go on to detail in Chapters 8 and 9, both sexes seek to escape the divisions described in Chapters 2 to 7 through fantasies of grandiosity and romance in which they aggrandise and idealise themselves or others as gods, heroes, and saviours. This returns me to the 'boy crazy' phrase with which I began. For, aggrandising and idealising themselves or others often involves women being crazy about men, and men being crazy about themselves. Boy craziness, in this sense, can be thrilling. But it can also cause problems as I will indicate in Chapter 10, before ending with solutions derived from theories illustrated and explained in earlier chapters.

One of the major factors impelling me to write this book, as I have said, was being reminded of my adolescence by that of my sons. This is in part why I will begin with men before turning to women. I will begin with men's adolescent memories and dreams of being self-divided, and with their precursor in the pressure often put on men as boys to detach themselves from others.

Part II
Divided selves

2 Detached sons

It has now become something of a commonplace to characterise men's early –
'Boys don't cry' – detachment from others (recently claimed to be genetically
determined)[1] as evidence of their 'emotional illiteracy'. The feminist therapist, Susie Orbach, claims that women and men are all relatively illiterate in
this sense. She writes:

> Emotional illiteracy exists because we have no shared language for
> emotional life. Words like love, hate, jealousy and competition reveal little
> more than the tip of an emotional experience whose depths we are unused
> to exploring. When we try to talk about our feelings directly ('How are
> you today?' 'Pretty awful actually.' 'Never mind, cheer up, luv, can't be all
> terrible') we both feel and engender shame and embarrassment. . . .
> Language for many of us has been a way of hiding our feelings from
> ourselves, and a way of not disclosing them to others.[2]

Some writers note that this guardedness is particularly marked in men. A
woman journalist reports with horror the refusal of a young man – an unem-
ployed 19-year-old, Mark – to countenance talking with others about the
miseries he encounters in being destitute:

> 'The lads I used to hang out with,' said Mark, 'are either locked up, dead
> or on the run from the law.' In 10 years' time, Mark thought he'd 'probably
> be dead. Someone could find me dead tomorrow morning.' Did he talk
> about these feelings with friends? 'Soccer, I talk about soccer.' Finally, I
> asked, was he depressed? 'I'm not depressed,' said Mark. 'There's a big
> difference between being depressed and not talking to anyone.'[3]

Many note the toll exacted from both women and men by men not knowing
about, being detached from, and being unwilling to talk with others about
their feelings, which, contrary to 19-year-old Mark's claim, often include
considerable depression and unhappiness. Commenting on this toll, another
journalist warns:

Emotional literacy is not the province of those born sadly 'unpenised'; the monolith of strong silent masculinity is in tatters and all of us have a stake in trying to reassemble something from the wreckage. . . . What comes over most strongly from reports about depression is the sheer loneliness of many men's lives. . . . As long as the power of essential masculinity is earthed to deathly silence, it will continue to mean greater numbers of depressed men and the unspoken corollary, depressed women.[4]

Why is it, though, that men are often so lonely, emotionally illiterate, silent about, and detached from knowing and talking about their feelings? What can we learn from Freudian and other theories about the causes of their emotional detachment?

Freudian explanations

Men's frequent early detachment from, and unawareness of, their emotional closeness with others can be understood in Freudian terms as an effect of their fear as boys that were they to enjoy continuing emotional closeness with their mothers they might be punished with loss of their masculinity – their penis. As evidence that boys might have good reason to fear losing their penis Freud quoted the example of a 3-year-old, now known in psychoanalysis as Little Hans, whose mother, catching him masturbating, reprimanded him by saying, 'If you do that, I shall send for Dr A. to cut off your widdler. And then what'll you widdle with?'.[5]

Boys, wrote Freud, often ignore such threats. But then they discover that girls are 'unpenised', as the above-quoted journalist puts it. This, according to Freud, makes boys terrified that they might suffer a similar fate. Fearful that this is the cost of wanting to be united with their mothers – expressed in Little Hans's case in his canoodling with his mother, and in his asking her to touch his penis – boys repress their wish for union with their mothers.[6] This repression accentuates an already existing division theorised by Freud in terms of the child being divided between his conscious and unconscious mind.[7]

US adherents of the version of Freudianism called 'ego psychology' argue that boys not only repress their wish for sexual union with their mothers out of fear of losing their penis, but that they *must* repress and distance themselves from union and closeness with their mothers so as to forge a different identity from their mothers – as men not women. Adopting the post-Freudian claim that babies initially identify with their mothers, the Californian psychoanalyst, Ralph Greenson urges that, in early childhood, the boy 'in order to attain a healthy sense of maleness, must replace the primary object of his identification, the mother, and must identify instead with the father'.[8]

The feminist sociologist, now psychoanalyst, Nancy Chodorow, adds that boys have to 'dis-identify' from those with whom they are closest in early childhood because of the continuing unequal assignment of childcare

primarily to women. The boy can therefore only forge a different male identity, Chodorow claims, by negating his initial closeness with the woman who
first mothers him, and by affirming instead his identity with men. But,
Chodorow adds, since men are relatively absent from the child's early life –
again because of the allocation of mothering primarily to women – the boy
cannot identify with men on a close personal basis. Instead they identify 'posi-
tionally' and 'instrumentally', as Chodorow puts it, with the roles socially
assigned to men at home and elsewhere.[9]

Nor, it seems, are Freudians and others wrong in thus characterising men
as early detaching themselves from closeness with their mothers in the interests of affirming their masculinity. Men often remember negating, and being
pressed to negate, their emotional attachment to, and closeness with their
mothers, in the name of their nascent manhood and masculinity. This is
particularly evident in men's memories of first going to school.

School memories

Again and again men remember being urged not to express their distress
about being detached from those to whom they are most attached on starting
school. In his autobiography, the psychoanalyst Wilfred Bion – sent away
from his family in India to boarding school in England when he was 8, after
which he did not see his mother again for over three years – recalls the
following conversation greeting him on his first arrival in the dormitory:

> 'What's the matter?' asked one of the three boys . . . 'I don't know,' I
> wailed . . . 'Are you homesick?'.
> 'Yes.' At once I realized what an awful thing I had done. 'No, B,' I
> hurriedly said.

Bion adds, 'As my powers of deception grew I learned to weep silently.'[10]

Recently the television announcer, Jon Snow, recalled in similar terms both
his and his mother's silence and inhibition about expressing their feelings
about being separated from each other when he first started boarding at the
prep school his parents ran. 'In that instant the heart-broken, bereft but independent new me was born,' he writes. 'The umbilical cord was finally broken'.
It is to that moment that Snow dates the origin of his continuing 'pathological
fear' of close relationships with women.[11]

Similarly, one man after another interviewed for a recent television series
about men and masculinity recalled how, as boys, they early learnt – in the
interests of proving themselves to be men – to repress, deny, and disconnect
themselves from expressing, or being caught by others expressing, their
distress at being sent to boarding school. A man in his seventies recalled:

> When I got to the school, the excitement of getting there, and the misery
> of being separated from my parents was very great. I was absolutely

miserable when I arrived. But once I was in the dormitory with other boys of the same age, though I do remember very much crying of homesickness, I did it under the bedclothes so that they wouldn't discover. I think probably we were all crying under the bedclothes if the truth were told. But one simply did not, and one should not, show emotion. And even at that age – at 8 – I wasn't going to let on to even the other little boys, who were probably feeling exactly the same as I was, er, that I was homesick, that I was blubbing, as we used to call it.[12]

Men who went to day school similarly recalled learning early on to stem their feelings of emotional closeness with their mothers and others to prove themselves to be men, not 'weepish' girls, as Geordie, another contributor to this programme put it. Geordie went on poignantly to recall how, having been taught since infancy not to express his feelings, he found himself, aged 11, unable to shed a single tear when his mother suddenly died of a heart attack.

When she died it was three parts of my life went. I wanted to cry but I couldn't. I just had the big lump in my throat, no tears. I don't think I knew how to do it. And, of course, on the other hand, there were quite a few neighbours at the funeral. And I didn't want to be classed as a softie and cry. None of me brothers cried. And you felt a sort of tautness around your chest. But you just couldn't get anything out. I think that was the feeling. It was an awful feeling happening, and you remember it to this day.[13]

Young men often still feel a 'tautness' about expressing their feelings. Many gag on their feelings even to the extent of stammering in keeping their feelings down. Psychologists find that stammering occurs almost three times more often in boys than in girls.[14] They also find that stammering often begins in boys, but not in girls, at the age when they are first separated from their mothers on going to nursery school.[15] The stammering effect on men of suppressing their feelings and fears has recently been movingly described by the novelist, Pat Barker, in her trilogy, *Regeneration*, about the shell shock suffered by officers in the First World War.

Shell shock

Barker draws attention to the frequency with which, having early learnt to 'keep a stiff upper lip' and to suppress their feelings, shell shocked officers in the First World War often stammered in stopping their feelings from showing. She recounts in these terms the first onset of the stammer of W. H. R. Rivers, famous for using Freud's 'talking cure' method to treat his officer patients. According to Barker, Rivers attributed the origin of his stammer to an occasion when he was 4 and his father took him to the barber's to have his hair cut, whereupon, much to his father's embarrassment, the young Rivers burst into tears. On their return home, however, when Rivers' mother asked if everything had gone well, his father said nothing of their young son's evident upset at the barber's. He denied it. He said everything had gone fine. It was from that moment, Rivers said, that, in imitation of his father's denial, he too learnt to deny and repress his feelings. It was then, he said, that his stammering began.

As for his shell shocked army officer patients, Rivers attributed their stammering and recurring nightmares to a similar cause – to their having been taught at an early age to deny and repress any expression or manifestation of their feelings and fears. He wrote:

> Fear and its expression are especially abhorrent to the moral standards of the public schools at which the majority of officers have been educated. The games and contests which make up so large a part of the school curriculum are all directed to enable the boys to meet without manifestation of fear any occasion likely to call forth this emotion.[16]

Having early learnt to deny and repress their feelings, Rivers concluded, men as officers similarly repressed the feelings evoked in them by the traumas they suffered in the trenches. These feelings could therefore only return when, falling asleep, their repression was temporarily relaxed. Hence these men's symptoms – their inability to fall asleep without being plagued by nightmares of the traumas they had suffered.

Rivers accordingly argued that the relative freedom from shell shock of soldiers fighting in close-knit units was due to their traumatic experience being mitigated by sharing it with each other.[17] As for treating those unprotected from shell shock by sharing and talking about their experiences with their fellow-soldiers, Rivers urged his medical colleagues:

> Instead of advising repression and assisting it by drugs, suggestion, or hypnotism, we should lead the patient to resolutely face the situation provided by the painful experience. We should point out to him that such experience . . . can never be thrust wholly out of his life. . . . His experience should be talked over in all its bearings.[18]

He urged his fellow-doctors to encourage their patients to talk about and share their feelings, just as he urged the shell shocked officers he treated to share their feelings with him. Barker writes: 'Every day of his [Rivers'] working life he looked at twitching mouths that had once been clenched. Go on, he said, though rarely in so many words, cry. It's all right to grieve'.[19]

Whereas Rivers noted his shell shocked patients' twitching and stammering, Freud, who also wrote about shell shock, said nothing about this aspect of the ills suffered by veterans of the First World War. He also said nothing about men's general repression of their feelings contributing to their war neurosis. Instead he implied, contrary to Rivers, that the war neurotic's ills – that his nightmares at least – were an adaptation to the traumas of war.

Today's Jungian psychologists argue much the same. They too argue that nightmares are an adaptation to stress. The Jungian psychiatrist Anthony Stevens cites in this context evidence that animals, operated on so that they can continue to move when they are asleep, often stalk prey or anticipatorily quake with fear during rapid eye movement 'dream' sleep. He argues that this shows that dreams are a means by which animals anticipate and prepare to attack and to deal with the stress of being attacked. He argues that nightmares in humans might serve a similar purpose. He claims that in humans, as in animals, nightmares mobilise 'archetypal components from the collective unconscious in order to promote the individual's better adaptation to life'.[20]

Freud claimed something similar regarding the repeated nightmares of soldiers with war neurosis. He argued that, in his recurring nightmares, the shell shocked soldier repeats the trauma he has suffered so as to abolish, master, and adapt to the feelings involved.[21] He likened the war neurotic's repeated nightmares to the scenes and games children imagine, invent, and repeat in adapting to separation and detachment, as I will now explain.

Dreams and nightmares of separation

Freud argued that dreaming begins with the hungry baby imagining himself sucking at his mother's breast in her absence.[22] 'Sucking at the mother's breast,' he wrote, is the starting-point of dreams, 'the unmatched prototype of every later sexual satisfaction, to which phantasy often enough recurs in times of need'.[23] As for war neurosis, Freud likened the shell shocked soldier's recurring nightmares to a game his 18-month-old grandson devised and repeated over and over again to master the trauma of being separated from his mother. In his game the little boy repeatedly staged his mother going away and disappearing by throwing a spool into his cot until it disappeared. He would then retrieve the spool by pulling on a thread attached to it just as he wanted to retrieve his mother when she was gone.

Illustrating children's response to separation from their mothers, the paediatrician and psychoanalyst, Donald Winnicott, recounts a similar example. It concerns a 7-year-old boy whom Winnicott treated at London's Paddington Green Children's Hospital. Adopting a method he often used in seeking to understand and treat the problems of his child patients, Winnicott made a number of squiggles for the boy to complete, whereupon the boy drew a lasso, a whip, a crop, a yo-yo on a string, a string in a knot, another crop, and another whip. Afterwards Winnicott asked the boy's parents about their son's evident preoccupation with string. They told Winnicott that they were glad he had mentioned it. String had become a veritable obsession with their son. 'Whenever they went into a room,' they said, 'they were liable to find that he had joined together chairs and tables; and they might find a cushion, for instance, with a string joining it to the fireplace'.[24] It turned out that this was their son's means of imagining himself reconnected with his parents, and

particularly with his mother from whom he had been separated for some ti
when she was hospitalised for an operation when he was 3, and again for tre
ment of depression when he was 4.

A 14-year-old boy in my secondary school study arguably resorted to a similar device in coping with separation from his mother. In her absence (he indicated that he lived with his father, brothers, and sisters, without his mother) he imagined being reconnected not by thread to a spool as in Freud's example but by rope to a statue of a woman. He wrote:

> My most repeated [childhood] dream was that I was hanging from a building trying to paint a statue of a lady gold. I only had 3 pots of paint and I had 24 hours before the sun came up. I then painted it completely apart from the legs, but I could not paint them as the rope was too short. The 24 hours was up and the rope holding me up snapped. I fell and as I reached the floor I woke up.

Try as he might he could not keep close to her.

Others tell similar tales. Whether or not they lived with their mothers as children, men often remember recurring nightmares of being separated from their mothers as children. Adolescent memories and dreams of maternal separation and reunion are the notorious starting point and central recurring motif of Proust's already mentioned autobiographical novel, *Remembrance of Things Past*. Early separation from his mother and others was also the first memory recalled, to his surprise, by a 70-year-old former managing director of one of England's leading insurance firms when he was interviewed for a recent book, *City Lives*. He told an interviewer:

> I remember being left behind at D . . . with my mother's parents when my mother and my brother and sister and my father all went off to Ireland [for eighteen months]. That is in fact my very earliest recollection of all. Seeing them drive away from the house and being left behind with my nanny. And feeling very deprived. It's extraordinary, I mean I was 3 years old then and I can remember it quite distinctly.[25]

It is an image that many are moved by – the image of the son separated from his mother, as in the often-remembered Disney cartoon of *Bambi* about a young deer separated from his mother by her death in a forest fire.[26] The anguished image of the son's separation from his mother was particularly movingly evoked in me recently by a friend describing the last day of her 70-year-old husband's life. She told me how, returning to his bedside after having to leave him for a couple of hours, he put his arms out to her, pleading: 'Hold me, hold me, I'm dying'. Again tears started to my friend's eyes at her husband's despair at his imminent and ultimate separation from those to whom he was closest, as he had been separated from his mother as a boy.

Young people recount similarly moving tales of early separation from their mothers. Surprisingly, perhaps, given men's reputation for being tough-minded and indifferent to the emotional upsets of separation and loss, several teenage boys (but no teenage girl) in my secondary school study wrote of recurring nightmares of losing their mothers. Examples include a 17-year-old who wrote:

> I used to have a dream about being separated from my mother as she was taking me to school. There was always a very strong sense of loss in this dream – it was particularly vivid, and at the same time quite frightening. It was a dream that reoccurred very frequently for some time.

They recalled nightmares of being separate and alone. Another 17-year-old told a dream in which 'I could see waves, not necessarily sea waves, but they were often like that. They created a horrible, distressing distance between myself and the object of the dream I was having'.

They told nightmares of being threatened in their aloneness and isolation by unknown hostile forces. A 12-year-old described himself in his best remembered dream 'walking along the beach. There is a clear sky and the water is clear and warm. Then I can feel a presence but I cannot see or hear it. The presence grows stronger tearing through me'.

Some recalled recurring nightmares of themselves alone, without any of the family and friends with whom teenage girls often imagined themselves surrounded in their dreams. They told dreams of themselves assailed, in their isolation, by amorphous and inanimate objects. A 14-year-old said:

> All that happened in the dream was me looking up towards the sun and everything went white. I then found myself walking in a place that was totally white. I couldn't distinguish between anything, and then a black spot appeared in front of me. The spot grew and grew until I was engulfed by it. I then found myself falling into nothingness with everything being black.

Another 14-year-old dreamt he was menaced – again alone – by a green mist hovering towards him. Still others, unlike any of the girls in my study, recounted nightmares of explosions – of 'fire blazing across killing everyone', of bombs blowing up, of 'alien laser ships . . . vaporising people'.

They remembered nightmares of being pursued by rocks. A 15-year-old wrote:

> When I was about five, I used to have a dream that very large boulders were rolling towards me. There were no humans or animals, landscape or sky. I can remember the dream being repeated 3 or 4 times. The dream was in slow motion and I can remember in the dream being *very* frustrated.

They told nightmares of being chased and destroyed by unidentified and unidentifiable objects. A 14-year-old recalled:

> I often had a strange dream in which there was a piercing noise. There was an infinitely small 'thing' – maybe me – and it was 'overtaken', crushed, by a much larger 'thing'. I had this dream maybe three times.

They dreamt of not being able to get away, or of only being able to move in 'slow motion', as if 'in glue'. In their dreams their feet were heavy. They could not put any distance between themselves and their pursuers. They wrote of not being able to make a sound, of not being able to speak or shout.

Like Freud's Wolf Man patient (whom I described in Chapter 1), they recalled nightmares of being threatened by sharp-toothed animals – wolves, dinosaurs, crocodiles, panthers, lions, tigers, dogs and cats. They described nightmares of being attacked by legendary, cartoon, film, video, and computer game figures – by witches, monsters, dragons, ghosts, elves, goblins, vampires, spirits, werewolves, fairy tale kings, trolls, the three wise men, by Ninjas, aliens, the devil, pacman and Robocop.[27] They remembered repeated nightmares of being attacked by 'baddies' – by skeletons, dead bodies, cannibals, soldiers, armies, the police, burglars, terrorists, and beggars. They recalled nightmares of being pursued or trapped by horror movie villains – by Freddy Cruger, for instance, from *Nightmare on Elm Street* – movies that, like recurring dreams, teenagers, particularly teenage boys, often watch repeatedly – over and over again – movies that are both informed by, and evidently inform, their recurring dreams.

When teenage boys recalled dreams involving identifiable figures, the figures involved were less likely than those in the dreams recalled by girls to be people they knew personally. Their recurring dreams more often featured people they did not know. They featured anonymous figures – often stereotyped tyrants and ogres. A 14-year-old wrote, 'My most repeated childhood dream was that I was being chased through some woods by a monster, and he kept gaining on me'. Another 14-year-old recalled a childhood dream of being 'on my own when someone with a mask and a long black cape glides across the water to me'.

Their dreams were similar to a nightmare the psychoanalyst, Carl Jung, in his autobiography, remembered from his teens:

> It was night in some unknown place, and I was making slow and painful headway against a mighty wind. Dense fog was flying along everywhere. I had my hands cupped around a tiny light which threatened to go out at any moment. Everything depended on my keeping this little light alive. Suddenly I had the feeling that something was coming up behind me. I looked back, and saw a gigantic black figure following me. But at the

same moment I was conscious, in spite of my terror, that I must keep my little light going through night and wind, regardless of all dangers.[28]

Today's Jungians, as we have seen, understand such recurring nightmares as adaptively preparing people of both sexes to cope with stress. Why then the greater frequency with which boys, compared to girls, recall recurring nightmares of being threatened by impersonal, unknown, uncontained, monstrous and explosive forces? Do they have more stresses to adapt to? One possibility is that this difference between the sexes can be understood in terms of non-Jungian, post-Freudian theories about the stressful and uncontaining effects of being early detached and separated from others.

Uncontaining detachment

The post-Freudian psychoanalysts, John Bowlby and Donald Winnicott, perhaps mindful of the ills done them by being early detached and separated from their mothers on being sent to boarding school (Bowlby when he was 7, and Winnicott when he was 13), and certainly mindful of the ills suffered by children evacuated and sent away from home in the Second World War, emphasised the importance to children of not being separated from their parents, particularly their mothers, if they are to feel unstressed, happy, and contained.

On the basis of this evidence and his early war-time study of children – mostly boys – separated from their mothers in early childhood, who were later diagnosed as 'affectionless' delinquents,[29] Bowlby emphasised that what is

essential for mental health is that an infant and young child should experience a warm, intimate, and continuous relationship with his mother (or permanent mother-substitute – one person who steadily 'mothers' him) in which both find satisfaction and enjoyment[30]

Bowlby and his co-worker James Robertson, who worked with evacuated children in the war nurseries run by Freud's psychoanalyst daughter Anna Freud, drew attention to the distress suffered by children on being similarly separated in peacetime from their mothers when, for one reason or another, they had to stay overnight in hospital. Winnicott suggested that the neglect by hospital doctors of the distress of their child patients might be due to doctors not wanting to be reminded of the distress they too suffered as children. Of the resistance of doctors and of the English generally to knowing about their feelings he wrote:

The Englishman . . . does not want to be upset, to be reminded that there are personal tragedies all over the place, that he is not really happy himself, in short – he refuses to be put off his golf.[31]

Winnicott insisted, by contrast, that the refusal of doctors to be put off by their feelings does not do their patients any good. He insisted that doctors must know about the feelings of their patients if they are to treat them effectively. Most of all, however, he insisted that mothers must not be put off by their children's feelings in bringing them up. He emphasised that mothers must hold their children not only physically but also emotionally. Through knowing about and anticipating her child's feelings, Winnicott maintained, the mother protects him from uncontained internal or external forces explosively impinging on and breaking up his nascent 'continuity-of-being'.[32]

Winnicott wrote of the importance to the baby and toddler of his continuing closeness with his mother as the means by which he discovers that his feelings are bounded and contained. He wrote of the importance to the child of learning – through his closeness with his mother and his impact on her – that she survives his anger, aggression, and hate-filled fantasies of destroying her.[33] Through surviving his attacks – both actual and imagined – the child learns that his mother is outside his omnipotent control, that his hatred has limits, that it is not unbounded, limitlessly destructive, and out of control.

Similarly the psychoanalyst, Wilfred Bion – perhaps also alerted to the importance of early mothering, and to the ill-effects of maternal separation by his experience of being sent away to boarding school when he was 8 years old (see p.19 above) – stressed the importance to children of their continuing emotional closeness with their mothers as the means by which they learn that their feelings, including their feelings of anger and hatred, are containable and contained. He wrote of the importance of the mother being affected by her child's destructive feelings. He wrote of the importance of her taking in, accepting, containing, and digesting her child's anger and destructiveness so he can take these feelings back into himself as bearable, delimited, and contained by her. Bion puts it thus:

> If the infant feels it is dying it can arouse fears that it is dying in the mother. A well-balanced mother can accept these and respond therapeutically: that is to say in a manner that makes the infant feel it is receiving its frightened personality back again but in a form that it can tolerate.[34]

Bion implied that the child's continuing emotional closeness with his mother is crucial to her sharing and converting his frightening, fragmented, and raw feelings and experiences into the containing images, or 'alpha-elements' as Bion called them, furnishing his thoughts and dreams. By himself, Bion maintained, the child cannot make use of the impressions – the 'beta-elements' as Bion called them – bombarding him both from outside and inside his body. He can only make use of these impressions by first evacuating or evoking them in his mother. He relies on her capacity for 'reverie', as Bion put it. The child needs his mother to experience and think about the bits and pieces of his experience so he can deal with them in thinkable, alpha-element form. These elements, Bion argued, can in turn only be joined together through being shared, just as the child learns through sharing his feelings with his mother to join up his otherwise fragmenting and fragmented feelings of love and hate.

In sum, Bion and others insist that experiencing our hatred as conjoined with and mitigated by love, and experiencing our fears and anxieties as containable and contained – rather than as uncontainable, monstrous, and overwhelmingly explosive (as in the above-quoted teenage boys' recurring dreams) depends on ongoing closeness with others, in the first place with the mother.

True, Bion was writing about babies and toddlers. But his emphasis on ongoing closeness with others surely also applies, even if only to a lesser degree, to older children and adults? Or, as one of my grown up sons said in response to my grumbling about worrying about him, 'But that's what mothers are for'. Yet, as we have seen in this chapter, boys are often denied the ongoing closeness with their mothers necessary, according to Bion, to their mothers doing the worrying for them. The nineteenth-century writer and designer, William Morris (sent away to boarding school after his father died), put it thus in versifying a mother's words to her baby son from whom she anticipates soon being separated:

> twixt thee and me
> Shall rise that wall of distance, that round
> each one doth grow,
> And maketh it hard and bitter each other's
> thought to know.[35]

The result, paradoxically, of mothers and sons being early separated from each other, and being early distanced from knowing each other's thoughts – in the name of such distance being necessary for making boys become manly, tough, and self-contained – is that boys often experience the adolescent feelings and changes involved in becoming men as quite the reverse. They often experience these changes as making them feel unmanly, weak, and uncontained. This in turn, as we will see next, often causes them to become even more distanced, detached, and divided, both from others and from themselves.

3   Divided adolescents

In illustrating some of the acutely felt divisions in adolescence between being and not being contained, I will begin with examples of men's memories of their early adolescent wet dreams as uncontained and out of control.

Wet dreams

In her novel, *The Secret Diary of Adrian Mole*, Sue Townsend depicts women's openness about sharing their feelings with others as precipitating 13-year-old Adrian into having and confessing his first wet dream. He writes in his diary:

> Tuesday February 3rd . . . My mother is reading *The Female Eunuch* by Germaine Greer. My mother says it is the sort of book that changes your life. It hasn't changed mine, but I only glanced through it. It is full of dirty words.
> Wednesday February 4th NEW MOON I had my first wet dream! So my mother was right about *The Female Eunuch*. It has changed my life.[1]

Perhaps it was Sue Townsend's openness in describing these experiences of adolescence that made her book so popular. For, more generally, contrary to women's openness with each other about their feelings, not least Germaine Greer's openness about sex in *The Female Eunuch*, and contrary to women's memories of sharing with their mothers and friends their first experiences of adolescence (as I will illustrate in Chapters 5 and 6), men do not usually remember sharing or talking with others about their first experiences of adolescence, certainly not their experiences of their first wet dreams.

This was not always the case. In 1948, the sex researcher Alfred Kinsey reported that 83 per cent of men interviewed in his study admitted to having wet dreams, with the majority saying these occurred most often in their teens and twenties.[2] Today's researchers however are almost entirely silent on the subject. Admittedly, a recent study of boys in Nigeria indicates that some experience their first ejaculation as upsetting.[3] Otherwise, in its listing of recent research (from January 1990 to March 1996), *Psychological Abstracts* reports ninety references to women's first menstruation (menarche) and 159 references to menstruation generally, but only one reference to men's first ejac- ulation (semenarche), two references to nocturnal emissions,[4] and only one reference to wet dreams – to a 1991 reprint of an 1886 article about wet dreams in women![5]

The only reported study of men's memories of their first ejaculation, based on a questionnaire and interview survey of thirty-six white middle-class camp counsellors aged 15 to 21, found that most did not tell anyone about it at the time.[6] An earlier study, based on interviews with a small sample of adolescent boys, similarly found that boys were extremely reluctant to engage in any discussion about their first ejaculation. Yet they also claimed it was a positive experience, albeit a bit frightening. Unlike the girls in this study, however, most of whom had discussed menstruation with their mothers, none of the boys had discussed ejaculation with their peers and only one had mentioned it to his parents – to his father.[7]

Perhaps it was his knowing me to be a Freudian, and as therefore liable to be given to talking about sex, that led a London friend of mine – Jonathan, a barrister in his early fifties – to tell me, as he stressed he had never told his mother at the time, nor his wife since, about his first wet dream. From what he said it transpired that, seldom if ever having discussed it with others either then or since, he experienced his first wet dream as completely uncontained. This was in stark contradiction with his image of himself as totally self-contained, as an 'upright citizen', as the man his parents made it clear they wanted him to become on his leaving prep school for public school, where they expected him to become head boy, win an Oxbridge scholarship, become a barrister and, eventually, a High Court judge.

Not having talked about his wet dream at the time, it remained blurred and confused, uncontextualised and uncontained by any certainty as to its content, his age, or the season when it happened. He says:

> I was 11 . . . it may have been later than 11 . . . probably in the spring . . . it might have been the winter . . . it could have been in the autumn, I don't remember. . . . I danced very close to a very attractive girl. I was a child. Nobody had ever told me about wet dreams. I didn't know anything about anything. And that night I had my first wet dream. . . . I think I put two and two together. But it is very disconcerting not to know quite what's happening . . . it was kissing, sexual stimulation, and then just falling apart.

The 'falling apart' reminded him of other occasions when he felt uncontained and out of control. It reminded him of an occasion when his scout master denounced him at camp as a 'dirty little brat' for leaving his bed in a mess. It reminded him of an occasion when his cousin caught him, aged 4, messing his pants. His cousin still teases him about it.

Erections

Many recall their early adolescent erections in similar terms. Just as Jonathan recalls the incontinence of his first wet dream dividing him between two images of himself – as an 'upright citizen' and as 'falling apart' – others recount the incontinence of their early adolescent erections as dividing and alienating them from their image of themselves, as men, as continent and contained.

Just as men are generally silent about their early adolescent wet dreams, they are generally silent about their early adolescent erections. True, one researcher, in a broad-ranging survey of adolescence, mentions that boys experience their early adolescent erections as embarrassing and humiliating, or cope with them by laughing and joking about them.[8] Others report that boys deal with this and other aspects of adolescence through avoidance, pretence, and humour.[9] More often researchers say nothing about this aspect of puberty.

Undergraduates in my study similarly either said nothing about their early adolescent erections or recounted them as happening to others, not themselves. A 19-year-old recalled being at boarding school in his early teens and feeling 'sympathetic/sorry for one friend who seemed 17, when 13. Everyone laughed, spied on him changing. Then another boy had erections in the showers – we/I thought this odd, alien'.

An acquaintance, now in his fifties, tells me he vividly remembers being inwardly divided when, going home on the bus from day school, he discovered he had an enormous erection. Fearing that if he were to stand up, he might betray his unruly Priapic state to his fellow-passengers, he stayed sitting. But this only resulted in further embarrassment, as it led to him being caught by the bus conductor for not having the money to pay the extra fare incurred by his staying on the bus and going past his usual stop.

Others recall going through similar, humiliation-risking contortions to avoid the yet more humiliating experience of others seeing the tell-tale signs of their ungovernable and unwanted erections. Recounting the manoeuvres he went through to avoid others seeing the signs when he got up to leave school assembly, a 19-year-old adds:

> There's one rule: boys don't talk. When I was 13 I could think of nothing but sex but I had no idea what or who might be involved. But one thing was certain: you didn't let others see any sign of your having a hard-on. And, as for talking about homosexuality, it was completely taboo.

In other respects, however, sex is far from taboo – adolescent boys seem to talk of nothing else.

Doing sex

Stopping themselves expressing their feelings, including their homosexual feelings, lest they thereby expose themselves to be emotionally uncontained, as women are often characterised as being, men are often more than happy to share experiences demonstrating them to be manly, contained, and in control – particularly experiences involving 'doing sex'. Or, as one feminist researcher found, men willingly regaled her with 'pubertal anecdotes revolving mainly around early heterosexual play or disconnected homosexual episodes like circle jerks'.[10] Men in my study did much the same. They were eager to report adolescent memories of phallic brag: one man, for instance, began his account of himself in early adolescence with 'Me and my friend showed each other our willies and had a sword fight with them'.

In his novel, *Cat and Mouse*, Gunter Grass celebrates men's teenage enthusiasm for showing off the size of their penises to each other:

'Measure it!' cried Jurgen Kupka. Tulla spread the fingers of her left hand. One full span and another almost. Somebody and then somebody else whispered: 'At least twelve inches!'. That was an exaggeration of course. Schilling, who otherwise had the longest, had to take his out, make it stand up, and hold it beside Mahlke's; Mahlke's was first of all a size thicker, second a matchbox longer, and third looked much more grown-up, dangerous, and worthy to be worshipped.[11]

Men are also often happy to write and talk about masturbating. Compared to young women, young men are much more likely to write in response to questionnaire studies that they masturbate.[12] One study found that 92 per cent of the men, compared to 64 per cent of the women questioned, wrote that they masturbated.[13] Another study found that twice as many men as women students said they masturbated, with men outnumbering women by three to one in the frequency with which they said they masturbated in early adolescence.[14] Yet another study reports that, among women and men who said they masturbated, the men said they did it more often.[15] Another researcher, who rejoices in the name of LoPresto, finds that teenage boys say they masturbate about five times a week.[16]

It was the only topic of conversation, recalls another man, in his English public school. He writes:

I had started my secondary school career at Marlborough, alongside 16 girls and around 850 boys, who talked of nothing else but masturbation. I can't remember a single conversation with a normal Marlburian which did not revolve around this pastime.[17]

Similarly men college students readily report fantasies involving masturbation. A recent study finds that, of forty-nine men and forty-seven women students, the men reported a significantly greater frequency of sexual urges and masturbatory fantasies than the women.[18] Another study finds that, in a sample of sixty-nine male and thirty-one female 18- to 20-year-old students, 98 per cent of the men compared to 83 per cent of the women reported sexual dreams and fantasies, with 91 per cent of the men compared to 29 per cent of the women reporting that they masturbated, while 10 per cent of the women did not reply.[19]

Similarly, several teenage boys, but no teenage girls, in my study told dreams ending in masturbation. A 15-year-old dreamt, or so he wrote, that:

> I was in some kind of public transport, either a bus or a tube, when this really attractive girl came up to me and asked if I wanted to come round her house to meet her friends. This place was massive, but there wasn't any people there. Then I forget what happens for a while, but I can remember performing oral sex with this woman in a '69' position. I woke up in the middle of the night and found myself masturbating.

Just as teenage boys, more often than teenage girls, tell recurring childhood nightmares involving people they do not know (as I have illustrated in Chapter 2), this 15-year-old and other teenage boys in my study wrote dreams involving sex with people they did not know or claimed to feel nothing for, or about. This brings me to another division in young men – between sex and love.

Sex and love

Early taught to equate love, feeling for, and emotional closeness with their mothers and others as feminine and not to be expressed or talked about, men talk less often about what they feel, as I have said, than about what they do. This includes talking about 'doing sex' while being inhibited from talking about the feelings involved.[20] They often report first having sex, as teenagers, with strangers or acquaintances with whom they have had no subsequent contact.[21] They boast of having casual sex.[22] They pride themselves on having sex with many different partners, most or all of whom they can hardly have known.[23] They pride themselves on first having sex at a younger age than girls admit to.[24] They claim to have had sex when they have not had sex at all.[25]

Psychologist Stephen Frosh and psychiatrist Danya Glaser explain the division in men between sex and love as follows:

> Traditional 'masculinity' focuses on dominance and independence, an orientation to the world which is active and assertive, which valorises competitiveness and turns its face from intimacy, achieving esteem in the glorification of force. The fear at the heart of this image is of emotion – that which makes us vulnerable and 'womanly'; emotion is dangerous not only because it implies dependence, but also because it is alien, a

representation of all that masculinity rejects. This fear of emotion in turn makes sex both over- and under-invested in by men. Sex is one of the few socially acceptable ways in which men can aspire to closeness with others, and as such it becomes the carrier of all unexpressed desires that men's emotional illiteracy produces.[26]

In keeping with this division between physical and emotional closeness, between talking feelings and talking sex, a group of working class 14- to 16-year-old boys, attending a Glasgow secondary school, recently told a researcher:

> If you ask any boy if he's a virgin every one will say 'No', 'I done it on holiday', and all that. That's the pure one: 'I done it on holiday at Ayr'. . . . You would not go and have a big conversation amongst all your mates. . . . You may come out with a joke and that. You never have a pure conversation at all. . . . You don't go and pour your heart out and all that. You keep your feelings to yourself.[27]

Talking about feelings – about love, at least – is too 'soppy' as a 19-year-old in another Glasgow-based study put it.[28]

Or they recount love – and longing for emotional closeness and commitment – as something that happens to others not themselves, typically to those with whom they make love. Remembering his first sexual partner, another 19-year-old grumbled:

> She thought like she owned me totally, you know. That is what like put me off her and that. Like she started like as if she owned us and that because the two of us had done it and that. Like that was the sort of thing.[29]

Nor is it any surprise that boys cut themselves off from knowing about any longing for love and commitment they might feel, given that they often ridicule any such talk of love in their friends. As another Glaswegian teenager puts it: 'One boy I used to hang about with, Joe his name is . . . he used to get loved up by just about every lassie. I used to slag him rotten about it.[30]

Given that they 'slag' off others talking about their feelings, it is no wonder that teenage boys complain that they cannot trust other boys not to similarly 'slag' them off were they to talk about their own feelings.

Not being able to trust their peers with what they felt and wanted was a frequent complaint of poor, working-class, African-American, Latino, and white teenagers recently interviewed in a US urban high school. Several lamented not having any same-sex friends with whom they could share their feelings. They lamented that, although they had confidantes when they were in elementary school, they dared not confide in anyone now they were at high school lest their confidantes think ill of them or give them away. Malcolm, an African-American, said:

I had a couple [of close friends] once when I was real young, around ten. . . . But right now, nobody really 'cause it seems that as I've grown, you know, everybody just talks behind your back and stuff. . . . With my girlfriend, I could relax . . . with a girl you can express certain feelings and stuff, you know . . . you can talk about certain things and with boys it's just harder to like . . . some of the things you may want make you seem you're gay or something[31]

Gay men are also diffident about sharing their feelings – including feelings of love – as opposed to bragging about their sexual conquests. In his autobiography, *A Boy's Own Story*, Edmund White recalls himself as a teenager falsely boasting his sexual prowess to Kevin, the son of friends of White's parents, when Kevin stayed overnight:

'How old are you?' Kevin asked.
'Fifteen. And you?'
'Twelve. You ever done it with girls?'
'Sure,' I said. I knew I could always tell him about the black prostitute I'd visited. 'You?'
'Naw. Not yet.' Pause . . .
'The guys back home? Guys in my neighbourhood?'
'Yes?' I said.
'We all cornhole each other. You ever do that?'
'Sure.'
'What?'
'I said sure.'
'Guess you've outgrown that by now.'
'Well, yeah, but since there aren't any girls around.'[32]

So they do it. They have sex. For White, contrary to his boast, it is his first experience of 'cornholing'. Knowing to talk up his sexual experience, he also knows to talk down his feelings. He knows not to let Kevin know of the love he feels for, and wants from him. It was the same with his father. White recalls never knowing for certain whether his father and he shared the same feelings and longings for closeness with each other. With Kevin, he knew he had to make do with horseplay – and sex. Kissing, romance, and love could not come into it. Their negation was signified for the 15-year-old White by a jar of Vaseline Kevin bought to ease their coupling. White writes of it as 'the application of method to sex, the outward betrayal of what I wanted to consider love, the inward state'.[33]

Self and other

Many men in their teens not only divide love and sex. Many attribute longing for sex, like longing for love, to others. This is nicely rendered by a Glaswegian cartoon of two young men saying to each other:

> 'You ever had sex?'
> 'Na! That's for lassies.'[34]

Perhaps this is surprising. So too, perhaps, is the finding that men, slightly more often than women, talk of being victims of others' longing for sex.[35] They talk of being seduced into sex by a stranger or by an acquaintance they scarcely know.

Toby, a graphic artist in his mid-forties, tells me he was initiated into sex by a girl he chanced to meet at a disco:

> She was much more experienced than I was . . . she was the one who took the lead role. I suppose, as boys of that age, you think about it. But, when it comes to doing it, you don't do anything. It was down to her the first time, and after a few drinks . . . just to give you courage to do it. It was after a disco, and we went to a park, and she started er, um, taking the initiative, so we ended up doing it there in the park. And I remember because I had white jeans on, and when I got home I had terrible grass stains all over these jeans, and I tried to scrub them off before my parents came home.

Today's teenagers tell similar tales – of being seduced into sex by an unknown girl or girls, as in the following dream from a 14-year-old:

> I meet a fairly attractive girl, about 17 years old and we go upstairs. On somebody else's bed, I don't know how we got there, she laid me flat on my back and started undoing my trousers. The next thing is me doing her from behind with some other attractive girl sitting on my face. I'm so happy and I just explode at the same time as the girls and cover them in semen. It is great!

Others tell dreams of being subjected to others' homosexual rape. A 19-year-old writes:

> A nightmare really. I dreamt I saw group male sex in a college toilet. Then I was raped from behind by another male whilst urinating. After leaving the toilet (the rapist had run off) in tears, someone I knew in the dream (the actor who plays Sgt Stubbs in *Soldier Soldier*) comforted me and sat me down and told me not to worry and then chased off after my attacker.

This dream seemed so real I woke up thinking I had been really raped in my bed and covered in sweat.

They describe anal sex as others', not their own, doing. A student in his late twenties writes of the penfriend, Pierre, who stayed with him when he was 14:

One day, Pierre stole a pornographic magazine which I had at home. He wouldn't admit it, but I knew it was him who had it. . . . Actually, it wasn't the whole magazine, just one picture that Pierre had torn out of the magazine. A picture of a naked blonde girl. One day when I was in Pierre's house, in Paris, I walked into his room and was quite shocked to see him lying face down on bed with a thermometer up his bum.

While some link anality and sex and attribute the linked activity to others, and while some attribute to others their impulses toward doing sex – both gay and straight – other men attribute their teenage wish for incest to others. A 15-year-old in my secondary school study candidly acknowledged this splitting off process in recounting a dream of which he wrote:

My most recent dream was last night – I dreamt I was with my sister. . . . She said she wanted to lose her vaginity [sic] but not to be a bastard. She asked me to have sex with her. . . . So I agreed, but I actually wanted to have sex with her! . . . She pointed to my trousers, and she took them off and pulled me down on top of her . . . I then got my penis and put it into her vagina and we started having sex . . . she reached her orgasm as I ejaculated. Then she got dressed and went to her bedroom. I am still a virgin!

Others – perhaps faced with similar divisions between wanting and not wanting sex and incest – choose not to remember or write down their dreams. A 14-year-old writes, 'The only ones I can remember are embarrassing'. Inhibited by embarrassment and by the wayward and transgressive unruliness of their dreams from sharing them with others, teenage boys arguably often experience their sexual dreams and fantasies as all the more embarrassing, wayward, transgressive, unruly, and uncontained for not being shared. This can lead to, or exacerbate, yet another division – between fact and fantasy.

Fact and fantasy

Freud described the division of fact and fantasy as a division between practical and psychical reality.[36] It was a division often eloquently written about by playwrights and novelists at the turn of the century when the division between social injunctions to young people to confess and not to confess themselves in terms of their sexuality became particularly pressing.[37] Writers at the time often expressed particularly well the adolescent's experience of this division not as social and interpersonal but as individual and intrapsychic – as an effect of a divided-off, guilt-inducing bodily force attacking their minds.

In his play, *Spring Awakening*, first written in 1890 but due to censorship not produced until 1906, the German writer, Frank Wedekind, depicted his drama's central teenage protagonist, Moritz, telling his schoolfriend, Melchior, about his sexual cravings and fantasies as though they were impelled by a split off foreign power. He recounts being hit by outrageous and alien sexual images and ideas:

> There were these legs in sky-blue tights climbing over the teacher's desk . . . I'd never felt anything like it before – such a craving – for such unbearable excitements. Unbearable! Why wasn't I left to sleep through it – and wake up when it was all over? . . . I can hardly speak to a girl without my brains going into a kind of spin down a drain – I think the most horrible things . . . I've been through the encyclo-pedia from A to Z. Huge, ponderous volumes, solid with words. Masses and masses and masses of words. But not one plain descrip-tion of what actually goes on.[38]

Internalising the division between common sense clarity and textbook obfus-cation, young men today, like Wedekind's Moritz, similarly experience this division and confusion as happening within them. A man in his early thirties, for instance, writes of himself in his early teens 'reading bits of a book called *Boys and Sex*, not understanding much (especially about "Public Hair")', and writing 'lots of poems about being in a cloud'.

Returning to turn-of-the-century writers, Wedekind's contemporary, the novelist Robert Musil, contrasted the 'being in a cloud' confusion of the sexual fantasies and cravings of teenagers of his day with the clarity of their mothers' feelings about being separated from them. In his 1906 novel, *Young Törless*, Musil describes a young teenager, Törless, sent to a military academy, similar to the one to which Musil himself and the poet Rilke were sent in their early teens. Musil describes Törless's mother, having just brought Törless to the academy, weeping at being separated from him on his leaving her at the railway station where she awaits her train home.

Meanwhile, Törless walks away, dry-eyed, along the street taking him from the station to his new school. Unlike his mother, and far from being mindful of, or dwelling on any sadness at their separation, Törless finds the emptiness filled with a confusing riot and 'mesh' of 'obscure' sexual images and longings:

> [He] looked through the little windows and the crooked, narrow door-ways into the interior of the cottages with a gaze burning so hotly that there was all the time something like a delicate mesh dancing before his eyes. Almost naked children tumbled about in the mud of the yards; here and there as some woman bent over her work her skirt swung high,

revealing the hollows at the back of her knees, or the bulge of a heavy breast showed as the linen tightened over it. . . . He was waiting for something . . . some monstrous sight of which he could not form the slightest notion; something of a terrifying, beast-like sensuality; something that would seize him in its claws and rend him, starting with his eyes; an experience that in some still utterly obscure way seemed to be associated with these women's soiled petticoats.[39]

Arriving at the academy, and through the next few days, Törless feels horribly alone. He associates his aloneness with being abandoned by his nursemaid as a child. Ungovernable sexual ideas fill the void – fantasies of the 'lure of woman', and of 'perverted lust in the secrecy of it'. He finds himself 'disturbed by the thought that his lustful imaginings might overwhelm and gain more and more ascendancy over him'.[40]

James Joyce wrote of sex similarly filling the void of being separated and alone. In his autobiographical novel, *The Portrait of the Artist as a Young Man*, written like *Young Törless* at the beginning of this century, Joyce described not only the separation of boys from their mothers on going to boarding school, but also the pressure on boys not to say anything about their closeness with their mothers. Writing of himself (or his father)[41] as Stephen Dedalus first arriving at boarding school when he was 8, he says:

> Wells came over to Stephen and said:
> – Tell us, Dedalus, do you kiss your mother before you go to bed?
>   Stephen answered:
> – I do.
>   Wells turned to the other fellows and said:
> – O, I say, here's a fellow says he kisses his mother every night before he goes to bed.
>   The other fellows stopped their game and turned round, laughing.
>   Stephen blushed under their eyes and said:
> – I do not.[42]

Divided from saying anything about his closeness with his mother, Stephen, arrives at adolescence constituting this division as an inner division between fact and fantasy, between sex as written and felt:

> On the desk he read the word *Foetus* cut several times in the dark stained wood. The sudden legend startled his blood. . . . His monstrous reveries came thronging into his memory. They too had sprung up before him, suddenly and furiously, out of mere words. He had soon given in to them and allowed them to sweep across and abase his intellect, wondering always where they came from, from what den of monstrous images. . . . The letters cut in the stained wood of the desk stared upon him, mocking

his bodily weakness and futile enthusiasms and making him loathe himself for his own mad and filthy orgies.[43]

Whereas some dwell on inner divisions of fact and fantasy – 'letters' and 'orgies', as Joyce put it – others dwell on inner divisions of past and present.

Past and present

This division has perhaps never been more exquisitely portrayed than by Alain-Fournier in his 1913 novel, *Le Grand Meaulnes*. In it he describes the enchantment of his novel's main character – 17-year-old Augustin – on finding himself in the middle of a wedding party of scarcely grown children in a chateau surrounded by woods. Augustin immediately falls in love with the groom's sister, Yvonne de Galais. No sooner done, however, than – as though it were a dream – the scene vanishes. Augustin finds himself back in his village school. Try as he might he cannot recover the enchanting woodland scene. Despairing, he leaves for a sordid liaison in Paris with the groom's abandoned bride. Years later, he dates the turning point between his past and present, childhood and adult, sexually innocent and guilty self to his 17-year-old discovery and loss of the de Galais chateau: 'I'm sure now that when I discovered the nameless domain I was at some peak of perfection, of purity, to which I shall never again return'.[44]

The New York journalist, Eva Hoffman, has recently depicted this self-same, past–present, child–adult division in terms of her 'exile', aged 13, on emigrating with her family from Poland to Canada. She likens the transition to 'being pushed out of the happy, safe enclosures of Eden'.[45] Writing as the teenager she then was she says:

> I am enraged at the false persona I'm being stuffed into, as into some clumsy and overblown astronaut suit. I'm enraged at my adolescent friends because they can't see through the guise, can't recognize the light-footed dancer I really am.[46]

Just as Hoffman describes being divided between her 'light-footed dancer' childhood self and a 'clumsy and overblown astronaut' adult self imposed on her by others, other writers describe being divided in their teens between their past and present selves, which they constitute as a division of true and false.

True and false

Whereas Hoffman recounts first becoming acutely aware in adolescence of being divided between a true and false version of herself, psychoanalysts more often date this division as beginning in early childhood. They attribute it to the mother experiencing her baby in terms of what she wants rather than in terms of what he truly wants so that, in order to survive, the baby has to comply with, and falsely make his mother's wants his own.[47]

Certainly the occasional Freudian notes that the reduction of what the child wants, to what the parent wants, often becomes acute in adolescence. They note that teenagers often vigorously seek to divide and dissociate their true selves from the false selves foisted on them by their parents. Therapist Paul van Heeswyk gives the example of 17-year-old Susan experiencing herself as 'the empty space, or place of reception, that feels obliged to offer sanctuary to her parents' unlived conceits. . . . She feels compelled to live out her parents' aspirations; but angry that they have outstayed their welcome'.[48]

Whereas, like Susan, Eva Hoffman writes of dividing her true childhood self from the false self she felt cast into by others when she was a teenager, men often portray this external pressure as an internal division within them. A striking example comes from a man whom I will call Julian. He is now a leading banker. Almost alone amongst the men interviewed for the recent book, *City Lives* (see Chapter 2, p. 23), Julian described his inner feelings as well as his outer sports and other achievements at public school. He described how, until he was 13, he lived alone with his mother, and attended school as a day boy only to be summarily sent away to board full time when his father returned home after the war. His father then added insult to injury by emphasising that Julian not only had to be got rid of, and sent away as a sexual rival, but that he was also no good. This was borne in on Julian particularly emphatically by his father's reaction to him being invited to become head boy. He recounts the incident thus:

> I received the letter for my last year from the High Master of Y, asking me to be Captain of the School . . . and I showed it to my father. He said that he was going to tell them what I was really like, because there was no way they'd make somebody like me in that position.[49]

Yet it was not in terms of his father's image of him as no good but in terms of an inner good–bad, true–false division that Julian most thought of himself. Interviewed in his fifties, he characterised himself as divided between an exterior 'confident and conformist' self and an interior self of 'quaking muddles'. He talked of being similarly divided in his teens between his inside and outside, true and pretended self:

> I had the good fortune, or misfortune . . . to be in the form with X [he named a leading film maker], people like that, who were intellectually so good . . . outstandingly brilliant . . . [whereas] it seemed to me then that I was always pretending . . . outwardly conformist, respectable, a good chap.[50]

Again and again, men, and to a lesser extent women, recall their teens as marking the beginning of a division within them between, as Julian puts it, a duplicitous 'outwardly conformist' and genuine 'quaking muddles' inner self. Another man, Brian, now in his early sixties and also a successful businessman – albeit not a top City banker like Julian – indicated that he attributes the origin of this inner–outer, true–false division within himself to anxiety in his teens about his sexuality. Still anxious, he tells me:

> Yes, er, well, I mean there was one [teenage experience] that was er was very important to my life, er, if you don't mind my getting a bit personal. I had an undescended testicle which had to be corrected. It was corrected. It's been okay ever since. But that, that was done when I was 17, in St Thomas's Hospital. That used to cause me agonies of apprehension, I think, all through my teens, about sex, and, er, whether I was abnormal, and so on. And I was never told anything about it. We lived in a household where these things weren't talked about. There was no one I could talk to about all this. . . . So I kept that all bottled up. . . . And, er, well, if I wasn't born with it, I don't know what happens in the early weeks, it became apparent at an early age. So I lived all through my puberty with this dreadful incubus hanging over me.

Like many other men, however, he remembers the division between what he could and could not talk about, and share with others as a teenager less as the effect of an outward, socially induced inhibition than as an inwardly imposed inhibition and division. He remembers being inwardly divided in his teens between his public image of himself as a success – as always having a girl-friend, as the boy his headmaster most expected to win an Oxbridge scholarship – and his private image of himself as a failure – both in sex and as a scholarship candidate. As for his 60-year-old self, he portrays himself as divided between being an 'outsider on the inside . . . a rebel in some ways, but also a bit of a conformist in others'.

Whereas the social and interpersonal determinants of Brian's continuing experience of being divided between his outside and inside, rebellious and conformist self include his and his family's inhibitions about voicing and sharing his teenage anxiety over the relatively uncommon late teenage condition of still having an undescended testicle, another man, Gordon, describes a more commonly occurring adolescent problem. He recalls puberty involving him being increasingly divided between his parents – between his mother pulling him in on her side in her feuds with his father, and his father's upset and fury with Gordon on this account. But, like Julian and Brian, Gordon recalls this less in terms of a division between himself and his parents than in terms of being divided against himself. He recalls his self-hatred as a teenager, his

> complete lack of understanding of sexuality, its problems, masturbation, etc. . . . feelings of guilt. The physical needs which aren't answered. Fantasies which have to substitute for relations with the other sex . . . I

don't think I would like to draw them in detail. They're pornography aren't they? They're mental pornography really. I wouldn't like to elaborate. It would take being on the psychiatrist's couch with a compensatory £1,000 cheque, and even then . . .

He locates in his still remembered, ungovernable-seeming, pornographic teenage fantasies – arguably rendered all the more hateful and ungovernable for not being shared either then or now – a continuing division within himself between his outwardly sane and successful journalist self and an inward sense of himself as insane and psychiatrically ill. He indicates in telling me the story of his life that, starting with puberty, he became and remained so guilt-ridden about sex he never had a sexual relationship until, years later, he was propositioned by an older woman whom he eventually married, but with whom it was then too late to have children. His teenage self-division between his true and false, innocent and guilty self still determines his life.

Teenagers today describe similar divisions between their true and false, good and bad selves. A 17-year-old dreams of mathematically doing away with the divisions. He writes of his best remembered dream: 'I would picture mentally a scale upon which the two variables were Goodness and Evil. This proved very successful and I rarely had nightmares again as I persuaded myself (using the scale) of omnipotent goodness'.

This, however, involves another division – between feeling and logic, passion and reason, often equated with a division between body and mind.

Body and mind

Experiencing oneself as divided between one's body and mind is rendered much more respectable than the interpersonal adolescent divisions often giving rise to it, by the mind–body dualism of Western philosophy authorised by the seventeenth-century French philosopher, René Descartes. Descartes defined the body, and matter generally, as characterised by extension, divisibility, and uncertainty. He defined the mind or consciousness, by contrast, as indivisible and certain. He maintained that the mind, unlike the body, can never be deceived. He declared, in effect, that the mind is self-authenticating. Hence his dictum *cogito ergo sum* (I think therefore I am).

Some argue that the sharp division of mind and body bequeathed Western philosophy by Descartes is rooted in the history of our social relations with others, specifically in the history of the transition from the communal ties of feudalism to the individualism of free market capitalism, in which, it is said, sensuousness was repressed and reduced to its rational exchange value.[51] Others – most recently post-modernist philosophers and literary theorists, notably Jacques Derrida – attack the Cartesian division of mind and body as spurious, as a false doctrine bequeathed us by Enlightenment philosophy.[52]

Whatever its philosophical validity, however, the division of mind and body remains an often acutely experienced reality in adolescence. The need of the adolescent to separate his mind and his body, and the terror of the young man of his mind being subordinated to his body, was graphically described at the turn of the century by the poet Rilke. In an autobiographical novel he depicts a young man terrified by seeing a man in the street ruled by the involuntary bodily tics of Gilles de Tourette syndrome. Rilke describes his fellow-pedestrian as driven by 'a sort of elemental force that bent him forward and dragged him back and made him nod and bow, flinging dance-force out of him in among the crowd'.[53]

In his novel, *A High Wind in Jamaica*, Richard Hughes attributes the division of mind and body, which is arguably a defence against the possession of the mind by the body like that described by Rilke, to a 10-year-old girl, Emily. He writes of her:

> it suddenly flashed into her mind that she was *she*. She stopped dead, and began looking over all of her person which came within the range of eyes. She could not see much, except a fore-shortened view of the front of her frock, and her hands when she lifted them for inspection: but it was enough for her to form a rough idea of the little body she suddenly realised to be hers. She began to laugh, rather mockingly. 'Well!' she thought, in effect: 'Fancy you, of all people, going and getting caught like this! – You can't get out of it now, not for a very long time: you'll have to go through with being a child, and growing up, and getting old, before you'll be quit of this mad prank!'[54]

Others recall divisions similar to that ascribed by Hughes describing Emily as divided between the 'mad prank' of her body and her experience in 'her mind that she was *she*'. A writer friend in his sixties tells me that, beginning when he was 13 and continuing through his teens, he found himself sometimes so horribly conscious of his body he would rush into the next room to get away, only to find, of course, that his body was still with him. He last found himself thus trying to rush away from himself when he was particularly upset on leaving home for college.

Men, it seems from the findings of other researchers, often tell 'out-of-body' stories about themselves.[55] Another example comes from the broadcaster, Melvyn Bragg. He writes as follows of his 'out-of-body' experiences:

> They began when I was about 13 and continued upwards of two years, at times intensively. . . . Usually they came at night. . . . What happened was this. Not *part* of me, but *what I was* left the boy's body on that bed and went above – it seemed to the corner of the ceiling next to the window. It hovered there. It stayed there. It, that thing, that object, was me. The huddle on the bed was controlled by it. There was no will in the boy's body. There was only, as it were, a holding state uninhabited, save for a

possessing aura of terror. . . . The desperate fear was – would these two fuse again or not?[56]

Whereas Bragg remembers this division of his mind and body as terrifying, a 17-year-old exults in a similar image. Dividing himself between his 5-year-old and 17-year-old observed and observing self, he writes:

> When I was five I had a dream which only happened once but I've never forgotten it, because it struck me as strange. I dreamt that I was asleep and standing by my self watching me sleep. Speech bubbles appeared. They said 'IS THIS ME?' At this stage the person who said the above woke up and was standing by another 'me' asleep. Again the 'This is me' reappeared and this kept on happening until I (real me) woke up! . . . very weird. GROOVY!

Writing in more obviously Cartesian vein, a 29-year-old student tabulates memories of his early adolescent self under two separate body-mind headings:

PHYSICAL	MENTAL
Developing hairy legs.	Always falling in love.
Permanent erection!	Becoming very political.
Aching legs.	Feeling isolated.
Sweating feet.	Sleeping a lot – always tired.
Voice breaking.	Always thinking about sex/women.

What are we to make of these and other divisions within themselves that men (more often than women) recall from adolescence? Despite the frequency with which men remember being divided as adolescents between their bodies and their minds, between their true and false, past and present selves, between fantasy and reality, love and sex, and between their controlled and uncontrolled erections and wet dreams, non-analytic psychologists write little about these divisions. Meanwhile, psychoanalysts, to the extent that they write about adolescence at all, often recount these divisions in terms of yet another internally-given division – between wanting and not wanting incest.

Incest

Freud argued that, learning from each other just prior to puberty about adult sexuality, children become preoccupied with their parents' sexual relations with each other.[57] They begin to want sex with their parents just as, according to Freud, they wanted sex with their parents when they were infants. Arrived at adolescence, Freud wrote, young people take revenge on their parents because they are not able to have sex with them. They depose them. They imagine much grander parents in place of their actual parents. They imagine their true parents to be aristocrats or lords.[58]

Wanting to have sex with their mothers in the way they learn adults have sex with each other, but faced with the conflict of this wish, both with society's taboo on incest and with fear of its realisation being punished with castration, Freud wrote, young men look for a substitute for their mothers with whom 'a real sexual life may be carried on'.[59] At first, as teenagers, they make do with fantasy. As for actually having sex, some young men, Freud claimed, horrified by the idea of being castrated, can only have sex on condition that a fetish stands in for the absence of a penis in the woman with whom they make love.[60] Alternatively, men turn to what Freud called 'psychical impotence, misogyny and permanent homosexuality'.[61] Some, Freud added, choose a man as their lover so as to rediscover themselves in him. They look to love their male sexual partners as their mothers loved them as babies.[62] More often, Freud argued, men resolve the division between wanting and not wanting incest by only having sex on condition that they feel none of the affection towards their sexual partner that they feel for their mothers, with the result that, as Freud put it, 'Where they love they do not desire and where they desire they cannot love'.[63]

Others, Freud claimed, women as well as men, find themselves sexually attracted as teenagers to women they imagine rescuing, just as they imagine rescuing their mothers from sex with their fathers.[64] Or, Freud wrote, quoting a story by Stefan Zweig about a widow who goes to bed with a young man who is the same age as her son to save him from gambling, young men imagine their mothers initiating them into sex to save them from the castrating-seeming perils of masturbation.[65]

For the most part, however, having begun his psychoanalytic work dwelling on the adolescent origins of neurotic symptoms in women, Freud later concentrated on the infantile origins of neurosis in men to the neglect of the neurotic-making impact of adolescence in either sex. It was left to his analyst daughter, Anna Freud, to develop his early ideas about puberty exacerbating a division in young people between wanting and not wanting incest.

Even more than her father, Anna Freud rooted this division within the self. She attributed it to internally-given instincts. She argued that the increase in the instincts in puberty revives the child's desire for incest, and that it is the contradiction between this desire and its prohibition that causes the mind–body divisions of adolescence. She wrote of adolescents maintaining tense vigilance over their bodily instincts and impulses so as to translate them into abstract thought and 'master' them 'on a different psychic level'.[66] The resulting division of adolescents from their bodies, she wrote, sometimes amounts to 'the ascetism of religious fanatics'.[67]

She attributed the widespread neglect of adolescence by psychoanalysts to the fact that young people seldom come for, or stay in, psychoanalytic treatment, because they prefer to act on rather than think about and talk through their problems. She also attributed the neglect by psychoanalysis of

adolescence to adults in analysis only recalling their adolescence, if at all, b
stripping the facts of their teens from the accompanying feelings.[68]

Seeking to counter the neglect of adolescence by her fellow-analysts, Anna
Freud comprehensively surveyed the divisions involved. In the process she
reduced these divisions, as her father had already reduced them, to a single
inner division – between wanting and not wanting incest. Her followers do
much the same. Psychoanalysts Moses and Eglé Laufer, notable for treating
disturbed young people at London's Brent Consultation Centre, argue that
the central division which they believe underlies all other divisions in adolescence results from puberty making incest biologically possible.[69] They argue
that resolution of the division thereby unleashed between incestuous fantasy
and its realisation determines whether teenagers become 'normal' or 'pathological' as adults.

The Geneva-based psychoanalyst, François Ladame, argues that dreaming
is one way adolescents resolve this division.[70] The Laufers, by contrast,
emphasise action. They argue, in effect, that the central inner division in
adolescence regarding incest is both due to sex and is best resolved through
sex – through masturbation. They advocate masturbation as the means by
which adolescents – girls as well as boys[71] – can best decide what they can and
cannot countenance and bear to realise sexually from their incestuous
fantasies.[72] Moses Laufer explains adolescent 'acting out' and delinquency in
these terms – as a reflection of the young person's efforts to find new ways of
integrating the divisions brought about by his desire for incest and expressed
in what Laufer calls the adolescent's 'central masturbation fantasy'.[73]

The Laufers argue that some use sex perversely to resolve a 'developmental
breakdown' already existing in the young person prior to puberty.[74] An
example is the sadist who arrives at adolescence with what the psychoanalyst
Mervin Glasser calls a 'core complex'[75] – involving the division between his
early childhood dependence on his mother and dread of being annihilated by
her resulting in him wanting to protect himself by destroying her. Glasser
suggests that the sadist resolves this division from puberty onwards through
sex. He converts his hatred of, and wish both to destroy and preserve his
mother, into sadistic pleasure in hurting and controlling his sexual partners.

Meanwhile Moses Laufer, as well as theorising the adolescent origins of
perversion, argues that some young people are unable to test out solutions to
the division between what they want and cannot allow themselves to realise
sexually for fear of being overwhelmed. Or they are prevented by fear lest,
were they to realise their desire for sex, they would unleash what Laufer calls
'violence that would destroy the sexual partner or the oedipal parent'.[76] It is in
terms of these dangers that Laufer explains the divisions of the mind and
body, and divisions within the body – between sexual maturity and immatu-
rity – experienced by young people in adolescence.[77]

On the basis of the Laufers' work with severely disturbed adolescents
Moses Laufer describes a variety of ways in which resolution and integration

of these divisions can go wrong. Some adolescents, he writes, live out a fantasy of integration

> of union with an idealized part of themselves (being male and female at the same time) through various forms of autoerotic activity which maintains the defensive withdrawal from objects (through anal masturbation in males, or through compulsive rocking, hitting one's own body, disfiguring one's own body through cutting, pulling out one's hair).[78]

Others reject their 'sexually mature body'. They divide it from an ideal image of their previous, pre-pubertal body. The Laufers and their Freudian colleagues attribute to this division adolescent suicide, attempted suicide, anorexia, drug-taking, bulimia, alcoholism, and obesity.[79]

Recently the Laufers' colleague, Kamil Mehra,[80] has illustrated the process by which resolution of the division within the adolescent between wanting and not wanting incest can break down. Mehra says that breakdown in men in adolescence is often due to their early adolescent fantasies being rendered traumatic by their childhood or teenage experiences. Mehra illustrates this outcome with three examples: first, a 26-year-old civil servant, Bob, isolated from others by his family moving home when he was 12 and by experiencing his adolescent sexual fantasies and masturbation as damaging and as still further isolating and making him different from others; second, a 23-year-old engineer, Charles, obsessed when he was 12 or 13 with his parents' sexual relationship, with compulsively masturbating, and with thoughts of suicide and murder rendered traumatic by his mother having died before he was 2, and by his father suddenly dying from a heart attack just after Charles started college; third, 25-year-old Dan who, from early adolescence, stifled any sexual feelings he might have for girls lest they die as his mother had died by committing suicide when he was 12. Mehra explains in these terms the psychosomatic, agitated, and depressed symptoms bringing all three men into therapy in their early twenties.

Others recount in terms of inner conflict about incest the fascination of teenagers with horror movies.[81] It is as though, inhibited from admitting to, putting into words, or sharing with others their private fears and anxieties, because these feelings contradict their public image of themselves as anxiety-free and fearless men, teenage boys are often driven to repeat these worries instead by watching them enacted by others on film. In this teenage boys are like shell shocked soldiers in the First World War who (as we have seen in Chapter 2) repeatedly watched in their nightmares horrors they had experienced in the trenches.

The Laufers' colleague, Donald Campbell,[82] attributes the fascination of teenage boys with watching horror movies to hatred of their bodies. He illustrates the point in terms of the film, *American Werewolf in London*, in which the film's central werewolf protagonist, David, lives out a dream of a dead friend telling him to kill himself so as not to kill others. The film thereby depicts, according to Campbell, the judgement of the suicidal adolescent against his instincts – that the only way they can be 'controlled is to kill the body of the hero'. Sadly suicide, as solution to mind–body and other self-divisions of adolescence, many of which I have illustrated in this chapter, is not confined to dreams, films, and fantasy. It is a tragic fact to which I will now turn.

4   Schizoid and suicidal splitting

Many more young men than young women kill themselves. They are also more likely to suffer schizophrenic self-division. Self-division is, of course, the essence of schizophrenia. Its name is derived from the Greek for splitting of the mind. Schizophrenia is now diagnosed by psychiatrists in terms of three 'first rank', 'positive' symptoms, all of which involve self-division: namely, hearing voices from inside one's head as though they were outside; imagining other people inserting, broadcasting, echoing, or withdrawing one's thoughts; or suffering the delusion of being persecuted by internal forces as though they were external attackers.

A mild example of this last symptom is a young man, Gary. He is terrified of having his identity stolen by a stranger. Therapy reveals that he experiences this aspect of himself as an external, divided-off, 'stranger' part of himself who orders him to 'have sex with loads of women; get roaring drunk in pubs and start fights, throwing chairs and tables over; run up huge bills and not pay them; knock the helmets off policemen and sprint off down the backstreets'.[1]

Conversely, another divided-off part of himself tells him to 'go to a football match, dressed as a woman, and scatter all my [the therapist's] headed notepaper in the crowd . . . get high on drugs; stick my bare bottom out of a taxi window and run off without paying'.[2]

As for the more severe self-divisions involved in the 'first rank' symptoms of schizophrenia, a recent world-wide survey found that these occurred more often in young men than in young women. Among those aged 35 or less diagnosed as schizophrenic, men outnumbered women by nearly three to two. Meanwhile, among those aged 15 to 54 in the UK sample diagnosed as schizophrenic, men outnumbered women by nearly two to one, with a particularly marked excess of men over women in all countries assessed in the age group 20 to 29.[3] Furthermore, a 1995 study found that the first rank symptoms of schizophrenic self-division increased in men, but not in women, through adolescence.[4]

Young men are even more at risk than young women of committing suicide. A recent survey finds that, amongst 15- to 24-year-olds, men are much more likely than women to kill themselves. Furthermore, it reports that, while the suicide rate in Europe in women and men aged 45 and older has recently fallen, the rate rose to an all-time high in young men, while remaining stable or decreasing in young women aged 15–24, through the 1970s to the early 1980s. Indeed, the suicide rate among young men in England was still rising in the late 1980s, to the point at which, in 1988, the rate for England and Wales was 11 per 100,000 in men compared to 3 per 100,000 in women.[5]

This increase[6] coincided with a time when, in England, unemployment – resulting in lack of regular social involvement with others – was also at an all-time high. That lack of closeness and involvement with others might contribute to suicidal and schizoid self-division is indicated by evidence of a negative association between adolescent psychosis and social competence,[7] and by the finding that adolescent boys who attempt suicide lack close relationships with their male peers, and that adolescent girls who attempt suicide have a history of having few or no friends as children. They also have a history of not being able to talk with others about their problems.[8]

The link between suicide and lack of emotional closeness with others is also indicated by evidence that many are driven to commit suicide by feeling cut off from others by what they experience as shameful, unmentionable, homosexual longings and desires.[9] Being cut off from others on account of equating masculinity with heterosexual success – not least at work – has been identified as a major factor contributing to the recent increase in the already much greater incidence of suicide in young men than in young women. One commentator attributes men's high suicide rate to the pressure on men both to prove their success and not to talk about their failures. He concludes that 'men have remained the silent sex and increasingly become the suicide sex'.[10] Suicide, it seems, remains linked to lack of confiding closeness and community with others just as the sociologist Emile Durkheim famously reported in 1888.[11]

Whereas Durkheim explained suicide in social terms – in terms of alienation from community with others – today's psychoanalysts explain suicidal and schizoid self-division in adolescence in individual terms. They explain it in terms of a division within the adolescent between his body and mind. Whatever its immediate precursors in failing exams, break-up of relationships, sudden job loss, or death of a parent, suicide in young people, writes Moses Laufer, is driven by the urge to silence an enemy or tormentor experienced by the adolescent as living within his mind or body. It is driven by the adolescent's hatred of his new-found sexual body, and of his homosexual, anal masturbatory, and other transgressive bodily urges.[12] Suicide, Laufer writes, is also driven by the wish to recover the otherwise divided off peace of mind – as 'calmer, happier, and friendlier'[13] – which the suicidal adolescent believes was his before puberty changed his body.

Mind–body

Laufer and other Freudians attribute schizophrenia, as well as suicide, in adolescence to an inner mind–body split. They argue that schizophrenic and psychotic episodes in adolescence involve the wish to destroy the body, experienced as divided from the mind. They argue that psychotic functioning involves hatred of the sexual body, whilst outright psychosis or madness involves a total rupture with reality in which both the body, and the adolescent's image of his parents, are destroyed and replaced by a fantastical 'neoreality' of incest and parricide.[14]

Laufer writes of adolescent psychosis as involving the adolescent's compulsive preoccupation with, hatred of, and destruction of his bodily-given desire for incest. Unconsciously, Laufer writes, madness in young people involves the wish 'to perpetuate a relationship to oneself and to one's own body as being nonsexual or nonincestuous'.[15] Laufer also claims that it often involves anal masturbation to cultivate the illusion of being non-sexual in the sense of being neither male nor female but both.[16]

Masturbation, Laufer maintains, is also a means of quelling the dread that having sex with others would incur destruction. As illustration Laufer describes a 19-year-old-student who said of his compulsive masturbation that he had to do it to rid himself of tension. Otherwise he feared he might rape a girl or be raped himself.[17] Or, splitting off into others his compulsive urge to masturbate, he became fearful of being masturbated into, and contaminated by them. He spent hours washing his hands to get rid of their contamination. He experienced his analyst's interpretations as similarly contaminating. He experienced what his analyst said as pushing contamination into him to drive him crazy. He became preoccupied with the idea that his analyst was masturbating behind him. He kept having to turn round to check that the analyst was neither masturbating nor penetrating his penis into him. With time, however, he felt less fearful. He was more able to experience his analyst's interpretations not as anally penetrating masturbation and buggery but as evidence that he understood him. This in turn, Laufer indicates, helped reduce the tension otherwise causing him to divide and project his aggressive sexual impulses from himself into others, including his analyst.

Laufer does not give any details of this young man's history. He gives more details about another young man, Paul, whose schizoid self-division seems to have been very much an effect of, or exacerbated by, early detachment and separation from those to whom he was closest as a child. Paul was 23 when he was referred for psychoanalytic help following his discharge from a mental hospital for persistently bringing drugs onto the ward. His history included two suicide attempts. Both occurred when he was away from home: the first at boarding school when he was 18; the second after his first few weeks at university. In telling his story, Paul dwelt on his childhood unhappiness at being separated from his mother. He told Laufer that:

> as a child he was terrified of the dark and needed his mother to be with him when he went to bed. When she left the room, he would have to hug his teddy, otherwise he was frightened that something might happen to him. At boarding school this was easier to cope with because there were

other boys in the room and he could feel safe with them; but he still needed his teddy in bed.[18]

Speaking further about his experience of boarding school, to which he was sent when he was 7, Paul said:

> Although he was very unhappy for a time, he 'got used to it'. He made some friends, but most of the time he spent alone. The picture he had of that period was of being teased and bullied, crying in his room, waiting for his parents to visit, and dreading the time when the visit would end.[19]

It was to his longing not to be alone and to be emotionally close to, and involved with others that he attributed his homosexual involvement with his fellow-pupils at boarding school.

His longing for closeness with others also impelled what Laufer calls Paul's central masturbation fantasy. From early adolescence this fantasy involved the following scenario:

> He would first drink or smoke hash; then he would lie on the floor in the dark imagining somebody doing something to him (he could not be sure what). He would then switch on the light and put on his mother's, and more recently his aunt's, dress. He would then undress, hit his back or buttocks, and masturbate. He could not be sure who was hitting him. This made him feel good because the alcohol, the masturbation, and the hitting deadened him for the rest of the day. The nearest he got to describing what fantasy was active during the time he was hitting himself was to say that he felt somebody was caring for him.[20]

Paul was divided, Laufer writes, between giving way to his childhood longing for somebody 'caring' for him – expressed in dependency on his teddy, his aunt, and his social security benefits – and feeling that realisation of this longing was impossible given that he was now independent and a sexually alive adult. He accordingly sought to do away with this latter aspect of himself. He was reassured by being sexually 'deadened' both in his fantasy, and by the drugs he took keeping his penis limp.

Laufer emphasises the importance of suicidal adolescents receiving skilled understanding so as to feel less alone and less driven – by feeling unable to share their fantasies and anxieties with others – into believing that to be dead is the only solution.[21] But, in concentrating on, and treating the inner division of the adolescent between his body and mind, and between his past and present, dependent and independent self, as the effect of instinct-driven incestuous drives, Laufer says little about the separation from aloneness, and not being understood by others first impelling these divisions.

Laufer says nothing about ways in which Paul's divorce from, hatred of, and suicidal attack on his body as a teenager might have been linked to his unhappiness at being detached from, not understood by, or close to others as a child. Yet Paul clearly expressed this unhappiness. He dwelt on childhood memories of longing for his mother 'to be with him when he went to bed'. He talked of 'waiting for her to have time for him so that they might go for walks or shopping'.[22]

Laufer also says nothing of the possible relation of Paul's pleasure in drugs reducing his capacity for sex, to fear of feeling anything – sexual or otherwise – due to being early inhibited from expressing or sharing his feelings with others on being sent away to boarding school when he was 7. Yet this inhibition was palpable. Paul and his parents were so inhibited from expressing or sharing their feelings with each other that, as Laufer himself acknowledges, they never expressed or took seriously, at least with Laufer, the feelings impelling Paul to try to kill himself at boarding school.

By contrast, Laufer's predecessors in psychoanalysis have attended to the inhibition of feeling, and to the lack of emotional closeness with others contributing to schizoid and suicidal splitting in young people. Particularly notable in this respect is the account developed by R. D. Laing in his books, *The Divided Self* and *Self and Others*.

Self–other

Taking issue with Freudian theories that root our psychology in internal instinctual factors to the neglect of our psychology's external interpersonal determinants, Laing insisted, using terms drawn from existentialism, that our 'being-for-others' is the precondition of our 'being-for-ourselves'. Normally the former guarantees the latter. Usually children arrive at adolescence experiencing themselves as whole and alive by virtue of their family's, and in the first place their mother's, aliveness to their aliveness.[23] Laing insisted that

> a necessary component in the development of the self is the experience of oneself as a person under the loving eye of the mother. . . . The child who cries when its mother disappears from the room is threatened with the disappearance of his own being, since for him . . . [it] is only in his mother's presence that he is able fully to live and move and have his being.[24]

But some mothers, Laing wrote, are not emotionally alive to their children. They are emotionally dead to them. Or the mother intrudes such extreme hatred into her child, as seems to have occurred in Laing's own case,[25] that, in order to survive psychologically, the child splits himself off, and walls himself against her. Or he grows up stripping everything she and others see him do and say of emotional significance.[26]

Either way, Laing suggested, children subjected to the annihilating seeming hatred or indifference of their mothers and other relatives are likely to grow up preoccupied with preserving themselves from the annihilation which seems inevitably involved in being emotionally involved with, and close to, other people. They risk growing up dreading 'engulfment', 'implosion', 'petrification', or 'depersonalisation' of their subjective existence by being emotionally involved with others.

Schizophrenia, Laing wrote, often involves reacting to this dread of emotional involvement and closeness with others by cultivating the illusion of being entirely split off, uninvolved, detached, isolated, and alone. The schizophrenic, Laing claimed, disconnects himself both from others and from himself. He 'uncouples' himself, as one of Laing's patients put it. He defends himself against annihilating-seeming interpersonal interaction by both detaching himself from others, and by uncoupling and dividing himself from himself. He imagines that he is divided in two, that he can keep his 'being-for-himself' divided from his 'being-for-others'. This often involves the idea of splitting his inner mind from his outer body. He imagines he can maintain his mind unsullied by, and free from crippling intrusion by others by absenting himself from his body.

He divides himself from his public, outer 'false self' behaviour, and cultivates an image of his private, inner 'true self' as innocent of, hidden behind, and divided from what he outwardly reveals of himself. But, Laing also insisted, the idea of an inner 'true self' divorced from outer 'false self' engagement with others is an illusion. Or, as Laing put it 'if he [the schizophrenic] does not exist objectively as well as subjectively, but has only a subjective identity, an identity-for-himself, he cannot be *real*'.[27] For our reality – our subjective identity – is constituted by our objective reality for others. To repeat: our being-for-others is the precondition of our being-for-ourselves. One cannot exist without the other.

In imagining himself to be divided from what he experiences to be his 'false self' interaction with others, the schizophrenic's 'true self', Laing wrote, becomes increasingly etherealised, 'volatilized', and 'phantasticised'. It loses all aliveness. The schizophrenic feels inwardly empty and dead. This makes him feel increasingly envious of others. He longs to fill himself up, and counteract his deadness, with the aliveness of other people. But his emptiness also leads him to dread more than ever the very implosion and engulfment by others that first led him to divide and cut himself off from them. Unable to conceive of a 'dialectical relationship', as Laing put it, women and men in this self-divided state of mind often experience interpersonal involvement with others as mutual devouring – as risking devouring or being devoured.[28]

Laing linked the self-splitting of schizophrenia to adolescence. Adolescence, he claimed, is on a continuum with schizoid splitting. It involves self-conscious obsession with seeing and being seen as part of a process of securing and preserving one's personal identity separate from others. He wrote of adolescence that 'The heightening or intensifying of the awareness of one's own being, both as an object of one's own awareness and of the awareness of others, is practically universal in adolescents'.[29] Hence the notorious self-divided self-consciousness of adolescence.

Laing did not relate the self–other, true–false, mind–body, or what he referred to as the 'embodied–unembodied' splits of schizophrenia specifically to adolescence. But the case histories he told indicate that experiences in adolescence were often a crucial trigger impelling his patients defensively to imagine themselves as divided and split in two. Certainly this was the case with the patient, Peter, in terms of whose story Laing most sought to illustrate his theory.

Peter first came for help, when he was 25, worried because he felt sure there was an unpleasant smell coming from him. He was not sure whether others noticed the smell. He was sure, however, that his parents did not notice him. His birth – after his parents had been married and remained childless for ten years – made no difference to them. He slept in the same room with them until he left school. But, although he was with them all the time, they 'treated him as though he wasn't there'.[30]

In other respects his parents did notice him, but only to resent him. Neither of them wanted him. They could not forgive him for being born. His mother resented her pregnancy having ruined her figure. She hated the damage and pain his birth had caused her. As a result she never wanted to get pregnant again. So she never had sex with his father after his birth. Peter supposed that that was why his father also hated him, told him 'I had been an eyesore since the day I was born', called him 'Useless Eustace', and lambasted him as 'a big lump of dough'.[31]

At home and at secondary school Peter felt obliged to become a credit to his parents and teachers. But he was convinced that all his efforts were phony, a play-acted façade, deception, and sham. He imagined himself severed in two – between his 'secret masturbator' self, and the 'paragon' of religious zeal his secondary schoolmistress paraded him as being to his fellow-pupils. It was his continuing investment in being other than the outer self he too paraded himself as being, it was his both dreading and wanting others to see him for what he was, in contradistinction to his usual play-acted perfect self, that, according to Laing, caused the symptoms for which he sought help.

Laing traced Peter's preoccupation with whether others did or did not notice the smell seeming to emanate from him to an incident at work, in the job he took after leaving school and the army, when he became convinced others knew that, far from being perfect, he was hateful. Laing wrote of this incident:

> At the office what he [Peter] regarded as his 'real feelings' were largely sadistic sexual phantasies about his female colleagues, particularly one woman there who, he thought, looked respectable enough but who, he imagined, was probably a hypocrite like himself. He used to masturbate in the office lavatory while evoking these phantasies and once, as had previously happened with his mother, just after he had been doing this, he

emerged and encountered the very woman whom he had been raping in his mind. She was looking directly at him so that she seemed to look straight through him into his secret self and to see there what he had been doing to her. He was filled with panic. He now could no longer believe with any assurance that he could conceal his actions and his thoughts from other people. In particular, as he said, he could no longer feel confidence that his face would not 'give him away'. At the same time, he became frightened lest a smell of semen should betray him.[32]

From the story he told of his life, it seems that Peter expressed – through both his adolescent masturbation fantasies and through his preoccupation with others knowing about them – the attack he wanted to make on his mother for either not noticing him, or for hating him if she did notice him. He also hated himself, identified as he was with his father's characterisation of him as useless. He felt guilty both about being 'a worthless lump of muck and dung' and 'at seeming to be anything worthwhile to others'.[33]

He was preoccupied with others not knowing about the badness of his masturbation fantasies, and with keeping hidden from them his contrary good self. For some time he kept from Laing the fact that, starting when he was 9 years old, he looked after a little girl the same age as himself who had been orphaned and blinded in an air raid during the war. He kept from Laing the value she attached to the help and friendship he had given her, to which, she said, she owed her life. He initially kept this, his good self, from Laing as he also sought to keep it from everyone else lest it be engulfed and ruined by the bad, phony, compliant, false self he mostly believed himself to be with others.

Above all Laing understood Peter's self-division – of which Peter first became acutely conscious in his teens – in terms of a division between his flawed masturbator and perfect secondary school self. Laing understood Peter's adolescent divided self as a symptom of his defensive disconnection and detachment of himself from others, stemming from his parents' annihilating seeming indifference to, or hatred of him.

Laing accordingly argued that the solution in therapy to the divisions within the self resulting from defensive division and disconnection from others depends on the therapist, through his love of the patient, enabling the patient to reconnect with others. This entails, Laing wrote, working with the obstacles the divided self patient erects against the therapist and others for fear of being overwhelmed by envy, longing, and dread of being close to, and involved with them. The division from others that Laing thereby sought to treat included the resulting illusion of being internally divided between being a man and being a woman.

Man–woman

Laing illustrated this division with the example of an 18-year-old, David. David came for treatment at the point where the man–woman division he imagined within himself was threatening to collapse. David was terrified that his sense of himself as a woman was no longer an assumed veneer but was intruding into, engulfing, taking over, and annihilating him as a man.

He told Laing that his woman self was modelled on his mother, that he was an only child and that, until her death when he was 10, he had striven to become whatever she wanted him to be. After she died he went on doing what she would have wanted. In her absence he took over from her. He did the housework, shopping, and cooking. He also took after his mother in doing embroidery, tapestry, and interior decorating as she had. In doing so, he severed his outward personality – 'what his mother wanted him to be', as Laing put it[34] – from his inner self.

Just before he came to see Laing, however, and as I have indicated, his inner self felt increasingly imploded on, and threatened with invasion by his outer self. Throughout his childhood, David told Laing, he had enjoyed acting in front of the mirror. He always acted women's parts. But now, aged 18, he found he could not stop playing the part of a woman. That was why he now dressed up as a man. The result, Laing said, was to make him look like 'an adolescent Kierkegaard played by Danny Kaye'.[35] Play-acting at being a man, it seemed from the story David told Laing, had become 'the only refuge he knew from being entirely engulfed by the woman who was inside him, and always seemed to be coming out of him'.[36]

A patient I saw in therapy some years ago told a similar story. I will call him Simon.[37]

Simon was a 19-year-old Modern Languages student. I saw him in therapy after he was referred for treatment following his hospitalisation after a serious suicide attempt. He began therapy, as many of Laing's patients began their therapy, by talking of his mother's indifference to him, and of her almost total physical and emotional absence from his life. His mother's indifference, Simon complained, included her not believing him when he told her a man in the train had grabbed him, pulled his head back, and spat into his mouth, leaving his intrusive stink inside him.

Most of all Simon complained of his father's hostile intrusion into him. He recalled his father calling him an 'alien', and 'the black sheep of the family'. He recalled his father ganging up with Simon's older brother and the two of them deriding, bad-mouthing, and labelling him 'schizophrenic'. It was to defend himself against his family's threatening and annihilating hostility and indifference to him that Simon depicted himself as a divided self. Or, as he later put it, 'I wanted to hide the real me behind something else'.

On the one hand he felt he was indeed the hated, alien figure his father accused him of being. He remembered himself, aged 12 or 13, going home from school with his younger sister and encouraging her to go to a sweet shop with a stranger who had been courting them, only to feel he was the same as this stranger who used the lure of the sweet shop to abduct his sister and abuse her. Simon felt he too was an abuser, a paedophile and a rapist, not least because he had several times gone along with his older brother's invitation to have sex with him.

On the other hand, Simon cultivated a contrary image of himself as a young woman – akin perhaps to the dead baby girl his mother had born his father early in their relationship, whom his father still very much grieved. Simon imagined himself being made love to as a young woman by another young woman. That was why he stole women's underclothes, he told me. Wearing them gave him sexual satisfaction. But he also hated himself for his cross-dressing. That was why he tried to kill himself.

He hated his sexual, bodily self. But he loved his intellectual, rational self. He regaled me with his near perfect achievements at school. But he had also begun worrying that he could not keep his body and mind divided. He worried that his bodily impulse to wear women's clothes had damaged his mind. He was convinced that a lump on his head was an effect of the bones of his skull being fed by his sexual drive – by excess sex hormone.

He had been to see his GP about it, but his doctor was no more understanding than his father. Simon could no more talk about his feelings with his GP than he could with his father or with anyone else. His doctor would not tell him honestly what was wrong with him. He regarded him as a 'pest'. He evidently felt uncomfortable being with Simon just as his father felt uncomfortable when Simon tried to talk about his feelings with him. Simon complained that he could not communicate with his fellow-students either. Nor could he share his feelings with his college tutors. He had tried, but, like his mother, they did not believe what he said. They laughed at him behind his back. They treated him as beyond the pale.

If only he could establish the closeness he wanted with me, free of the division between being a hated man and a loved girl – the division that it became apparent was the legacy of his parents' destructive indifference to, and hatred of him, in contrast to the love his father felt for Simon's dead baby sister. Simon signalled his longing for closeness with me, for me to recognise his worth, by bringing a school photo of himself, aged 8, handing his work – a beautifully detailed poem, quirkily about a poisonous snake – to a visiting woman dignitary, famed for her motherliness.

He wanted to be close to me, but he was also inhibited from emotional closeness and talking about his feelings with me, just as he was inhibited from talking about his feelings with others at home and at university. Instead he often wrote long letters to me about what he felt. He wrote about his hated, sexual self; about his suicidal self-loathing at giving way to his urge to wear women's clothes; and about his rapacious, murderous thoughts about women and children. He wrote about his attempt, aged 11 or 12, to kill and punish himself for stealing his father's typewriter and outdoing him as a poet in composing verses that had earlier won him the motherly woman dignitary's approval and attention at school.

He felt diffident about being with me, and about confiding in me. He left sessions early. Later he wrote to me about his anger at my not taking in the fact of his initial 'crush' on me. Long since alienated and separated from his mother, he wrote, 'I wanted to be close with you'. His longing had evidently been a major source of his nervous laughter when he was with me. I had not noticed. He told me he had concluded that I did not take him seriously, that I had distanced myself from him out of fear lest he become too intimate and emotionally involved. He was angry that I seemed not to understand. But he was also more confident than with his parents that I might understand and withstand 'the mess' of his trying to convey what he felt. He became hopeful that I might withstand his longing and hatred without rebuffing him. He wrote between sessions saying, 'I know that if I tell you what bothers me you will try to help'.

Perhaps it was his confidence about both of us being able to retain something of the closeness that – despite its conflicts – he had shared with me that enabled him to leave therapy to pursue his university studies, first in England and then in Germany. Many months later, before going abroad, he wrote saying, 'You probably remember me. . . . You are one of the few professional people who has known me.'

He wanted to see me – the manifest reason being that he wanted me to endorse his identity card photo. When we met it transpired that he also wanted to renew his previous closeness with me – just as he renewed the closeness he experienced with the motherly figure at school by repeatedly returning to the photo of the two of them together. It was his answer to the disruption and separation from emotional togetherness with his parents, and his resulting 'keeping secrets and bottling things up', as he put it, that he had cultivated in the divided man–woman story with which he had begun therapy on first coming to see me when he was 19.

His divided self story, as I have sought to show, was on a continuum with many men's experience of being divided within themselves in adolescence. Women, by contrast, who are the main subject of the following three chapters, often describe the divisions of adolescence very differently – not as divisions within themselves but as love–hate divisions in their closeness with others.

Part III
Divided loves

5   Attached daughters

Unlike Simon, whose detached divided self story of adolescence I have just told, women often talk of their attachment to others, particularly to their mothers and friends, through childhood and adolescence. Does their talking more about their attachments stem from a genetic factor making women more emotionally involved than men?[1] Or is their talking more about their attachments, and about their feelings generally, a result of their mothers talking to them more as babies?[2] Is this why girls, on average, learn to speak earlier than boys?[3] Is this why they grow up to be better at talking,[4] and communicating with others both verbally and non-verbally,[5] with girls from age 3 onwards being more emotionally coherent and better able to situate and evaluate relationship issues than boys?[6]

But why do mothers talk to their daughters more than to their sons? And why are girls often more ready than boys to talk about their emotional closeness with others, and about the divided love and hate involved? What have psychologists and psychoanalysts made of this difference between the sexes?

Love and hate

Freud wrote elegiacally of the freedom from hate of the boy's early love of his mother, and of her love of him. He claimed that 'A mother is only brought unlimited satisfaction by her relation to a son; this is altogether the most perfect, the most free from ambivalence of all human relationships'.[7]

He noted, however, that his women patients often dwelt on the hatred as well as love they bore their mothers as toddlers. They talked of hating their mothers for disappointing their longing for love. They complained that their mothers did not suckle or feed them enough as babies. They complained that, as children, they were frightened of being cruelly treated, poisoned, or even killed by their mothers; that they remembered their mothers and other women – their nursemaids, for instance – sexually seducing and abusing them.[8] They talked of despising their mothers for being women, not men. And, however illogical it might seem, they also talked of hating and blaming their mothers for bringing them into the world as girls, not boys.[9]

Freud wrote that his women patients' childhood hatred of their mothers drove them to look to their fathers for love. This, he said, often added another factor to his patients' hatred of their mothers – hatred of them as rivals for their fathers' love. Freud concluded, however, that since, unlike men, women have no reason to dread their intense love and hate of their mothers and fathers being punished with castration, women have no reason to give up their intense closeness with their parents either as children or adolescents. Nevertheless, he wrote disparagingly of women who continued this closeness into adolescence. He deplored as pathological, girls who

> with an exaggerated need for affection and an equally exaggerated horror of the real demands made by sexual life have an irresistible temptation on the one hand to realize the ideal of asexual love in their lives and on the other hand to conceal their libido behind an affection which they can express without self-reproaches, by holding fast throughout their lives to their infantile fondness, revived at puberty, for their parents or brothers and sisters.[10]

Just as Freud attributed the persisting 'fondness', beyond puberty, of girls for their relatives to their having no reason, like boys, to fear their fondness being punished with castration, Freud's US ego psychology followers today argue that women's attachment to their relations, at least to their mothers, persists because, far from threatening to un-sex them, their attachment to their mothers fosters their gender development. Adopting the New York analyst Margaret Mahler's account of the child's initial psychological attachment to, and 'symbiotic identity' with the mother, the feminist sociologist Nancy Chodorow claims that, while boys early negate their initial attachment to, and identification with, their mothers so as to forge a different male identity, the little girl, being female like her mother, has no need to negate or divide herself from continuing attachment to, and identification with, her mother in establishing her identity as a woman. Rather, Chodorow indicates, girls learn to become women through remaining close to, and identified with their mothers in copying and sharing what they do, feel, and think.[11]

Feminists have made much of women's awareness of their closeness with others, in the first place with their mothers, as the source of what is now often referred to as women's 'emotional literacy'. Feminists and others, however, have made less of the divided feelings involved – of the fact that, in remaining aware of their emotional closeness with others, girls and women are often also aware of the hatred as well as love they bear those to whom they are closest. Yet this division of love and hate was long ago noted by Freud's follower, the psychoanalyst Melanie Klein, whose work has been very influential, at least in British psychoanalysis.

It has been suggested that, in drawing attention to the divided love and hate characterising the early attachment of boys as well as girls to their mothers, Klein drew on her own intensely divided love and hate of her mother as an adolescent.[12] Certainly, in her theories she drew on her own experience of being mothered, and of mothering her children. She also drew on her child, adolescent, and adult patients' divided love and hate for her, in being a woman like their mothers.[13] On this basis she hypothesised that babies have fantasies, consisting in the first instance of mental or psychical representation of their instincts which pervade everything they feel and do. Or, as Klein's follower Susan Isaacs emphasised, 'There is no impulse, no instinctual urge or response which is not experienced [by the baby] as unconscious phantasy'.[14] And the first object of the baby's fantasies is the person who is closest to him – the woman who first mothers him.

Klein argued that, experiencing their hatred as threatening to annihilate them, boy as well as girl babies get rid of this feeling into the nearest available person, usually the mother.[15] The baby experiences the mother, not himself, as the source of the hatred he would otherwise recognise as his own. But he also experiences his mother as a source of love as well as of hate. To protect one image of her from the other he divides them.[16] He experiences his mother on the one hand as loving and loved, and on the other hand as hating and hated. Seeking to obliterate this latter aspect of his mother, he idealises her as full of everything he most longs for and wants. But this evokes fantasies of greedily scooping out, appropriating, or enviously destroying everything in his mother that makes him feel so empty by contrast with her.[17] This in turn evokes fear lest she retaliate by greedily and enviously scooping out, appropriating, and destroying everything in him.

Perhaps this is the cause of the recurring childhood nightmares both sexes bring with them into adolescence – of maternal figures as vengeful ghouls and witches. Girls in my secondary school study described nightmares of witches coming to get them, and wanting to kill them. One girl told a nightmare of witches grabbing her to boil her up in cauldrons 'steaming with green smoke'. Boys told similar dreams. One remembered dreaming of 'three witch-like creatures' chasing him. Another imagined being attacked by a hostile army led by 'SHE . . . a woman with jet black hair'. Another described a dream of a queen operating 'giant balloons that went around eating people whole'. Another dreamt 'an evil old woman' was standing over him shouting to her friend and throwing things. Still another recounted a nightmare of wanting to warn his grandfather about a dangerous 'mad cow' in the next room.

To judge from what they wrote, many boys dread having a 'mad' or 'dangerous' cow-like maternal figure inside the rooms, towns, or countryside of their dreams, and inside their bodies and minds. But, whatever damage they imagine these hateful figures doing to their bodies and minds, Klein maintained, boys reassure themselves with their masculinity, with the fact that their penis remains intact. They make much of being boys not girls. One might add that they are also reassured by their masculinity on account of the high status accorded men in male-dominated society.

Girls have no such reassurance. Overlooking the social factors involved, Klein attributed to biology the lack of reassurance and confidence of girls faced with nightmares of their mothers attacking them in retaliation for their hatred of them. Klein argued that since the female sexual organs – the vagina and womb – are internal, girls cannot reassure themselves, as boys can, that their sexuality has not been irreparably damaged by their mothers' actual, imagined, and dreamt-of witch-like revenge and attack.

Klein explained in these terms the continuing clinging closeness of girls to their mothers from infancy into adolescence. Through keeping close to their mothers (in imitating them in looking after their dolls, cooking, and sewing) and through looking after their mothers (by drawing, writing, and making presents for them), Klein claimed, girls seek to reassure themselves that, whatever their mothers' attacks on them, their creativity remains intact. By helping her mother, and by making and giving her presents, Klein maintained, the girl also seeks to repair and make amends for any damage she does by hating as well as loving her.[18]

A nice example of just such concern, linked to early mothering, comes from a student's observation of a 4-year-old girl attending a local playgroup. 'Oh, it's raining,' the little girl said, noticing the increasingly gloomy weather outside. 'We'd better put up an umbrella for the dolls,' she added. Then, concerned lest the student feel abandoned and alone, she gave her a toy phone saying, 'It's your Mummy. Do you want to speak to her?'. She then went on to look after the student by getting together with another girl to make her pretend things to eat.[19]

But remaining emotionally attentive to others – in the first place remaining close to, and concerned for their mothers – brings in its wake love and hate of this self-same togetherness. Or, as psychologists put it, girls often arrive at adolescence experiencing more loving and hating ambivalence than boys about their identity and difference, and about their autonomy and individuation from those with whom they are closest, particularly their mothers.[20]

Ambivalent togetherness

While boys are often early pressed to 'dis-identify' from their mothers so as to acquire a different male identity, the pressure on girls both to identify and not to identify, to remain and not to remain close to their mothers is often delayed until adolescence, following a childhood in which, unlike boys, they are often relatively free to be androgynous – to be both masculine tomboys and feminine girls. Perhaps this accounts for some of the differences in the imagined images girls and boys recall in adolescence, with boys more often recalling recurring childhood dreams of maternal separation and reunion (as illustrated in Chapter 2), while girls more often recall recurring dreams of suffocating and comforting maternal togetherness.

The latter include the following dream from a 12-year-old:

> I was outside my house and this white dragon came and was chasing me, so I ran up our road and I kept jumping into the sky, trying to fly but I

couldn't. I kept thinking why I couldn't fly. Then I was in my Mum's arms when I woke up. My Mum said that I had been walking along the landing.

Another girl, aged 13, recalled a recurring dream of getting her finger caught in the brakes of her bicycle, her fingernail coming off, and her mother looking after her and taking her to the hospital.

Some recall dreams of comforting closeness with cuddly toys. A 12-year-old dreams:

I was in this kind of field place where there was just me and a basset hound and I was playing games with him, and I was really happy. Then when I woke up I was cudderling [sic] and squeezing tight my toy dog. I have always wanted a dog and I'm sure that's what made me have my dream.

A 13-year-old remembers imagining being 'a teddy bear and a child was cuddling me and I was so happy'. Another 13-year-old dreamt she was 'sitting on a chair in a dark room without Mum or Dad'. She then crossed out this dream, and replaced it with another in which she was 'sliding down a rainbow with a care bear'. Still another 13-year-old tells a dream of 'riding "My little pony" through the pretty fields, with a long river running through'.

Others, by contrast, recall nightmares of stifling togetherness. They tell dreams of pleasure ruined by their mothers' presence. A 14-year-old dreams of paradise destroyed by her mother being there:

I was on a beach under a palm tree relaxing in the hot shade, watching the sea lap up against the warm sand. As I sat there I ate a huge double ice cream. When I finish I get up to run down to the beach to the sea and my Mum suddenly appears and tells me to sit down and let my ice cream go down or I'll be sick!

Others describe nightmares of maternal and female figures smothering, swamping, enveloping, and ensnaring them. A 12-year-old dreams:

I am on a giant web and there is a giant spider coming towards me. She is smiling but as she gets nearer she lets out a horrible scream, so high it hurts my ears. She becomes scary and ugly. She gets really close to me and I am stuck on the web unable to move. She looks like she is going to kill me and then she scuttles back to the beginning, puts on a smile, and it begins again. It goes on for ages.

Her dream is akin to the image with which the Freudian analyst, Jacques Lacan illustrated primary anxiety as the sensation of being swamped by 'the desire of the other' as 'a gigantic, man-sized, praying mantis'[21] devouring her mate on being fertilised by him.

Others write of nightmares of maternal figures imprisoning or being imprisoned by them. A 12-year-old recounts a dream of a witch imprisoning her family's goats. A 14-year-old recalls a recurring dream of a witch running 'headless' round the garden after first being kept 'chained up' in the family loft. A 16-year-old tells a dream of being crowded by her mother 'sitting on the top of my cupboard amongst my teddybears . . . shouting down at me . . . whilst a bird mobile . . . would be swinging round violently, because the birds were alive trying to escape'.

Others remember dreams of wanting to escape being crowded, imprisoned, and suffocatingly confined with their mothers, or with their friends' mothers. A 13-year-old writes:

> I had this dream about 12 times. I was walking through a bricked tunnel with my friend and her mum. Each time I took a step the tunnel got thinner. In the end it was so thin I couldn't breathe. Then either the dream ended or I woke up.

Teenage girls in my secondary school study, who lived alone with their mothers, without their fathers, were particularly likely to record recurring childhood dreams of being dangerously cooped up with their mothers, or of being besieged with them. A 14-year-old dreamt:

> My mum and I were in a house at the bottom of a hill. There were also about 5 cocker spaniels in the house. Suddenly brown liquid started to roll down the hill towards the house. We were now stuck in the house because of the brown liquid – there was no way out.

Another girl remembered a nightmare of a women teacher, in place of her mother, taking her and her classmates swimming and forcing them to stay under the water. Others describe recurring nightmares of being crushed, just as therapist Susie Orbach says adolescents liken being with their parents to being crushed by 'a massive boulder that needs to be pushed off'.[22]

Novelists similarly depict the horror of adolescent girls of being crushed, incarcerated, or confined with their mothers on becoming women like them. In her novel, *An Experiment in Love*, Hilary Mantel relates the agonising sensation of her novel's pre-teen protagonist, Carmel, on feeling trapped with her mother – with whom she is already locked in conflict – in the changing room of a department store where she tries on the clothes she needs for secondary school. Carmel writes:

> I was shut up with my mother in my own cubicle, at dangerously close quarters. But she was all simpering smiles now: for the duration, I was her darling. She took off her coat and hung it on one of the hooks supplied, and at once her woman smell gushed out and filled the air: chemical tang

of primitive deodorant, scent and grease of Tan Fantastic, flowery scent of face powder, emanation of armpit and cervix, milk duct and scalp.[23]

Others describe their horror at the closeness not so much of their mothers as of their grandmothers ensnaring, embracing, and celebrating their burgeoning womanhood. One teenager talks of armouring herself against her family's 'swooping' endearments:

> I kind of put on a mental suit of armour. I clamp myself in it, and then walk into the room. Grandma opens her arms up and cries 'You're beautiful! Isn't she a beauty? Look at my beauty!' and I want to scream. I feel like my nipples are sticking out for everyone to see, and I can feel my thighs sticking together, and I think of little things, like whether there are any of those gooey specks of dirt between my toes. That admiration is excruciating! It swoops down on you. . . . All those eyes on you, thinking 'Ooh, ah – hasn't the little girl gone and got all developed?'[24]

Often adolescents feel more ambivalent. They both want and do not want to remain within their family's, particularly their mother's, containing orbit. This is particularly evident in women's memories of their mothers' response to their first menstruating.

Mothering menstruation

Whereas men are often singularly silent about their early adolescent wet dreams, unruly erections, and wayward sexual fantasies (as I have illustrated in Chapter 3), women write and talk a great deal about their early adolescent menstruation. Frequently, in their autobiographical reminiscences, women recall both love and hate, pleasure and grievance at their mothers' response. In her autobiography the New Zealand poet, Janet Frame, recalls her grievance thus:

> 'There's blood between my legs,' I said tremulously. 'It's the monthlies,' Mother said. . . . [She] cut an old bath towel into rectangular strips. . . . 'It will show,' I said, looking at the bulk. . . . I knew it showed. For the remaining years at school I suffered those bulky strips of towelling with the blood seeping through so that by the end of the day, if I bent my head toward my desk, I caught the smell of stale menstrual blood, and realizing that others could smell it, I felt unceasing shame.[25]

In a recent account of women's complaints about their mothers' reaction to their first menstruating, the psychoanalyst, Kirsten Dahl, emphasises the division in adolescent girls between wanting and not wanting their mothers' intimacy with them in this respect. Dahl writes that first menstruation revives in girls longing for continuing closeness with their mothers – longing to be physically looked after by their mothers just as their mothers looked after them as babies.

Women's complaints about their mothers' response to their first menstruating, Dahl claims, are due to their mothers' response inevitably falling short of the closeness they imagine having enjoyed with them as babies. The adolescent girl's complaints are also due to dread lest, were her mother to meet her longing to be babied by her, she would overwhelm her. Dahl argues that adolescents are accordingly angry with their mothers and blame them for evoking this dangerous-seeming longing in them. Disowning and projecting their anger into their mothers, they experience their mothers, not themselves, as angry and neglectful. An example, says Dahl, is 12-year-old Mary:

> [She] recounted to her therapist how she had gotten her period for the first time on a school field trip: 'Ugh! It was *disgusting*! I was running, playing catch, and all of a sudden I felt, you know, something wet – I knew something was happening. I grabbed Sally and told her I had to get to the bathroom. We used all the toilet paper. I didn't want anyone to see what had happened. I felt so embarrassed, like people would think I was a baby or something! . . . It was the worst moment in my life. I mean, I wanted to get my period but not on a field trip. I didn't want to get my clothes all dirty and everything. And my Mom wasn't even there.[26]

Grown women recount similar feelings of being let down by their mothers not being there. They complain of their mothers' lack of response. True, some praise their mothers. But they also criticise them.[27] An 18-year-old writes of talking 'extremely openly with my best friend and Mum about it. I wasn't shy of it at all'. But she also writes of feeling 'absolutely disgruntled' about first menstruating. Others remember triumphing over their mothers. A student in her late twenties recalls 'thinking it was the best thing that had ever happened to me'. She adds:

> It was also a big deal getting my first packet of tampaxes. No one in my home used them. So when my Mum found out that this was what I used it was the equivalent of a parent finding his/her daughter with a vibrator.

More often women recall not feeling triumphant and happy but defeated and unhappy at their mothers' downbeat response. A student in her early twenties writes:

> When I was about 12 years old I started my period. I had two older sisters who had already started and I remember being extremely jealous that I hadn't. I remember not wanting to take a bath because I thought it would fill up with blood. When I told my Mum she seemed really disappointed and this dampened my enthusiasm.

Another student recalls her mother's sneering attitude in keeping with still pervasive, woman-hating, misogynist, and dismissive attitudes to women's bodies.[28] She remembers herself aged 11:

> wondering how I was going to tell my Mum that we had been told about periods at school. This took me weeks and I was expecting some big adult discussion with her after my revelation. She simply replied, 'Ah you know it all now – boobs and bums!'

Others remember wanting 'to avoid the subject'. They found it too embarrassing. Many blame their embarrassment on their mothers not speaking to them about 'these things'. They blame their distress on their mothers never warning them about, or discussing menstruation with them. They complain that their conversations with their mothers about menstruation were both too little and too much.

US psychologist, Elizabeth Kissling, finds that teenagers report first learning what little they know of menstruation from their mothers – albeit one girl she interviewed grumbled, 'I didn't hear it from my mom'.[29] But the girls Kissling interviewed also hated their mothers making too much of their menstruating. And as for their mothers celebrating their first menstruation, most were horrified at the idea. 'No way!' exclaimed one girl. 'I wouldn't do that. I'd say, "Skip it, Mom!"'[30]

A teenager in another study talks of her misery at her mother's excitement:

> my mom thought it was like . . . the beginning of a new world. She told everybody her daughter was a woman now. I was really embarrassed. I can remember that. That was a nightmare. . . . At first I thought the whole world had come to an end 'cause I didn't under. . . my mom didn't go into depth. She just said, 'This is your period. You get it once a month.'[31]

While this teenager disliked her mother's 'new world' celebration of her beginning to menstruate, another teenager resented her mother's far from celebratory attitude:

> Umm; my mother just told me her experience, and she goes through hell with her period. She's like, 'I hope that doesn't happen to you.' She'd never really told me about it before. I was worried that it would happen to me.[32]

Women remember their mothers' reaction as worrying, anxiety-making and damaging. They also remember experiencing menstruation itself as damaging. They remember thinking that they must have cut themselves, that the blood indicated that they were 'very vulnerable'. They recall feeling 'frightened' and 'scared'. They remember 'horrifying pain', and terror at not knowing 'what was happening'. Again they blame their mothers – for leaving them in ignorance of what to expect.

In her autobiographical novel, *Prozac Nation*, Elizabeth Wurtzel blames her teenage depression, at least in part, on her mother's gloomy reaction to her first menstruating:

> It seems to me that I was about eleven when it happened. Maybe I was ten or maybe I was twelve, but it was somewhere in my preadolescence. . . . I remember the exact date, December 5, 1978, when I was eleven, and noticed some dry spots that were obviously blood on my little white cotton briefs. . . . Whatever she [mother] said gave me the strong and distinct impression that suddenly I was going to become different and morose, which already seemed to be happening.[33]

Perhaps it is anger at their mothers' negative response – linked in some cases to projecting into their mothers anger at the negative lot assigned women in our still sexually unequal society – that contributes to teenage girls, more often than teenage boys, recalling dreams of anger with their mothers, of their mothers angrily attacking and being attacked, and of themselves not being able to make them better. Or perhaps their dreams associating their mothers with anger and attack are due to the widespread image, purveyed by Freud and many others,[34] of women as attacked and attacking, castrated and castrating, damaged and damaging.

Damaged and damaging mothers

A particularly dramatic example of the attack of teenage girls on their damaging-seeming mothers is depicted in the New Zealand film, *Heavenly Creatures*. Based on a true story, it tells how two 15-year-old girls came to believe that all their problems were due to the mother of one of them stopping them being with each other, to which the only solution seemed to be to kill her, which they duly do.[35]

Killing hated and damaging-seeming mothers is less often a matter of fact than fantasy. So too is experiencing the mother as repressive and confining. Just as one of the two teenagers in *Heavenly Creatures* experiences her mother as damagingly confining her, a 14-year-old in my secondary school study imagined being damagingly confined with and by her mother. She dreamt of 'being squashed in a tupperware box' with her mother. Then, in her dream, she found herself 'left alone' with another woman who proceeded to attack her – 'a shop mannequin with no arms or legs. . . . I remember her taking the dufflecoat I was wearing. Then she grabbed my arms'.

Whatever led to this dream, its manifest content – 'being squashed', 'left alone', and 'grabbed' at by a limbless, lifeless 'mannequin' woman – is an apt emblem of the divided feelings of many girls about being both abandoned by, and damagingly cramped and attacked by women on donning the 'dufflecoat', as it were, of the mature femininity that with adolescence they come to share with their mothers.

Perhaps it is laying the blame on closeness with their mothers for the upsets of adolescence that contributes to many girls disposing of their mothers in their dreams. In her novel, *Bonjour Tristesse*, written when she was in her late teens, Françoise Sagan imagines a teenager engineering the death, in an automobile accident, of her would-be stepmother. Pre-teen and teenage girls today similarly kill, and imagine their parents being killed, in their dreams. A 12-year-old tells a dream of arguing with her parents, wanting them to die, and of their being killed in a car crash. Pre-teen and teenage girls imagine their mothers in their dreams being eaten, poisoned, rotting, murdered, and pushed over cliffs.

They describe nightmares of not being able to put the damage right, of not being able to save, or recover their mothers from the damaging attacks they imagine being visited on them in their dreams. A 12-year-old writes that in her most memorable recent dream:

> We are at the beach going for a walk by the cliffs. My Mum, brother and dad are there and then suddenly my dad runs over to my mum and pushes her off the cliff. He then laughs. My brother screams and I jump off the cliff to try and safe [sic] her. As soon as I jump I stop in mid air and see my mum splattered on the rocks. Then I wake up in a cold sweat. I've had this dream about 4 times.

Perhaps it is fear of not being able to save or repair the damage they dream of themselves or others doing to their mothers that leads teenage girls, more often than teenage boys, to recount nightmares of women judging them as useless and undeserving. A 13-year-old tells the following repeated dream: 'Every night before my birthday this fat lady would walk up to me . . . carrying a pair of boots . . . [and] say "You don't deserve these boots". And I would always be sad'.

Others recall dreams of implacable maternal and older women refusing to be mollified by their efforts to please. A 15-year-old recalls a dream in which:

> my boss forgot to get my wages, so she made me run to her house and then I came back with it. When I opened it there was no money. There was a note saying that my work was not good enough and that she never wanted to see me again. I ran home crying.

They dwell on their divided love and hate of their mothers and other women. A 13-year-old dreams:

> we were changing in the cloakroom and Mrs S came in (who I really hate) and said, 'Sorry girls, Mrs R isn't teaching you, I am' . . . it was a bit of a

nightmare . . . your worst teacher saying she was going to teach you
instead of the one you like.

A few psychologists, writing about adolescence, attribute the divided feelings
of teenage girls for their teachers and mothers to their both looking to them to
be close and look after them, and to their hating their shared low status as
women in male-dominated society. They write of the ambivalence of adolescent girls about their and their mothers' shared loves and fates.

Shared loves and fates

In her autobiography, and in her pioneering account of women's psychology
which she began not with childhood but with adolescence, the psychoanalyst,
Helene Deutsch, drew attention to the way in which pre-teen and teenage girls
look increasingly to their sisters and female friends as refuge from hated identification with their mothers on becoming women like them.[36] She recounted
adolescent girls' dread of becoming as oppressed, down-trodden, and
confined to the home as their mothers.

Deutsch wrote of her own divided love of her mother – of her hatred of
her mother for disappointing her longing for love. She remembered hating
her mother for not loving her. She remembered hating her mother for
beating her for not being the son her mother wanted in place of her feckless
older brother. She remembered hating her mother for expecting her, when
she left school at 14, to devote herself to finding a husband so as to become
a stay-at-home wife and mother as she was herself. Hating her mother – as
both snobbish and slavishly submissive to her father – Helene rebelled by
becoming a political activist. She ran away from home, and courted scandal
by having an affair with a married man – a prominent socialist leader.[37]

More often women recall warmer, albeit still ambivalent, memories of
teenage closeness with their mothers. They recall memories of their mothers
being those in whom they most confided their loves and hates in their teens.
Like Deutsch, however, they too recall their teenage horror of their mothers'
subjection to their fathers. Unlike Deutsch, who adored her father, many
remember dreading becoming as subject as their mothers to their fathers'
tyranny. They also luxuriate, however, in memories of their mothers siding
with them against their fathers. An example is Gwen, in her early fifties. She
tells me:

> My father was very Victorian in his attitude. . . . I wasn't allowed to go
> out with boys. I wasn't allowed to wear make up. I wasn't allowed to wear
> high-heeled shoes . . . and my mother was my ally in so much as she knew
> exactly what I was doing and kept quiet about it, and got into trouble
> afterwards if it was found out, which made it difficult for me because I
> would have preferred if it was me who got most of the flack. She got into
> a lot of trouble because I was disobeying my father and she knew about it.

Other women tell a different story. They talk of their fathers' response to their becoming adolescent not so much as bringing them together with their mothers, as dividing them from their mothers. Eileen, in her early sixties, complains that her father, having beaten her as he had her brothers and sisters when she was a child, became excruciatingly attentive to her in her early teens. His previous physical punishment of her now threatened to turn into sexual abuse. But what Eileen most hated was that his increasingly blatant fondness for her threatened to divide her from her mother. She says:

> he used to come in and give me big hugs, and my mother used to get very resentful, and I even got to the stage, I can't remember, perhaps 15, 16, when I seriously thought I'd run away and become a nurse to get away from this very tense situation . . . from the atmosphere that it created . . . because I wanted my mother to like me. My mother was there more. I was very fond of my mother. . . . I would have rather he didn't pay me as much attention, so Mummy would have. . . . She used to get very cross. Whether he was neglecting her or not, I don't know.

Unlike Eileen, many women remember knowing what their mothers felt when they were teenagers because their mothers told them. They remember their mothers telling them, amongst other things, about feeling cross and irritated with their fathers. Today's teenagers describe the similarities and differences they discover between themselves and their mothers on talking with them about their feelings, not least about the men in their life. One girl says of her mother:

> Umm (pause), she's a lot like me in good ways and bad ways. She's funny; she's good with people; she tends to be too sarcastic; I think that her experiences have made her kind of negative about men, about relationships and I think that's rubbed off on me and in a way it's good because, because I think I'm more wary, but I think it's also bad because I'm living through her experiences instead of making my own judgments. We get along very well, but the older I get and probably the more similar we get the less we get along. But we definitely go through phases. I mean she's been my best friend probably since I can remember[38]

Others find that girls not only confide in their mothers but also become increasingly involved with their mothers in other ways through their teens.[39] Or they name their mothers equally with a same-sex friend as those to whom they feel closest and to whom they talk most about their feelings.[40] Interviewing teenage girls and their mothers in England and America, the feminist psychologist Terri Apter finds that mothers and daughters are often intensely involved with each other in sharing their divided loves and hates.[41]

On the other hand, like Helene Deutsch as a teenager, the girls Apter interviewed dreaded having the same domestic fate as their mothers. They also dreaded having the same no-good jobs their mothers had. Like Deutsch, they also complained that their mothers were repressive and interfering. Like other researchers,[42] Apter also found that mothers complained about their daughters.

Alongside their complaints about each other, the mothers and adolescent daughters Apter interviewed also valued each other. Daughters valued the fact that, unlike their fathers, who only seemed to relate to them 'from the outside',[43] they and their mothers shared their inner feelings and thoughts. They appreciated their mothers understanding what was going on in their minds. They also valued knowing what was going on in their mothers' minds whereas, they grumbled, they had no idea what their fathers thought or felt. Unlike their mothers, they said, their fathers seldom said anything about their feelings. They complained that their fathers never reassured them by expressing or talking about their love for them.

Fathers made excuses for their silence. They told Apter of their uneasiness and inhibition about expressing or enabling their daughters to express and share their feelings with them. They explained their unease in terms of their daughters' increasing need for privacy through their teens. They said 'I don't want to intrude.' 'I have no business prying into that sort of thing.' 'It hasn't changed our relationship, I don't want her to think it has. But I can't barge in her bedroom like I used to'.[44]

Women often describe their distress as teenagers about becoming divided from their fathers because of their fathers' diffidence about remaining physically or emotionally close to them on their becoming women. The novelist, Carson McCullers, puts it thus in her novel, *The Member of the Wedding*, about a motherless young girl, Frankie, who, until her pre-teens, shares her father's bed:

> One night in April, when she [Frankie] and her father were going to bed, he looked at her and said, all of a sudden: 'Who is this great big long-legged twelve-year-old blunderbuss who still wants to sleep with her old papa?' And she was too big to sleep with her father any more. She had to sleep upstairs in a room alone. She began to have a grudge against her father and they looked at each other in a slant-eyed way. She did not like to stay at home.[45]

Daughters distance themselves from their fathers. Fathers distance themselves from their daughters out of fear of sexual intimacy and of the abuse that closeness might incur, and out of fear lest talking about feelings make them appear feminine or weak.[46] The teenage girls Apter interviewed complained that their fathers often restricted their talk to issuing orders. Or, if they did talk, they often seemed to regard this as a matter of reason not passion, of finding a cut-and-dried answer to their daughters' problems which, once discovered, meant there was no need for further talk, that there was nothing else to talk about. Or, if they did go on talking, they preferred to talk to their daughters about facts and ideas, not about feelings.

Daughters felt that their fathers often regarded what they said as boring or pointless. And indeed their fathers often dismissed what their daughters said as empty and tedious. One father candidly admitted:

> No, I don't talk to her for hours on end like her mother does . . . but most of what she talks about is drivel. You try to listen to it. You've listened to it! It's nothing. It goes on and on, and it's nothing.[47]

Furthermore, Apter found, if their daughters have an argument with them, instead of staying and talking things out, their fathers stalk off. They seldom return to pick up the threads. Nor do they stay to try to chivvy themselves or their daughters out of a huff, or out of being inhibited from talking. Apter puts it thus:

> Whereas mothers do tend to notice when a girl is reserved . . . fathers normally take a silent girl at face value. Mothers pry and nag and cajole a sulky daughter into speech, however negative; fathers are likely to let a girl remain silent if she wants to. They see it as 'her choice'.[48]

In keeping with the equation of femininity and masculinity with being and doing, the fathers Apter interviewed preferred action to words. They preferred not talking but doing things with their daughters. They preferred doing sports with them, and helping them with their school work, especially science. Their daughters often appreciated them in this respect. But when it came to sharing feelings – including their divided loves and hates – the girls Apter interviewed told her they usually got further with their mothers. And when it comes to sharing their feelings about sex and their divided relations with their peers, teenage girls often prefer talking with their friends,[49] as I will indicate next.

6　Divided friends

Feminists have increasingly investigated women's friendships with each other, not least to document the solidarity between women that feminism might draw on to get women collectively to expose, confront, and challenge the wrongs done them as women. With the revival of feminism in the late 1960s women's proclaimed 'sisterhood' became a by-word for their togetherness in campaigning for a better deal for their sex.

Whatever its feminist implications, recent research into women's friendships with each other reveals that from nursery school onwards – while boys often engage in more or less sophisticated 'rough and tumble' play, group games, and sport – girls more often get together in intimate and mutually confiding groups of two or three.[1] This continues into adolescence, with researchers finding that adolescent girls' friendships involve more self-disclosure, discussion of problems, sharing of emotions, and more mutual support, than the friendships of adolescent boys.[2]

Less often commented upon is women's awareness, again from their pre-school years, of divisions not only in their closeness with their mothers, but also in their friendships with each other as I will illustrate in this chapter, beginning with Margaret Atwood's particularly acutely observed fictional example in her novel, *Cat's Eye*.

Cat's Eye

Atwood tells her novel's story in flashback, through the eyes of its central protagonist, a middle-aged artist, Elaine. Elaine recalls, as though it were still going on, her teenage horror at her mother's depressed-seeming neglect of what she looks like to others:

> She is becoming even more indifferent to fashion, and strides around in improvised get-ups, a ski-jacket, an old scarf, mitts that don't match. She says she doesn't care what she looks like as long as it keeps out the wind.[3]

Mentioning her father only to dismiss him as 'largely invisible',[4] Elaine dwells at length on her and her friends' shared adolescent preoccupation with their mothers' and, more often, with other women's bodies:

> We look surreptitiously at the breasts of women on the street, of our teachers; though not of our mothers, that would be too close for comfort. . . . We can't ask our mothers. It's hard to imagine them without clothes, to think of them as having bodies at all, under their dresses.[5]

Elaine describes her own and her friend Cordelia's disgusted teenage fascination with:

> old ladies, or we think of them as old. . . . Some are respectably dressed, in tailored Harris tweed coats. . . . Others are poorer and foreign-looking. . . . Others are bulgy, dumpy, with clamped self-righteous mouths, their arms festooned with shopping bags; these we associate with sales, with bargain basements. Cordelia can tell cheap cloth at a glance. 'Gaberdine,' she says, 'Ticky-tack.'[6]

She remembers their shared pre-teen and teenage speculation about, and revulsion at the thought of, their teachers' underwear:

> My own teacher is Miss Lumley. It's said that every morning before the bell rings, even in late spring when it's warm, she goes to the back of the classroom and takes off her bloomers, which are rumoured to be of heavy navy-blue wool and to smell of mothballs and of other, less definable things.[7]

She describes her fear of the womanliness Miss Lumley's underwear signifies:

> I am afraid of these bloomers. I know it will be the worse for me if I ever actually catch sight of them. They're sacrosanct, at the same time holy and deeply shameful. Whatever is wrong with them may be wrong with me also, because although Miss Lumley is not what anyone thinks of as a girl, she is also not a boy.[8]

Elaine reviles the body and ungainly attire of her friend Grace's mother. She derides her appearance as a woman with the hint of also being a man:

> Over the dresses she wears bibbed aprons that sag at the bosom and make it look as if she doesn't have two breasts but only one, a single breast that goes all the way across her front and continues down until it joins her waist. She wears lisle stockings with seams, which make her legs look stuffed and sewn up the backs. She wears brown Oxfords. Sometimes, instead of the stockings, she has thin cotton socks, above which her legs

rise white and sparsely haired, like a woman's moustache. She has a moustache too, though not very much of one, just a sprinkling of hairs around
the corners of her mouth.[9]

In her paintings the adult Elaine mocks Grace's mother's breasts, as she
remembers them from her teens. She also remembers the teenage preoccupation of herself and her friends with their own womanhood – with their
growing breasts and first periods.

Above all, however, she remembers her dependency on her closest friends –
Grace, Cordelia, and Carol. She remembers their mercilessly exploiting her
dependency on them. She recalls their teasing and taunting her, knowing that
she will go along with whatever they make her do to keep them as her friends.
Their cruelty culminates in the novel's central episode in which the three girls'
bullying of Elaine ends in near disaster.

Walking home from school one day, through a snowstorm and growing
darkness, Cordelia throws Elaine's knitted hat into a gully. Then, together
with Grace and Carol, Cordelia dares Elaine to go down into the gully to
retrieve it. Terrified – given the gully's reputation as a haunt of the dead, and
of all the 'bad men' of the neighbourhood, 'the shadowy, nameless kind who
do things to you',[10] and even more terrified of being rejected and scorned by
her friends, Elaine descends. Slipping, she falls into the icy water of the creek.
She nearly drowns. It is only with great difficulty that she gets away – her shoes
are so waterlogged. But then she has a vision of the Virgin Mary cradling her
in her arms as though she, Elaine, were a cat's eye marble, exotic, 'clear glass
with a bloom of coloured petals in the centre',[11] 'valuable as a jewel'.[12] 'You
can go home now,' the figure says. 'It will be all right. Go home.'[13]

Somehow Elaine clambers out of the creek and gets herself home. Her
mother nurses her back to health. But it is the image of the Madonna that
most stays with her, and the impossibility, with the onset of adolescence, of
ever re-finding this icon of motherhood save as a remembered childhood
mirage. Grown up, she remembers this figure of the Virgin Mary as the
talisman protecting her from the triumvirate of her primary school friends,
still jeering at her from across the years, still watching over her from her pre-
teen and teenage years, solemnising over her adult fate as though they were
the reflected observers in Van Eyck's painting, *The Arnolfini Marriage*.

Recalling being bullied by her teenage friends, Elaine also recalls her
discovery, whilst still scarcely more than a child, that their tormenting her was
an attack on what they most hated and feared in themselves – their clinging
dependency on each other. Atwood fictionalises this dynamic. Others recall it
for real.

Bullies, enemies, and friends

Recalling the bullying and enmity she meted out when she was a teenager,
33-year-old Sophie describes herself as being:

such a relentless tormentor of a girl at secondary school that her victim's mother telephoned her to try to get her to stop. 'I just laughed,' says Sophie. 'To me, this girl was a nonentity with a bland personality. I didn't even hate her – she was there, like a dog waiting to be kicked. I bullied with indifference. . . . In some awful way, being horrible was a safety valve. . . . My parents were unpredictable, possessive and explosive. I never had tantrums or got angry. I was so nicey-nicey and desperate to please that there was no room for the vicious side of me.[14]

So she viciously attacked and bullied her 'nicey-nicey', 'bland', 'desperate to please' self in her fellow schoolgirl victim.

Perhaps it is women's emotional knowingness about their fellowship and mutual closeness with, and dependence on others that often makes their cruelty so well-honed. Interviewing students attending a private girls' school in Cleveland, Ohio, the feminist psychologist Carol Gilligan and her colleagues document the perspicacity of 7- and 8-year-old girls regarding their dependence on each other. They also document the girls' forthrightness in voicing their mutual likes and dislikes and differences which, they say, were they not voiced, might drive them apart. An example is Marianne who says:

There was someone that was a new girl and moved into someone else's house . . . and I didn't really like her that much, but my friend did, but then I learned to like her. . . . I just played with her a lot. It was because she always was like the boss, but then I told her, 'Hey, I don't like you being the boss,' and so, 'And I know another friend who played with you before, and she doesn't like you being the boss.' And then she stopped being the boss and I liked her.[15]

Whereas boys and men often cut themselves off, remain silent, sulk, or stalk off rather than stay and talk about the feelings of distress others arouse in them (as indicated in Chapter 5), Marianne and other 7- and 8-year-old girls in Gilligan's study talked of staying and talking with their friends about their divided loves for each other so as to promote their continuing togetherness. As another girl in this study, 8-year-old Jessie, put it in speaking about what happens when she feels excluded by her friends:

I would just go over to them, and go in the other friend's ear, I would kind of take them over somewhere else where the other of her friends couldn't hear, and I would say, 'This is really making me feel bad, for leaving me out. Can you please play with me too?' That 'I will go home if you don't, cause this isn't any fun for me just sitting here.'[16]

Returning to interview these girls three or four years later, however, Gilligan and her fellow-researchers found that their precision and candour, aged 7 and 8, about airing and detailing similarities and differences with each other in the

interests of securing and promoting their continuing friendship was regarded
by them, when they were 11 and 12, as endangering their continuing togetherness and as therefore not to be voiced. Whereas, when they were 7 and 8, they
emphasised the importance of openly sharing with their friends their likes and
dislikes so as to get on better with each other, they were much more diffident,
when they were 11 and 12, about voicing disagreements with each other lest
they offend or alienate their friends by thereby betraying themselves not to be
the 'perfect girl . . . the girl who speaks quietly, calmly, who is always nice and
kind, never mean or bossy'.[17] The above-quoted Jessie, for instance, says when
she is 11:

> Sometimes when you have friends and they are being real nice to you and
> you are trying to be nice to them and usually when you are nice to them,
> they are nice to you and sometimes when other people say something that
> everybody likes, and they say, 'Oh, that's a good idea,' and you have the
> exact opposite, you feel like 'Oh oh, they really won't want me to do this,
> or they won't want me in the club since I don't have good ideas,' and you
> sort of get afraid to say it. And sometimes you get afraid to say things like
> 'I hate you' when you're mad at somebody. . . . Because a lot of times they
> get really mad and it really terrifies you because you feel like they are
> going to tell somebody and they are going to get almost the whole class on
> her side and it would be one against, I don't know, ten.[18]

Gilligan and her colleagues say little about the increasing divisions in adolescence between girls and their parents contributing to girls increasingly turning
through their teens to dependency on, and closeness with their peers. They say
little about this as a factor contributing to girls in adolescence being increasingly wary of risking their togetherness with their friends by voicing
differences between them. Yet there is now considerable evidence of increasing
divisions in adolescence between girls and their fathers, and even more
between girls and their mothers,[19] and of these differences provoking many to
look to girls their own age as their closest confidantes,[20] albeit some find that
adolescent girls still experience more satisfaction from talking with their
mothers.[21]

Whatever the truth of the matter, women often talk of increasing divisions
between themselves and their parents on reaching adolescence. And they link
these divisions to friendships with other girls becoming increasingly important to them through their teens. One student writes of 'mental distance from
parents' leading her, aged 13, to 'wanting friends'. Another recalls 'wanting to
be independent from my parents . . . feeling that being accepted by my friends
was the most important thing in the world'. Others recall 'long talks' and
'chatting for hours'. A 20-year-old remembers break times at school:

> The boys used to play football and the girls would spend a lot of time
> walking around the school grounds. We would be split up into small

groups and would talk about how we felt about other people and tentatively about ourselves.

They remember their adolescent preoccupation with making and remaking friends. A psychology student writes of herself aged 14, 'Friends came and went. I had 2 "best friends" – we fell out and sometimes one was more "best" than the other'. Another student in her early twenties describes similar switchback advances and reverses in her friendships with other girls on starting secondary school. She describes being

> friends with Lucy and Nina at first. . . . Then moved on to Harriet as my best friend. . . . Also had fights/quarrels with her – she was quite weakwilled. Remember music lessons and conversations with other girls, telling me off for being nasty to her. 'Broke up' with her after silly argument. . . . Then hanging round with Delia (Nicole, Sally and Jane whom I didn't really get on with).

Recalling their teenage sensitivity – hyper-sensitivity even – to getting on and not getting on with their friends, women also remember their teenage longing to be reassured that not getting on with other girls had not lost them as friends. They remember their preoccupation with 'wanting to be liked'. They remember dreading 'not being one of the "in" group at school', and dreading not belonging to the 'popular group'. They remember 'falling out with friends being a major event, with everyone taking sides for what always became a major battle'. Like Elaine in *Cat's Eye* they remember learning, in early adolescence, that 'best friends can be treacherous when their own self-confidence and popularity is threatened'.

Teenage girls describe nightmares of their peers turning against them on sleepovers and school trips. They tell dreams of their best friends betraying, tricking, or laughing at them. A 13-year-old dreams:

> I was looking forward to going to Italy but as we were leaving, my friend said she couldn't go and if I went I would be wrong. I wanted to go to Italy but didn't understand my friend. In the end I got off the coach. It drove away and my friend's face was grinning at me through the window.

Less distanced and detached from their feelings of closeness with others than boys often are in growing up, more mindful of their feelings both of love and hate, girls often arrive at adolescence acutely aware that, just as they are driven by divided feelings, so too are their friends. Perhaps this is why, just as adolescent girls remember dreaming of turning against their friends, they remember dreams of their friends turning against them. They remember nightmares of 'evil children' taunting, catching, and threatening to beat them up, of girls at school ganging up on them – stabbing them, pushing them through windows, and laughing at them. They also remember dreams of themselves ganging up

on, and attacking their friends. A 14-year-old, after recalling a childhood
dream of a witch attacking, chasing and wanting to kill her, recalls a dream of
herself doing the witch-like, blood-sucking attacking:

> I was with my best friend and some other people in my class and we were
> all vampires. We all owned a shop but we were normal people in the day.
> Once, I went into our shop and said I was thirsty. We were the only people
> who knew what I was going on about. At night we would change into
> cloaks and go suck some blood. We had a morgue in the back of the shop
> where we kept our coffins.

Such dreams have recently become the subject of movies about teenagers – of
the film *Heathers*, for example, in which a group of schoolgirls, signalling
their togetherness by all adopting the same name (Heather), gang up on their
fellow-pupils. Just as this film recognises and depicts the closeness of teenage
girls with each other in sharing their feelings, both good and bad, so too does
the film, *Nightmare on Elm Street*, and its sequels, in which teenage girls share
their dreams just as they do in real life.[22] A 13-year-old writes of both having
the same dream as her friend and of the risk of being attacked by a girl like
her. She writes that in her most memorable recent dream:

> My Mum was very ill and my dad and sister were being kept in an old
> Edwardian house. . . . One night, I peered down the drive and saw a girl in
> a long white nightgown, big brown plaits, eyes, vampirish teeth, blood red
> lips and a pale white face . . . as soon as I got to the back door she pressed
> against me from behind. I ran again but she followed me. . . . I ended up
> along the glass corridor at school and she pressed me against the glass and
> columns. She pushed me through the glass. . . . She came down and
> stabbed me over and over again. . . . I woke up terrified. I had this dream
> 13 times, and then a little while ago, my friend had the same dream.

While this teenager and other teenage girls write about sharing their dreams,
others write about sharing and mirroring with others their feelings about their
changing teenage bodies.

Mirrored bodies

Summarising her findings regarding young women's memories of mirroring,
and talking with each other about their bodies, the psychologist Elizabeth
Kissling writes, 'The girls I spoke with especially value the information they
get about menstruation from their girlfriends'.[23] Kissling adds that talk about
menstruation and other taboo subjects increases solidarity between friends
and decreases their discomfort with such issues.[24] Other researchers report
that girls do best if they are maturationally 'in sync' with their peers.[25]

But, of course, being 'in sync', mirroring, and sharing their experience of becoming women, not only brings solidarity and togetherness. It also risks its opposite. Making bids for solidarity and togetherness with others risks their rejection. But their commitment to having friends often makes teenage girls resilient to such rejection. This was particularly eloquently expressed by Anne Frank when she and her family were in hiding, confined in an attic, during the war. In her diary, confided like the diaries of many other teenage girls to an imaginary friend, she wrote when she was 14:

> I remember that once when I slept with a girl friend I had a strong desire to kiss her, and that I did do so. I could not help being terribly inquisitive about her body, for she had always kept it hidden from me. I asked her whether, as a proof of our friendship, we should feel one another's breasts, but she refused. I go into ecstasies every time I see the naked figure of a woman, such as Venus, for example. It strikes me as so wonderful and exquisite that I have difficulty in stopping the tears rolling down my cheeks. If only I had a girlfriend![26]

Anne Frank was writing in January 1944. Over fifty years later Judy, in her early sixties, recalls in similar vein her teenage pleasure in lying together with her friend:

> She used to come back with me after school. These endless afternoons where you trail back from school, and decide whose house you'll go to. And I used to simply lie with her, on my bed. We'd talk about Keats or whatever. And we'd lay with our arms round each other. It was so lovely. And then we'd talk on the phone for three quarters of an hour. . . . I was in love with the girls at school and they with me. . . . Then I was also in love with someone called Rosalind. You just absorb somebody with your eyes. . . . In a sense you were looking at yourself, with a sense of pleasure in your own body, looking at them.

Writing about women's adolescent pleasure in looking at themselves in their friends, Terri Apter says that the young girl 'not only uses friends as mirrors, to persuade them to respond to what or who she is, but also chooses mirrors as friends, seeking to understand herself more by looking at girls very similar to her'.[27]

In *Cat's Eye* Margaret Atwood fictionalises the conflicts in adolescent girls resulting from their friends actually, as well as metaphorically, mirroring them:

> Cordelia brings a mirror to school. It's a pocket-mirror, the small plain oblong kind without any rim. She takes it out of her pocket and holds the mirror up in front of me and says, 'Look at yourself! Just look!' Her voice is disgusted, fed up, as if my face, all by itself, has been up to something, has gone too far.[28]

Teenage girls write stories of their preoccupation with their mirrored reflection. A 14-year-old tells a dream of 'walking around in a maze of mirrors'. Another tells a nightmare of going to a seaside arcade and getting 'attracted to the funny mirrors, which make you look all out of proportion (short and very fat, etc.)'.

In her book, *The Second Sex*, the pioneering feminist, Simone de Beauvoir, similarly emphasised the preoccupation of adolescent girls with being mirrored, with being surveyed by others, and with surveying themselves. She wrote that 'above all the lie to which the adolescent girl is condemned is that she must pretend to be an object, and a fascinating one, when she sees herself as an uncertain, dissociated being, well aware of her blemishes'.[29] The adolescent girl worries lest others see and reflect her to herself, as the above-quoted 14-year-old put it, 'all out of proportion'.

The art critic John Berger puts this preoccupation less in terms of women's relationships and togetherness with each other – the terms Apter and Atwood use to describe their mutual mirroring. Instead Berger puts it in terms of inner divisions in women. He assimilates their experience of mirroring to men's experience of being divided within themselves. He writes:

> A woman's being is split in two. A woman must continually watch herself. She is almost continually accompanied by her own image of herself. Whilst she is walking across a room or whilst she is weeping at the death of her father, she can scarcely avoid envisaging herself walking or weeping. From earliest childhood she has been taught to survey herself continually.[30]

Women themselves, however, describe this preoccupation not as an intrapsychic but as an interpersonal division. They describe their adolescent preoccupation less with surveying themselves than with being surveyed by others. Teenage girls recall dreams of wanting others to survey and look at their changing bodies – equated, in some instances, with being wounded or dismembered. A 13-year-old writes a dream of being shot 'four times in the chest' and 'showing my wounds off to my friends'. They write of their distress at others not noticing. Another 13-year-old dreams:

> I got to school and I didn't have my left arm. I told Dr Smith and she said all the science teachers would make me a new arm. I went to the lab and they made me an arm. They fixed it to my shoulder. I went back to my classroom and I was upset that no one knew about my new arm.

They dream of both wanting and not wanting others to know about and see their changing bodies and looks. Still another 13-year-old remembers dreaming of herself:

walking down the road and all I had on was my nightie. I went back home to change, but as I walked out the door and down the road again, I still only had my nightie on. No-one seemed to notice me though – it was as though they thought I was fully dressed. I also have had dreams about buying really unfashionable clothes.

They recall being picked on by other girls for being unfashionable or over-weight. One woman charts the ups and downs in her teenage friendships in terms of similarities and differences between herself and her friends mirroring their size and shape to each other. She writes:

When I was 14 I had a very tortuous friendship with somebody who even-tually turned anorexic. I yo-yoed in my weight but ended up increasing while she went the other way. That year the friendship broke up irreparably . . . it was a horrible, lonely year with no friends. . . . I felt as though there was nobody for me out there in the world. . . . I felt trapped in a golden cage . . . an awful year.

They remember talking with each other about their changing bodies. A 19-year-old remembers 'showers at school where everyone talked about how they were developing. Bras, periods, etc.'. They remember envying others starting menstruating before they did. Another student writes:

When I was 12/13 years old everyone at school was fascinated by periods and sex. There was a book that went round the whole class about a boy who had his first girlfriend and they called his willy Ralph. Book – *Forever Judy Blume*. I can't remember much else apart from everyone waiting for the book – hiding it from their parents.

They remember mutual 'drooling over film stars'. They remember sharing with each other their first experiences of romance and sex.

Romance and sex

They remember the likes and dislikes involved. A 21-year-old writes of herself aged 14:

I used to go around with three very good friends and we used to spend a lot of time doing each other's hair and make-up, lot of time at each other's houses, talking about men (boys!) who we fancied, who we didn't fancy but thought would like us, who liked us, who we thought liked each other. Gossiped about other people, what they did, who they were going out with.

Women remember sharing with each other their experience of their first kiss. Having talked extensively with their friends about it at the time, they often remember the occasion in detail. Nina, in her early forties, remembers she was 13, that she was staying with her grandparents, and that the kiss happened when they took her to a dance. She still remembers the name of the hotel. Her memory only becomes patchy when it comes to the lad who kissed her. She thinks he was probably a trainee chef, but she isn't sure. She didn't talk to him much. But she did talk to her friend immediately after he kissed her. And she remembers exactly what she was wearing:

> this white outfit. It had no sleeves, which was very unusual for me, because I don't like anything without sleeves now. I was completely flat-chested. That's right. We bought my first bra as well, and my grandma stuffed it with hankies. And I think it was only a 32A then. But I think she stuffed it with hankies. And I had this outfit. And culottes. It was this all-in-one piece with culottes.

As for the kiss, what she emphasises most was its value as shared currency with her friends. She says:

> All we talked about [when we were 13] was had you been kissed, and had you had your periods. All the girls were desperate to be kissed. I don't think it mattered if it was a gorilla that kissed them. It was more a thing to tell my friends – that I'd had my first kiss – rather than the kiss itself.

Others remember 'the kiss itself'. Again, they remember the occasion in detail, having talked about it with other women both then and since. After all, as Cathy, another woman in her forties points out in sharing it with me, as she had with her friends as a teenager, her first kiss was done mainly to impress her peers. She remembers it all – 'what he tasted like' – her fear and most of all the kudos it gave her with other girls. She also remembers her mixed feelings about the bodily togetherness involved:

> I probably blocked out the sense that it was quite frightening by, probably what I did for quite a long time, was actually standing in its place was the fact that this was a very high status activity that I was engaging in here, being kissed in the double seats in the pictures, by a boy, which put me ahead of the game as far as other girls were concerned. . . . And it was frightening, kind of strange, as in like this is very odd. . . . I suppose it's very vivid because it's the first intimate encounter with another human body . . . a real feeling of being a grownup, a strange grownup experience. And I didn't dislike it because I was so transfixed by how meaningful it was.

A 13-year-old similarly shared with me, her unknown reader, her ambivalence about being kissed. She wrote of her best remembered recent dream:

> I was at home sitting on the sofa in the kitchen with everything in the kitchen as it should be. My mum, dad and older brother were also in the kitchen and a boy called Shane was sitting next to me. Then we started kissing each other and while he was kissing me, my mouth had disgusting flavoured herbs and spices in it and felt really dry. I didn't want to stop kissing Shane so I carried on.

But girls are also mindful that, in sharing with others their actual as opposed to their dreamt-of experience of being kissed and of having boyfriends and sex, they risk alienating and becoming divided from their friends. They risk making themselves or their friends feel uncomfortable, triumphed over, or left out. They fear lest their friends reject them on this account. No wonder. Many teenage girls do indeed reject their friends on their getting involved with having boyfriends.[31]

The mindfulness of adolescent girls of this possibility – and of the possibility of others rejecting, disapproving, or thinking ill of them for having a boyfriend – was nicely expressed by a 12-year-old who wrote of her best remembered recent dream:

> I was in bed in my dormitory [at camp] and I heard a handful of gravel hit the window. I went over and opened it. Kevin and his friend climbed up a tree and got in. I slept with Kevin and I thought 'I wonder what Anna will think I am two years younger than her and I am sleeping with a boy and she hasn't kissed one yet'.

Others recall nightmares of being irrevocably divided from their friends by having boyfriends. Fifteen-year-old Amanda tells a researcher of an awful fight between her friend and herself regarding her friend's boyfriend:

> Like the other night she called me and I was just so mad. I was like, 'I'm just fucking friends with him!' And I was yelling 'cause I have a big mouth and then she said something, something . . . I can't remember but something 'cunt' and then she was like, 'I'm gonna nail you'. And I was like, I'd kill her. She's so stupid, I could kill her. But like I wouldn't touch her unless she touched me first.[32]

Like Amanda, other young women recall nightmarish battles with their friends about their boyfriends. They also recall wish-fulfilling dreams of mollifying or being mollified by their friends for having or not having boyfriends. They recall dreams that, far from having boyfriends dividing them, they and their best friend are united by both having boyfriends, as in the following 14-year-old's dream:

My best friend (V. J.) and I were going on this camp with other people from our year. My younger brother and lots of his friends went too. V. J. and I went to see them and I fell in love with this older kid. He was really cute. Then we all went to the pub and V. J. also fell in love. It was nice.

Perhaps it was a similar wish-fulfilling longing for sex not to divide them from their family and friends that impelled the only two teenage girls in my study, who described manifestly sexual dreams, to describe them in terms of group sex. One girl, aged 17, told a dream of:

A sex-session between my parents and me and my brother. I remember questioning the moral tastelessness in the dream, but everyone else was saying: go on, go ahead. Never reached full blown sex (thank God!).

Meanwhile a 13-year-old wrote:

This is quite rude but we were all having sex. I was with Steve, Sue was with Ben and Anna was with Simon and Brian. And then Anna, Sue and I started running, hopping, and jumping with orange and pink scarves around us and nothing else on.

But as these two teenagers' *caveats* about the 'rudeness' and 'tastelessness' of their dreams indicate, teenage girls are wary of sharing their dreams about sex lest they thereby excite others' disapproval and dislike. Perhaps this was why, unlike boys, and unlike the above-quoted girls, no other student from the girls' school in my study wrote an explicit dream about incest, masturbation, or sex – lesbian or straight. Instead, if they told dreams of romance, they couched them in terms of holding hands, hugging, and 'general comforting contact . . . but not in a sexual way', as one 17-year-old emphasised.

Some deplore the unwillingness and resistance of teenage girls to write or talk about sex, or to discuss it only in covert terms, or in terms of guilt, anxiety about pregnancy, and fear of being found out.[33] The US feminist psychologist, Michelle Fine, deplores 'the anti-sex rhetoric' conditioning adolescent girls into talking about sex in terms of exploitation and abuse – a rhetoric which, she says, also silences girls about their pleasure in sex.[34] Doubtless their inhibitions about alienating others by talking about their agency in sex contributes to adolescent girls often portraying themselves as passive victims of, or as passive participants in sex, with many talking about their first experience of sex as painful, boring, or disappointing.[35]

Yet they are often not at all inhibited about talking about their agency in sex. Certainly researchers have recently concluded that their findings indicate that young women are wary of revealing what they feel and think about sex. Yet their findings also indicate that, as well as being wary, teenage girls are often very willing – and are often much more willing than teenage boys – to talk honestly and openly in one-to-one conversation with young women researchers about their first experiences of, and mixed feelings about, sex.[36]

This might be an effect of teenage girls being seduced into confessing and thus producing themselves in terms of currently dominant ways of speaking about ourselves that equate our subjectivity and individuality with what we are and do sexually. Some, moreover, modelling themselves on men's phallic brag, talk about themselves in its terms, thereby seeking to subvert through parody its male-centred alienation of women from what they want sexually as female-centred individuals.[37] More often, however, as I have sought to illustrate and explain, women talk about their experience of adolescence less in terms of their individuality than in terms of their togetherness with, and ambivalence about, their togetherness with others. It is in these terms, as we will now see, that women also often describe the depression and eating disorders many first begin to suffer in their teens.

7   Depressed and eating disordered ambivalence

Young men, as I have said, are more at risk than young women of schizoid and suicidal self-division and self-destruction. Young women, by contrast, are more at risk of depression and eating problems, which, as I will illustrate later in this chapter, they often explain in terms of divided love and hate for those to whom they are closest in adolescence. Possibly young women's mindfulness of their divided feelings is due to their becoming generally more mindful than young men of their feelings in their teens. Certainly teenage girls more often than teenage boys describe themselves in terms of what they feel rather than in terms of what they do.[1] This includes more often describing themselves as dispirited and depressed.

Depression

Perhaps girls more often talk about being depressed because they anticipate more adverse, depressing-making experiences as adults. They learn at an early age that, as women, they are likely to be expected to sacrifice and subordinate their needs to those of others, both at home and at work. They can see the loneliness and poverty of many women in looking after their children and other dependents in their family. They can also see other problems women suffer – including poor pay, discrimination, sexual harassment, violence, and abuse.

The above might well contribute to the increased rate of depression in girls compared to boys through adolescence. Whatever the cause, researchers find that, although there is little difference in the rates of depression in girls and boys before the age of 11 (with any difference tending in the direction of boys more often being depressed),[2] girls in their teens are much more likely to be depressed. By the age of 16 they are twice as likely as boys to suffer significant depressive symptoms.[3]

Some argue that the increased rate of depression in girls through their teens is due, at least in part, to puberty.[4] Interviewing black and white, working- and middle-class 14- to 19-year-olds, US psychologist Karin Martin concludes that depression and decreasing self-esteem in girls in adolescence is due to puberty exacerbating their lack of sexual agency at a time when their sense of themselves as sexual is first being consolidated. Martin argues that this is compounded by prevailing negative stereotypes of women's sexuality as dirty, taboo, 'scary', and dangerous. This contributes, she maintains, to many teenage girls being unhappy with themselves, their bodies, and their first experiences of menstruation and sex.

The only exceptions, Martin finds, are girls who gain a sense of agency through sport and school, and through being affirmed by their mothers.[5] Martin illustrates this in terms of a 14-year-old, Erin, who comes from a predominantly working-class state high school. She talks of her mother affirming her good looks, sharing with Erin her experience of menstruation, and talking with her about sex. Erin indicates that this is a major factor contributing to her feeling good about herself, not least in asserting herself with her boyfriend in telling him she is not yet ready for sex.

By contrast, says Martin, others suffer the depressing-making injuries to their self-esteem of not being affirmed by their mothers. Other researchers similarly argue that the depression suffered by girls in their teens is not due to puberty *per se*,[6] but to associated interpersonal factors and stresses[7] – particularly to stresses interpreted by girls as threatening their closeness with others. Some find that the two most powerful predictors of depression in girls are paternal rejection and maternal control,[8] with the self-esteem of girls being crucially linked to the quality of their interaction with their mothers.[9] While boys are found to link depression with factors unconnected with others – for instance, with not being as intelligent as they want to be – girls link depression with falling short of their ideals regarding their closeness with, and attractiveness to others.[10] Similarly, whereas researchers associate self-poisoning in teenage boys to their not having a job, or to their use of alcohol and drugs, they associate similar self-harm in teenage girls to interpersonal relationship difficulties.[11]

It is not only researchers and teenage girls who relate their ills to their relationships with others. So too do grown women. Repeatedly women referred for psychiatric help trace the first onset of their ills to the depression they suffered in their teens on losing those to whom they were then closest, and to not being able to share with others their feelings and unhappiness at the time.

Twenty-five-year-old Carol[12] tells her psychiatrist that the eating disorder for which she now wants help is linked to the depression – indeed the 'major trauma' as she puts it – that she experienced when her father died when she was 14. He died of lung cancer and brain secondaries after two and a half years' illness during which, although Carol was attending school, she spent much of her time nursing him, and getting up in the night to look after him. Following his death, she says, she could not bring herself to talk about him. She banished all photographs of him from the house, and, according to the psychiatrist's report, still misses him dreadfully.

Similarly a woman GP, referring a 13-year-old girl, Mandy, for psychiatric help, describes the loss of her father, and her inability to talk about her feelings about it, contributing to her depression. She writes:

Her parents separated a year ago. Very depressed and withdrawn. Doesn't see father. Mother says Mandy still wants 'things to be as they were'. Father is with another woman who has three children. Mandy sees them being driven to school every day in father's car, while she has to walk several miles to school. So withdrawn difficult to communicate with her.

Writing generally about women's psychological ills, Freud long ago noted that, whereas unhappiness in men and boys is often due to inward division and fear of losing their masculinity and being castrated, unhappiness in women is often due to fear of losing the love and closeness of others.[13] Today many young women, like Carol and Mandy quoted above, still trace their teenage unhappiness to loss of their fathers. Many more trace their teenage depression to loss of their mothers. Or, rather, they trace their teenage depression to loss of the possibility of sharing and talking with their mothers about their feelings because of their mothers' depression.

Depressing mothers

Examples include Sonia, whom I saw in therapy some years ago when she was in her early thirties. She traced the first onset of her continuing depression to her mother's depression through her teens. It was when she was a teenager, she said, that she lost all hope of ever sharing what she felt and thought with her mother. It was then, with the psychological-mindedness of adolescence, that she first became aware of not making any emotional impact on her mother, of not being able to bring her back to life from the misery and gloom she now increasingly experienced as her mother's pervading state of mind. She experienced herself, as a teenager, as being as miserable as her mother and as therefore being unable to do anything to help her.

Increasingly through her teens Sonia despaired of herself and her mother ever confiding and helping each other by sharing and thereby resolving their likes and dislikes of each other. She despaired of ever sharing their similarities and differences, their loves and hates. She despaired of ever establishing the mutually confiding togetherness with her mother or with other girls that (as we have seen in Chapters 5 and 6) young women often regard as crucial to their continuing closeness with their mothers and friends through adolescence.

Sonia's mother either ignored her, or agreed with whatever Sonia said. There was no sharing, no communication between them. Sonia could not bear being with her mother, either then or since, so much did their being together evoke both Sonia's longing to be emotionally close to her mother, and her hatred of her mother's continuing distance from her in never talking to her about what she thought, felt, or did.

Ann, whom I met through her referral for social work help in her mid-forties, told a similar story. She too dated the first onset of her continuing depression to deteriorating closeness with her mother from early adolescence onwards. She attributed the first onset of her depression to her mother's response to her failure, aged 11, to secure the grammar school place her mother wanted for her. From being a wonderfully comforting mother – whom Ann remembered as previously always singing and kind, cuddly and close – her mother now changed, in the 11-year-old Ann's mind, as she now remembers it, into an imprisoning monster.

Ashamed of Ann's failure, as though it were her own, her mother kept her home from school. Thereby separated from other girls with whom she might have shared her woes, Ann was also unable to share what she felt with her mother, because her mother now increasingly withdrew from Ann into depressed misery. She also persecuted and imprisoned Ann. She would not let her out of the house. She provided her with no heat or light, apart from candles. She barely fed her, and in her more mad moments she even threatened to kill her.

Fearful lest she might indeed kill her, Ann's mother wrote to the School Board to warn them. Years later, still muddling herself with her mother as though they were both as guilty as each other, Ann remembers her mother's letter provoking the School Board into punishing both of them by taking them in a 'Black Maria' to a police station, from where Ann was sent first to boarding school, and then to live with her father, long since divorced from her mother.

Her father told her that her mother was evil, that she had wanted to kill her. It seemed that her father felt Ann, too, was evil, or at least that he no more liked her than he liked her mother. Why else, but through dislike of her, Ann asked herself, did he send her away to foster parents almost immediately she arrived to live with him and his new family? He said he wanted Ann out of his house because his new mother-in-law was coming to stay and he did not want her to know of his previous marriage, and of Ann's existence. Evidently he did not want Ann to be with him.

But, whatever her father's rejection of her, it was above all in terms of her mother, not her father, that Ann remembers the depression she suffered in her teens. She tells me that when she was 13, and learnt from her father that, because of her mother's murderousness, she would never live with her again, she became bitterly depressed at thereby losing all hope of ever being close with her mother as she had been as a child. She became so depressed she could not talk. She became dumb with grief. In her silence she became fused and confused with her mother – not with the cuddling mother she remembered from her early years, but with the nightmare image of her mother she remembered from when she was 11. She found herself identifying with her mother as the horrible, persecuting witch she pictured her as being in punishing and imprisoning her for failing her grammar school entrance exam.

Ann blamed her hatred of her mother for losing her both her mother and her mother's love. Had she not hated and complained, to her older sisters for instance, of her mother's cruelty and murderous threats, she told herself, she might not have been sent away. Had she not complained her mother might not have nearly starved herself to death, as Ann later learnt she did, out of grief at losing her.

Separated from her mother, and unable to talk either with her or others about her mixed feelings of love and hate, Ann sought to comfort herself with sex, into which she was initiated, aged 13, when she was living with her father, and a stranger sexually assaulted her in the park. Ann felt it was her fault. She also hated herself for wanting sex and the stranger's physical closeness with her again. She had a succession of one-night stands. She also sought to comfort herself with food, as babies are comforted by their mothers breast- or bottle-feeding them.

But, seeking to replace lack of physical and emotional closeness with her mother with food and sex made Ann hate and despise herself all the more. Neither food nor sex consoled or filled her need for comfort. Neither allayed the depression she felt at losing her mother whom she both longed to be together with – so much so she cultivated the same Welsh accent as her mother – whilst also remembering her early adolescent togetherness with her as hatefully frightening and oppressive.

Ann felt similarly beleaguered by the idea of being with me. That was why, it transpired, she never answered my appointment letters. That was why, when I made a home visit, she initially ignored my knock at the door. It was only later when, having let me in, and having gradually begun to assimilate me to her childhood image of her mother as comforting and reassuring, that she began to relax. It was only then that she began sharing with me, as she had been unable to share with her mother, or with other girls when she should have started secondary school, her mixed feelings of love and hate. Eating, she told me, was still a problem. But it was, and always had been, peripheral to her other woes.[14] For many, however, eating is central to their experience of adolescence.

Eating problems

Retaining from infancy awareness of the importance to them of their closeness with others, and early taught that to secure others' closeness and love they must be beautiful and thin, many girls in adolescence worry lest eating and puberty make them unlovably ugly and fat. Every teenager, except one, interviewed in a recent US survey said she was too big or too fat.[15] Unlike boys, girls regularly report being dissatisfied with their bodies, following puberty.[16] Physically mature girls are more likely than physically mature boys to describe themselves as being unhappy about being too heavy.[17] While early maturing boys often declare themselves satisfied with their height and weight, early maturing girls are often particularly dissatisfied with their size, with the majority wanting to be thinner.[18]

It is no surprise therefore to find that the incidence of eating disorders sharply increases in girls in early adolescence. The rate of both anorexia and bulimia is approximately ten times higher in women than in men in their teens and early twenties.[19] Some find that these disorders are more likely to occur in early maturing girls.[20] Others dispute whether biological maturation – puberty – is the main cause.[21] Rather it seems that a variety of psychosexual changes involved in girls becoming women contributes to their increasingly succumbing to eating disorders through their teens.[22]

Classically, psychoanalysis has attributed eating disorders in teenage girls to their defensive regression, with adolescence, from adult sexuality to child-hood preoccupation with being close to their mothers through food,[23] and with their equating baby-like closeness with their mothers with incest. Thus, for example, therapist Rosalind Joffe,[24] working with 16-year-old Mary at London's Brent Consultation Centre after Mary became anorexic and attempted suicide, attributes Mary's anorexia to puberty causing her to experience as sexual, and therefore incestuous, her continuing longing to be looked after physically by her mother. Defending against this longing, Joffe argues, Mary experienced not herself but her mother and Joffe as seducing her into wanting to be close to them. Joffe also traces Mary's teenage dread and yearning for continuing closeness with her mother to adolescence exacerbating her experience of her mother as threatening to intrude her depression into her, as she felt she had done ever since Mary was 2 years old.

Some therapists explain adolescent girls' experience of their mothers as intrusive and depressed as a legacy of their having resolved their innate, instinctually- and internally-given feelings of love and hate for their mothers as babies by getting rid of their hatred into their mothers. Girls then grow up experiencing their mothers, not themselves, as hated and hateful, and as retaliating by intruding back into them both their hatred and the depression it causes them. Hence Mary's and other anorexic girls' feeling that their mothers intrude their misery into them, against which they defend themselves by not taking anything in, least of all food.

Whereas some therapists understand young women's eating problems as stemming from instinctually-given feelings of love and hate, independent of whatever the mother herself does, others understand these problems as primarily the mother's fault. They argue that young women's eating problems stem from their mothers depriving them emotionally or physically as babies. They argue that, as babies, both girls and boys seek to manage deprivation by their mothers by internalising and controlling them as divided – exciting and frustrating, tantalising and depriving – figures within them.

Whether or not the original cause of young women's eating disorders lies in innately-given instincts or in their mothers depriving them as babies, Freudians claim that adolescence exacerbates the girl's image of her mother as a longed for, tantalising, and hated internal and intrusive figure, not only in her mind but also in her body, in so far as she experiences adolescence making her physically the same as her mother. Some argue that the experience of being bodily the same as their mothers is the cause of adolescent girls resorting to anorexic and bulimic self-purging and self-starvation as a means of attacking their mothers in themselves.[25]

Although Freudian therapists recognise that women's problems (including their eating problems) often differ from those of men in involving them, ambivalently, both wanting and not wanting to be the same as their mothers,[26] these therapists often overlook the wider social factors contributing to girls not wanting to become women like their mothers. They often overlook the extent to which the pervasive social devaluation of – or, at best, ambivalence about – women as sexually and reproductively mature beings, contributes to the negative or ambivalent feelings of many teenage girls on becoming women. Feminists are more mindful of these and other social factors contributing to the eating problems in which these mixed feelings often eventuate.

Susan Bordo explains young women's ambivalent anorexic restraint and bulimic excess in terms of the contradictory injunction by capitalist society to women, as well as to men, both to restrain and discipline themselves as workers, and to indulge themselves as consumers.[27] Bordo also draws attention to the prevailing misogyny about women's bodies, and to current media pressure on women both to indulge and to discipline their bodies which, she says, makes this contradiction particularly acute for them.

In the past, as Mary Wollstonecraft observed at the end of the eighteenth century, women were pressurised to look good so as to win a husband to support them. Now that women are increasingly supporting themselves they are still pressurised into making themselves look good. Or, as the US feminist Naomi Wolff puts it in her book, *The Beauty Myth*, discrimination against women in terms of their appearance has become a new means of controlling them in today's backlash against the gains won by feminism. As a result, women often equate their problems with what they look like. For many teenage girls, as one research report puts it, 'feeling fat has become synonymous with feeling bad'.[28]

A student in my study describes herself, aged 13, as 'feeling fat, ugly and unloved at home'. Similarly 17-year-old Jennifer, referred to a clinic for treatment of her bulimic response to her father leaving home in her early teens, describes not her unhappiness at his going away but her unhappiness about being fat:

> Every time I ate I made myself sick because I think I'm fat. . . . Every time I look at myself I think I'm ugly and fat. I see all these beautiful girls and models who are popular and good looking. They have all the guys and then I look at myself. Ugh! What a horrible sight. No guys wanted to go out with me and complete strangers come up and tell me how ugly and fat I am. They really hate me because of the way I am.

Feminist therapists draw attention to the possibility that one factor contributing to women's hatred of themselves for being fat might be their interpreting their mothers' depletion in mothering – due to the social discrimination exercised against them as mothers – as an effect of their having enviously spoiled and greedily drained them in feeding from them as babies, and as an effect of them growing up and leaving their mothers. Daughters, therapist Kim Chernin claims,[29] feel more guilty than sons in this respect because, whereas society encourages boys to grow up and become independent and different from their mothers, society encourages girls to remain close to their mothers, and to become women like them. It is young women's resistance to this pressure, writes Chernin, that contributes to their anorexically and bulimically seeking to become as thin and unmotherly-looking as possible, whilst at the same time punishing themselves for their urge to be different with self-starving and purging atonement.

Other feminist therapists, notably Susie Orbach,[30] argue that women's eating problems are due to their mothers teaching them as girls to deny and subordinate their needs to others in preparing them to look after their partners and children as women and mothers. Women, Orbach and others argue, often suffer anorexic self-denial and indiscriminate bingeing in ignorance of what they want, or self-purging out of guilt about indulging their needs because they have been taught as children to deny what they want.[31] Girls learn this lesson from their mothers, it is argued, not least through their mothers not feeding them as much as they feed their sons,[32] and through their mothers being less sensitive to their feelings and moods than they are to those of their sons as babies.[33]

Orbach argues that, in face of the relative lack of responsiveness of their mothers to them as babies, women learn early to sacrifice their wants to those of their mothers. Orbach likens this process to that by which the psychoanalyst Donald Winnicott says both sexes learn in infancy to comply with, and go along with what their mothers want, in so far as their mothers are too depressed or preoccupied with their own needs to take in, or respond to what they want.[34]

Unlike Winnicott, Orbach and other feminist therapists draw attention to the sexual inequalities involved. They draw attention to the fact that, because childcare and mothering are still assigned primarily to women, women as mothers are the most immediately obvious people to blame when things go wrong.[35] This includes women blaming their adolescent anorexia and bulimia on their mothers failing to share with them their feelings, including their divided feelings of love and hate, as I will illustrate with two examples from my work as a therapist. They concern two women whom I will call Eva and Daisy.

Bulimic mother-blaming

Eva was in her late twenties when she was referred for therapy. She had been urged to come for help by her husband because she had spent all their savings financing her bingeing and purging, which she now did six or seven times a day. Like many women, Eva attributed her bulimia to having been sexually abused.[36] She first became bulimic, she told me, after her uncle (her father's brother) sexually abused her in her early teens. But she did not blame her uncle for sexually abusing her. Nor did she blame her father. Like many sexually abused women, she blamed her mother, not the men who had abused and connived in her abuse.

Just as many women link their negative experiences of menstruation to their mothers not sharing with them and warning them about this aspect of their becoming sexually mature (as I have illustrated in Chapter 5), Eva linked her uncle abusing her to her mother not sharing with her, preparing her for, and warning her about sex. Had her mother warned her, Eva felt, she might have been more ready to anticipate and protect herself against her uncle's advances. As it was, she said, since her mother had not shared her feelings about sex with her, she felt inhibited from sharing with her mother her experience of sex – the fact that her uncle had abused her. Anyway, even if she had tried to talk to her mother about it, Eva complained, her mother would not have believed her. Her mother reckoned herself to be so 'perfect', such a 'queen', so above it all. She never noticed, or credited other people with having wants, needs, failings, or weaknesses. Had Eva tried to confide in her mother, her mother would not have wanted to know.

Feeling abandoned by her mother, Eva sought to recreate the closeness she looked for with her mother through mothering herself. That was why she first started making herself sick, she told me, so as to mother and protect herself. She made herself sick so as to have an excuse to stay home rather than go out with her parents when they visited her abusive uncle. She continued to make herself sick. She also spent hours exercising. Otherwise, with all the food she ate, she explained, she would become hideously fat, and then nobody would love, care for, or be emotionally close to her. She would become divided not only from her mother but also from her friends and everyone else.

As for her eating so much, she blamed that, too, on her mother. She told me she first used food to comfort herself when her mother left her when she was 5, to go out to work. It was then, Eva said, that she first began bingeing – on ice cream. Not only had her mother not been home to look after her, Eva complained, she had also never given Eva half the treats she gave Eva's brothers. And she ruined what little she did give Eva by insisting she be grateful. Forced thanks ruined what little her mother gave her. Nothing her mother gave her was any good. It never filled her up. Nor, in taking her mother's place, was she able to fill herself up. That was why her appetite was so insatiable. That was why it knew no bounds. That was why she binged.

She longed for her mother to mother her. Perhaps that was why she also could not bear to be with her mother – because of the unbearable longing for closeness that her mother's physical proximity to her provoked. She also found being with her mother unbearable because it reminded her both of her longing to be with her and of her contrary longing to get away. She could not abide being with her mother. They were so horribly alike. Her mother, she said, thought of herself as a queen. But in fact, said Eva, her mother was 'common'. So was Eva. Her mother was 'petty'. So was Eva. It was the little things, Eva said, she hated most about being with her mother. She hated the way she scratched at her legs. But Eva also scratched. She scratched at the arm of the chair in which she sat through her sessions with me.

Divided between wanting and not wanting to be close to her mother, she sought to escape. That was what drove her, starting in her early teens, to have one boyfriend after another. That was what drove her into marrying the father of her children. Now she wanted to escape from him too. He had become just like her mother. He no sooner suggested something she might do than, like her mother, he put obstacles in the way of Eva doing what he suggested. She was finished with him. There was no point, therefore, in the two of them having family therapy.

As for individual therapy with me, I too was no good. I too was just like her mother. Women had never been any use or help to her. She was not 'a woman's woman,' she said. Men had always been much kinder and more understanding. Anything I gave by way of help was useless, just as whatever her mother gave her was useless. Therapy with me left her still having to look after and mother herself even though she was patently not up to the job, as she made obvious in always arriving for her therapy sessions in a terrible mess. She complained that she was eating more than ever. It was my fault, just as it was her mother's fault when she was a teenager, that she remained as messy and bulimic as ever.

Mothering anorexia

Whereas Eva made abundantly clear the disorderliness and mess of her life, Daisy, a lawyer whom I saw in therapy when she was in her mid-thirties, presented herself as being entirely orderly and in control. She linked her presenting symptoms – her depression at so often disappointing her ideal of herself as perfect wife and mother by angrily shouting at her husband and children whenever they did not do her bidding – to her anorexic control over herself and others, beginning in her mid-teens.

Freud attributed the anorexic and other symptoms of his 18-year-old patient Dora (whose case I described in Chapter 1) to a division he assumed to exist within her between wanting and not wanting incest with her father. He attributed Dora's anorexia to her displacing and changing her incestuous desire for her father into oral preoccupation with feeding and food.[37] By contrast with Dora, Daisy said little about her father in explaining her problems save to dismiss him as useless for not protecting her from her mother. She complained that her father only related to her 'on the surface' – superficially.

It was not her father but her mother whom she blamed for her teenage anorexia. She talked to me of her divided teenage longing for, and loathing of, her mother's closeness with her. She talked again and again of her mother never cuddling her, and of her being 'forbidding', and not 'warming to her'. She remembered her mother letting her know that she found Daisy's yearning for her love 'insatiable' and an 'encumbrance'. She assumed that it was because her mother found her longing for love so encumbering that, when Daisy was 15, her mother left the family – to get away from Daisy.

Just as her mother seemingly could not bear, and seemingly sought to get away from, the encumbering ambivalence of being with Daisy, Daisy could not bear the ambivalence of being with her mother. She remembered her teenage dread of being overwhelmed by, or fragmented by, being with her mother. She could not bear to be too close to her. Her mother's emotional 'intensity', she said, threatened to do away with her image of herself as free as air, as 'happy-go-lucky'. As a teenager, she dreaded being enmeshed with her mother. She likened being with her mother to a film of a Russian and an American trapped in each other's countries.

Daisy talked of her spurned childhood love of her mother turning in her teens to virulent hatred of her. Like Gwendolen Harleth in George Eliot's novel, *Daniel Deronda*, confessing to Deronda her conviction that she had willed her husband's death, Daisy confessed to me her conviction that she had willed her mother's death. Her mother dying when she was 20, Daisy told me, was her (Daisy's) doing. How else but by making her mother die could she get away from her? Rather than staying together to sort out their divided love and hate of each other, she said, the only solution she felt as a young woman was to get rid of her mother.

As well as remembering wanting her mother dead, Daisy also remembered her mother wanting her dead. She described her mother's eyes as 'laser beams' murderously penetrating into her. She remembered her mother's hateful 'physicality', her gestures, mannerisms, and 'thereness'. She remembered her mother imprisoning her in a suffocating cupboard, and 'in the bathroom, a small room'. She remembered 'not being able to get away'. These images were so frightening, Daisy indicated, that she fled them at the time rather than talk about, share, or seek to allay and resolve with her mother the problems giving rise to them.

Unlike many of the mothers and adolescents interviewed by feminist psychologists (as described in Chapter 5), Daisy remembered feeling completely unable, as a teenager, to share with her mother their divided feelings about and for each other. Years later, however, she shared her love and hate of her mother with me. She told me of her teenage longing both to be and not to be the same as her mother.[38] She told me how she had recently tried on an all-in-one slip of her mother's only to be bitterly disappointed that, despite now being a woman and a mother herself, she still remained so different from her mother – a child, not 'rounded ... womanly ... grown up', she said, like her.

She also told me of her teenage dread of becoming a woman like her mother; of her horror of the uncontrollability of menstruation; of her dread of suffering the same emotional and bodily ills and needs that led to her mother repeatedly being hospitalised through Daisy's teens. That was why, Daisy said, she reacted to her mother quitting home when she was 15 by anorexically controlling her own needs. Otherwise, she said, in the face of

being abandoned by her mother, her need and longing for her mother's closeness would have become too excessive and out of control. It would have been
'anarchy', she said.

So she controlled, disciplined, and drove herself to become 'self-sufficient'.
She urged herself to become 'the thinnest of the thin . . . the cleverest of the
clever'. Her survival, she told herself, depended on excelling. It also depended
on exciting herself, when she was 13, by imagining herself as a hero saving
others in their hour of need, thereby evoking in them every ounce of their
longing and desire for her, their saviour and protector.

As for her divided feelings about her mother, unable to share these feelings
with her mother as a teenager, she shared them twenty years later as they arose
in her therapy with me. On the one hand, she told me she had no need of me.
She arrived late for sessions. She only came, she said, because her appointments with me were scheduled in her diary. She distrusted me. She said she
feared I might control, 'label', 'classify', and hurt her with words just as her
mother had done when she was in her teens. She worried I would use words
not to help understand what was going on between us but to distance myself
from her, as she used words to distance herself from me. On the other hand,
she wanted to be the same. She wanted to be a mirror of me. She wanted to be
close. Often she ended her sessions in floods of tears – she was so loathe to
leave.

I felt similarly divided. Her unhappiness made me want to hold and
comfort her. But her cloying female sameness with me – her detailing of her
periods, the 'yuckiness' of it all as she put it – made me want to get away. So
too did her dismissiveness of therapy, and her intellectual superiority. They
made me feel unskilled, stupid, and useless.

Perhaps it was my being there for her, nevertheless, week after week to
share with her, rather than flee these divided feelings, as she and her mother
had fled them when she was a teenager, that led to her becoming more relaxed.
She began therapy with memories of her teenage unhappiness at not being
able to share and talk freely with her mother about their divided love for each
other for fear of 'all hell breaking loose' and her mother being 'taken away'.
She began with her mother's illness stopping her mother staying with, and
trying to understand what was going on between them. She talked of how, not
being able to confide in her mother, she confided in her aunt until she too gave
up on her. She told me how she had never had a brother or sister to confide in.
She talked of not being able to share her divided feelings with other girls at
school because she always felt too unwanted, rejected, excluded, and snubbed
by them. Nor, when she was grown up, could she confide in other women.
Talking with them about the ups and downs in their closeness with each other,
she said, made her feel too 'uncomfortable'.

But, as she increasingly shared with me her divided feelings about her
mother, her friends, and about me, she began to change. She talked of not
wanting to get away. She talked of wanting to stay to sort out differences both
between us and between herself and other women. She talked of both not

wanting and wanting to be with them, and of wanting them to want her to be with them. She talked of wanting to get back in touch with the good as well as bad, caring as well as uncaring figure she now began remembering her mother being to her through her childhood and teens. She talked of making new friends. She talked of a confidante she had recently acquired. Unlike her account of her mother and herself with which she began therapy, she talked of her new confidante's willingness to stay with rather than flee the divided loves and risk of being 'overwhelmed', as Daisy put it, of their being together.

More often women remember escaping the divisions involved in their 'overwhelming' togetherness with their mothers and others not through anorexia, as in Daisy's case, but through boy craziness. Women remember escaping divided love and hate of their mothers, and men remember escaping the divided bodies and minds of their teens, through 'boy crazily' aggrandising themselves or others as gods, heroes, or saviours, as I will illustrate and explain in the following chapters.

Part IV
Grandiosity and romance

8 Gods and heroes

So far I have been concerned with women's and men's memories and dreams of their attachment to, detachment from, and resulting divisions within and between themselves and others in adolescence. Turning to the fantasy of escaping these divisions through male-centred, teenage aggrandisement of oneself or others, it is worth noting that psychologists have recently described something similar in characterising adolescence as involving 'intensification of masculinity'.[1] But few psychologists note the divisions impelling this development. Yet these divisions were addressed in detail by one of modern psychology's leading founding fathers – William James. It is therefore with his now often forgotten insights bearing on the divisions impelling young people to deify others, that I will begin before going on to recount more recent theories and examples bearing on this aspect of our psychology.

William James

In lectures which he gave in Edinburgh in 1901–2, and which were published in his book, *Varieties of Religious Experience*, James drew attention to the way that, through the centuries, young people have often been precipitated into sudden intensified faith in God by what James called their experience of being a 'divided self'. As evidence he quoted the confessions of a number of religious writers.

He quoted St Augustine writing of his self-division as a young man:

> So these two wills, one old, one new, one carnal, the other spiritual, contended with each other and disturbed my soul. I understood by my own experience what I had read, 'Flesh lusteth against spirit, and spirit against flesh'. It was myself indeed in both the wills, yet more myself in that which I approved in myself than in that which I disapproved in myself.[2]

James also quoted the French writer, Alphonse Daudet. Daudet remembered himself, aged 14, divided between what others subsequently might have termed his authentic and inauthentic, true and false self. He writes:

> The first time that I perceived that I was two was at the death of my brother Henri, when my father cried out so dramatically, 'He is dead, he is dead!' While my first self wept, my second self thought, 'How truly given was that cry, how fine it would be at the theatre'. . . . Oh, this terrible second me, always seated whilst the other is on foot, acting, living, suffering, bestirring itself. This second me that I have never been able to intoxicate, to make shed tears, or put to sleep. And how it sees into things, and how it mocks![3]

Others too remember being divided between a suffering and mocking, sincere and insincere theatrical self. They too remember being divided between a loved and hated, good and bad or evil self. As illustration James quoted a nineteenth-century evangelist, Henry Alline, who recalled himself being driven as a young man by a divided off, hated part of himself:

> the devil and my own wicked heart drove me about like a slave, telling me that I must do this and do that, and bear this and bear that, and turn here and turn there, to keep my credit up.[4]

James went on to observe that it was precisely this sense of being divided between his tormenting and tormented inner self that drove Alline to seek refuge in God. Alline describes the result as follows:

> At that instant of time when I gave all up to him to do with me as he pleased, and was willing that God should rule over me at his pleasure, redeeming love broke into my soul with repeated scriptures, with such power that my whole soul seemed to be melted down with love; the burden of guilt and condemnation was gone, darkness was expelled, my heart humbled and filled with gratitude . . . filled with immortal love, soaring on the wings of faith, freed from the chains of death and darkness.[5]

James similarly quoted a French Protestant, Adolphe Monod, who, after recalling being divided as a young man between sickness and health, happiness and corruption, wrote of escaping this division and finding unity, peace, and strength through turning to God:

> Renouncing then all merit, all strength, abandoning all my personal resources, and acknowledging no other title to his mercy than my own utter misery, I went home and threw myself on my knees, and prayed as I never yet prayed in my life. From this day onwards a new interior life

began for me: not that my melancholy had disappeared, but it had lost its sting. Hope had entered into my heart, and once entered on the path, the God of Jesus Christ, to whom I then had learned to give myself up, little by little, did the rest.[6]

James drew these and many other examples from Starbuck's book, *The Psychology of Religion*.[7] Starbuck claimed that the average age of religious conversion is 16. James, however, rejected any attempt to explain sudden intensified faith in God in terms of teenage psychology.[8] Furthermore he insisted that, whatever psychological motives impel religious belief, its validity can only be determined by other, independent criteria.

James also did not seek to explain the origin – teenage or otherwise – of the divided self which he claimed to be the mainspring of belief in God. By contrast a few psychoanalysts – notably Anna Freud and her followers – have sought to understand the teenage origins of the divided self which, like James, they observe often drives young people to idealise others, not so much as religious but as secular idols and gods.

Anna Freud

Anna Freud claimed that the inner divisions impelling young people to deify themselves or others result from an increased drive for sex in adolescence reviving and intensifying a divide between wanting and not wanting incest. She described how she resolved this division in her own case by imagining herself and her father as quasi-gods.[9] She thereby also sought to resolve, she wrote, a further division within herself between masturbatorily exciting herself and hating herself for masturbating. Faced with this conflict, she wrote, she gave up the 'ugly beating fantasy' with which she excited herself in her early years for 'nice stories' in middle childhood.

Then, beginning when she was 13 or 14, she resolved the conflict involved by idealising herself and her father as a medieval knight and lord in which she drew on a book of stories lent her by a boy she knew. It enabled her to cast her beating fantasy in culturally acceptable, non-incestuous form. In her daydreams she now thought of herself as a knight, imprisoned, tyrannised over, and tortured to within inches of her life by a sinister and violent lord. Then, just as the lord was about to kill her, he would nurse her back to health. Or, in another version of her daydream, she would imagine herself, again as the knight, straying from the lord's castle, whereupon the lord would threaten her with public humiliation and, again at the very last moment, spare her.

In each version of her teenage fantasy, Anna Freud wrote, she experienced all the excitement of the knight's anxiety and strength and, at the moment when the lord's rage and wrath turned to pity and benevolence, she found her excitement turning to calm content. And when this failed – when, instead of becoming calm, she found herself becoming excited to masturbatory pitch –

she allayed her excitement by distancing herself from her daydream by writing it down.

She turned her fantasy into a novella, which she called *Heinrich Mühsam* (*Painstaking Henry*). She thereby sublimated, she said, her erotic fantasy. By casting it in publishable form she escaped the self-dividing masturbatory and incestuous impulses fuelling her fantasy by subordinating these impulses to the respectable aim of becoming a published writer – an ambition arguably modelled on an idealised 'superego' image of her writer father.

Later she wrote generally of the superego and god-like resolution by young people of the division wrought in them by the increased drive for incest which she claimed to be brought about by puberty. She maintained that many young people seek to resolve this division by turning away from incest-risking attachment to their parents through instead becoming attached to, identifying with, and idealising others as superego gods. Young people, she wrote, often model themselves on idealised 'leaders' intermediate in age between their own and their parents' generation. Often the adolescent's copy of their new-found deity is so perfect, Anna Freud wrote, one can immediately tell from the young person's 'handwriting, mode of speech, way of doing their hair, their dress, and all sorts of habits . . . the older friend whom he admires'.[10]

Writing at the same time as Anna Freud began developing her theories about young people's identification with others as deified leaders, the novelist François Mauriac wrote in his novel, *Thérèse Desqueyreux*, of an older woman's recognition of this self-same tendency in her daughter's boyfriend, Georges:

> she knew in advance precisely who he was; the wonderful object of hero-worship who is almost always present in the lives of men of Georges' age, the friend who had read everything, can play any piece of music, and follows a mysterious star of his own; the marvellous person whom you simply *must* meet.[11]

As for Anna Freud, she maintained that, beyond hero-worship, many young people resolve the division within themselves between wanting and not wanting incest by withdrawing their sexual desire for their parents into themselves with the result that they love and idealise themselves, to the extent that some entertain grandiose 'fantasies of unlimited power over other human beings, or of major achievement or championship in one or more fields'.[12] Or teenagers turn love of their parents into hate. They imagine their parents as their main persecutors and oppressors. They imagine themselves, Anna Freud claimed, as their parents' benighted Christ-like victims, 'with corresponding fantasies of saving the world'.[13]

Anna Freud advanced this theory in 1958. If her work on adolescence remains known today beyond psychoanalysis this is largely thanks to the popularisation of her work by her one-time analysand, Erik Erikson, to whose theories I will now turn.

Erik Erikson

Unlike Anna Freud, Erikson did not describe the divisions impelling deifying idealisation of self and others in adolescence as an effect of biology, sex, or incest. Instead he explained these divisions as an effect of pressure on young people to conform both with the roles attributed to them by their families and those socially available beyond their immediate families of origin. He argued that conflict between these different roles precipitates adolescent girls into seeking to unify the resulting inner divisions through hero-worship, and adolescent boys into identifying with heroes, or with the idealised heroic images of themselves mirrored to them by those with whom they fall in love. He wrote of young people:

> To keep themselves together they temporarily overidentify with the heroes of cliques and crowds to the point of an apparent complete loss of individuality . . . in this stage not even 'falling in love' is entirely, or even primarily, a sexual matter. To a considerable extent adolescent love is an attempt to arrive at a definition of one's identity by projecting one's diffused self-image on another and by seeing it thus reflected and gradually clarified.[14]

Erikson warned against young people becoming prematurely fixed in their new-found, reflected, heroic identities. He warned against their identity's premature 'psychosocial foreclosure'. He also warned against its opposite – 'identity confusion'. Nevertheless, he celebrated the 'moratorium', which he said was accorded young people in the US, to experiment with a variety of identities before installing 'lasting idols and ideals as guardians of a final identity'.[15]

He celebrated US individualism, including its promotion of the belief that both women and men can become whatever heroes or gods they want and choose to be. He was enthusiastic about the stand of US individualism against totalitarian collectivism. He approved the claim of US individualism that, provided they apply themselves, each and every young person can realise the ideal of 'the self-made man'.[16] He deplored any obstacles to adolescents achieving 'the freedom of self-realization' promised by what we might now call enterprise culture.[17] But whatever its resonance with what has sometimes been called the 'me generation', Erikson's work has now been superceded by the theories of Peter Blos – a childhood friend of Erikson, and the man who first introduced Erikson to Anna Freud.

Peter Blos

Like Erikson, Blos wrote of adolescents resolving divisions within themselves through idealising themselves and others as heroes or gods. Unlike Erikson, however, Blos based his theory on his adoption, after leaving Vienna for the

US, of the version of psychoanalysis developed in New York by the Hungarian-born analyst, Margaret Mahler.[18] Mahler argued that the baby is initially symbiotically identified with the mother (see p.64). She claimed that the baby subsequently individuates from, and becomes independent of, the mother's external containment and control through internalising her as a containing and controlling figure within him.

Adopting Mahler's theory, Blos argued that in adolescence young people must yet further individuate from the mother by getting rid of the 'archaic' and 'omnipotent' image of her formed within them in earlier childhood.[19] But, in getting rid of the mother as an internal containing and controlling figure, Blos noted, all manner of divisions within the adolescent, which this maternal figure previously contained and held in check, are unleashed. These include divisions in young people between love and hate, activity and passivity, masculinity and femininity, and between homosexual and hetero-sexual desire for their parents.

These divisions can only be escaped, Blos suggested, attending primarily to young men in adolescence, by the young person identifying with an idealised hero- or god-like image of his father and of other men idealised in his place.[20] Blos accordingly approved what he called the 'proverbial hero worship' of youth, the 'personalities on posters and albums . . . inhabiting the inner sanctum of the adolescent's world'. He argued that these idols serve less as figures of sexual desire than as figures of identification. The adolescent thereby boosts his self-esteem, as Blos put it, in 1984, through

> admiration, idealization and devotion to the respective hero's qualities of excellence and perfection, most frequently attached to personalities in the field of sports, music or stage . . . predominently acclaimed performers and almost exclusively male.[21]

The novelist Milan Kundera describes something similar in his novel, *Slowness*, in which he characterises as follows what he takes to be the pre-conditions of the self-esteem involved in idealising others:

> When a person sees himself as elect, what can he do to prove his election, to make himself and others believe that he does not belong to the common herd? . . . Through a worshipful fixation on famous people. . . . [They] have become a public resource like sewer systems, like Social Security, like insurance, like insane asylums. But they are useful only on condition of remaining truly beyond reach.[22]

With less scepticism than Kundera about young men's 'worshipful fixation on famous people', and undaunted by his feminist[23] and Kleinian critics,[24] many of Blos's followers continue to reiterate Blos's injunction to young people to build up their self-esteem on a self-idealising basis through worshipping and modelling themselves on famous men, idealised as gods. Like Blos, his followers insist that boys in adolescence should idealise their fathers, and other men in their stead, so as to acquire the masculinity necessary, they claim, to engaging in sex. They argue that heterosexual intercourse yet further enhances young men's masculinity by enhancing their 'phallic prowess', and male 'gender-role identity'.[25]

Ironically, in approving the idealisation of men which they claim to be necessary to adolescents acquiring adult masculinity, Blos and his followers develop an account of adolescence that is remarkably similar to that developed by Jung and his followers, from whose work Freudians like Blos more usually dissent.

Carl Jung

Just as Blos and others write of the divisions young men suffer within themselves in adolescence, Jung wrote of the divisions he suffered as an adolescent. He wrote in his autobiography of intense self-division in his pre-teens. He recalled becoming suddenly aware of this division when, aged 12, his friend's businessman father told him off for standing up to steer a rowing boat as he had learnt to steer his family's punt as a boy. It provoked Jung to divide his know-nothing boyhood self from his know-all adolescent self as though they were 'two different persons' within him. He wrote of these two selves:

> One of them was the schoolboy who could not grasp algebra and was far from sure of himself; the other was important, a high authority, a man not to be trifled with, as powerful and influential as this manufacturer.[26]

Like the writers quoted by William James, who recalled being impelled by the inner divisions of youth into sudden intensified belief in God, and like the young people Blos praises for resolving adolescent divisions within themselves by identifying with pop stars as though they were gods, Jung wrote of cultivating an image of God as escape from his divided teenage self:

> Somewhere deep in the background I always knew that I was two persons. One was the son of my parents, who went to school and was less intelligent, attentive, hard-working, decent, and clean than many other boys. The other was grown up – old, in fact – sceptical, mistrustful, remote from the world of men, but close to nature, the earth, the sun, the moon, the weather, all living creatures, and above all close to the night, to dreams, and to whatever 'God' worked directly in him.[27]

Divided between identifying with, and hating his outer-directed, egotistical schoolboy self – his 'Personality No. 1' – Jung remembered taking comfort as a teenager in the idea of an integrating, inwardly-given, God-like self – his 'Personality No. 2'. He likened this second aspect of himself to 'a temple in which anyone who entered was transformed and suddenly overpowered by a vision of the whole cosmos'.[28]

He described himself as launched by his adolescent quest 'to overcome the inner split in myself, my division into two worlds' into the unifying and transcendental path that was to govern his subsequent life. He recalled being driven out of his 'ordinary, everyday existence into the boundlessness of "God's world"'. He remembered being 'lifted' beyond his teenage craving 'to be up and doing' into the harmony of God as 'a single eye in a thousand-eyed universe', high above 'the incoherent fortuitousness' and everyday fragmentation of 'study, money making, responsibilities, entanglements, confusions, errors, submissions, defeats'.[29]

Blos attributed the impression of young people of being divided and fragmented within themselves to their dethroning and distancing themselves from previous closeness to, and internalisation of, their mothers as a containing and controlling figure within them. Jung similarly wrote of the mother as a containing figure. He wrote of his mother as his 'strongest support' and bulwark in his teens against inner division between 'paternal tradition and the strange, compensatory products which my unconscious had been stimulated to create'.[30]

Like Blos, Jung also argued in effect that, far from seeking to further the containment of their divided feelings through continuing closeness with their mothers and others, young people should distance and free themselves from all such closeness. Like Blos, Jung insisted that 'the son needs to separate from the mother in order to individuate'.[31] Many regard this as the major enduring tenet of Jung's founding text of analytical psychology, *Transformations and Symbols of the Libido*.[32]

This book was first published in 1912. Writing over seventy years later, Blos recommended, as we have seen, that young people should escape or integrate the inner divisions resulting from individuating from their mothers by identifying with an idealised image of their fathers and other men publicly acclaimed as idols. Jung similarly recommended young people to forge an integrated identity separate from their mothers through modelling themselves on culturally given mythic and legendary heroes. Just as Blos many years later warned against the ill-effects of not doing this, Jung warned that failure to follow this path and to realise himself as a hero risks the adolescent remaining a child – a *puer aeternus* – merely the puppet, the insubstantial incarnation, the 'fleeting existence' of his mother's fantasies and dreams, nothing but the 'anticipation of something desired and hoped for' by her.[33]

The Jungian analyst, Marie Louise von Franz illustrates this outcome in terms of the life and fiction of the French aviator, St Exupery. The fascination of the perpetual adolescent with dangerous sports – with mountaineering, exploration and flying, in the case of St Exupery – results, says von Franz, from an image of getting as high and as far away as possible from the mother, equated with the earth and the humdrum daily grind. St Exupery's story, *The Little Prince*, she writes, both expresses the perpetual adolescent's wish not to grow up and leave his childhood and early mothering world, and the terror of remaining incorporated within it, represented by the Prince's drawing of an elephant eaten inside a boa constrictor. The elephant, von Franz claims, is 'the model fantasy of the grown-up hero . . . swallowed by the boa, the devouring mother'.[34]

The fate of the eternal adolescent, von Franz warns, is to remain forever enchanted by the illusion of escaping this fate through imagining himself to be the hero of his mother's dreams. He does nothing to transform fantasy into fact. He remains the figment of his mother's imagination, fabulous but evanescent, a butterfly-like playboy creation of her unconscious. He refuses reality and its limits. He refuses to become 'just a petty little bourgeois who goes to his office'.[35]

Escape from the merely illusory or 'provisional' existence of the eternal adolescent depends, according to Jung and his followers, on young people engaging with the world to realise themselves as men, just as the heroes of myth and legend free themselves from the suffocating and engulfing mother – the 'dragon of death'[36] – through proving themselves in outward trials of bravery and strength. Or, as Jung also put it, adolescents must 'overcome the monster of darkness', representing the mother, so as to realise 'the long-hoped-for and expected triumph of consciousness over the unconscious', of masculinity over femininity.[37]

Only later, in middle age, Jung maintained, can men give up seeking to realise themselves through outward worldly achievement. This was the path into which Jung claimed he himself was launched in middle age by a dream he then had of the teutonic hero, Siegfried, being killed. Jung interpreted his dream as signifying that he must now turn from pursuing outer achievement to pursuing his inner truth.[38] By contrast, like Jung, his followers recommend young people to pursue outer goals. They urge young people to cultivate our culturally-received myths and legends of men as heroes. They argue that these images serve as beacons inspiring young men's outward- and forward-looking development and change.

The Jungian psychiatrist, Anthony Stevens, writes that myths of men as heroes:

> express in symbolic form the experience of Everyman: to embark on the adventure of life . . . to win a bride, he [the young man] must undergo a second birth from his mother – a final breaking of the psychic umbilical cord. Victory over the dragon-mother often involves entry into her. Then, after a period in her belly, he succeeds in cutting his way out or causes her to vomit him up. Failure to overcome the monster signifies failure to get free of the mother: the hero languishes in her belly for ever, and the princess (the *anima*) is never liberated from the monster's clutches.[39]

It is the myth of young Siegfried in Wagners' opera, *The Ring*, slaying the dragon, Faffner, in his cave, and going on to awaken, liberate, and win himself the sometime goddess, Brunnhilde, from the fire with which she is encircled and entrapped.

For Jung, like Blos, growing up involves a two-fold process. It involves following the path of the hero freeing himself and his bride from the clutches of the monster, signifying the mother. It also involves unifying the otherwise divided self of adolescence through turning to, and submitting to God or His secular equivalents. This is a path many men still remember pursuing in seeking to escape the divided selves of their pre-teen and teenage years.

Remembered gods

Examples include Gordon. Now in his seventies, Gordon still remembers feeling acutely divided within himself as a teenager. He tells me of how he felt divided then between the guilt-free boy he experienced himself as being until puberty and his post-puberty, guilt-ridden, pornography-obsessed, adolescent self:

> I think probably before the age of 10 I probably was an innocent child. There's always a time in one's life when one had a clean sheet, that has no burden. I think I was at about 10. Puberty came at about 11 – that's pretty early. . . . I also think there's a sexuality, pre-puberty. I do seem to have experienced it in a mild way. I had certain experience of that – in a very mild way. This teenage sex thing was a heavy load. There was no advice, not from my family. They didn't speak about sex at all.

Whereas Gordon is uncertain whether he had sexual feelings before puberty, he is quite certain that, faced with self-loathing of his teenage sexual obsessions, he turned to God. 'I certainly prayed a good deal about being relieved of the burden of sex, and my guilt about sex,' he says. 'I certainly prayed about that.'

A 19-year-old, Alex, tells a similar story. He tells me that many of his fellow Christian students left the Church after getting confirmed. They regarded confirmation, he disapprovingly declares, as 'a Church-leaving exam'. He then remembers he too experienced a lapse of faith when he was 11. Or perhaps he was 12. He is not quite sure. But he is sure that this was followed, when he was 13, by his becoming more religious than ever. Of the comfort it gave him he says:

> It is always reassuring to think that there is a supreme being who cares about you, if you are in trouble, or if you have serious worries, or if you're feeling depressed. If you suddenly realised He didn't exist, then I just don't know where we'd be.

Mark, also 19, similarly remembers his sudden, intensified certainty and faith in God in early adolescence. It happened when he was 11, he says. Or perhaps he was 12. Like Gordon, confused about whether he did or did not have sexual feelings before puberty, like Jonathan (see p.30) uncertain when he had his first wet dream, like the above-quoted Alex, Mark cannot remember his age or the precise moment when his religious faith suddenly peaked. All he remembers is that it happened at one of the many funerals which, as the son of a vicar, he often attended. Like many funerals the service included a Bach fugue. That was what did it. 'It was one of those magic moments,' Mark recalls, 'difficult to describe – things suddenly clicked.' Ever since, he says, he has repeatedly returned to his then heightened faith in God whenever he is faced with self-dividing doubt between 'right and wrong', and between wanting and not wanting 'selfishly' to pursue what he wants. 'Prayer gives you peace of mind,' he tells me, 'a sense of purpose, strength.' Without faith, he goes on, 'You'd be so encumbered by worrying about everything you'd not done right . . . you just wouldn't be able to do anything'.

Others remember looking to non-ecclesiastical gods. Tim, in his early twenties, remembers himself in his late teens fragmenting after failing his school-leaving exams. Self-division, he says, drove him to look to two older men, Nat and Jake, to guide him. He met them doing karate. He says of them:

> They were near enough to gods. . . . Nat is a formidable character in everything – he seems to be inscrutable, ineffable. He's travelled the world once or twice. He's got an extraordinary IQ, and a near photographic memory. And he's an artist. . . . And when I met them I thought they saw me to be young and aspiring, but in somewhat of a quagmire, with various indoctrinated views of what was good, and what was bad, and what was right and wrong. And slowly but surely they tended to help me lift myself out of it. . . . Nat was about 30, Jake was 6 years older than me. . . . He's probably the cleverest person I've ever met, or ever likely to. . . . And I suppose Nat was so formidable. . . . They're both incredibly charismatic.

Tim – like Mark, Alex, and Gordon – is now grown up. All four men, nevertheless, still vividly remember the gods of their teens. So too do teenagers. A 17-year-old remembers a dream about a god-like religious figure saving him from division between good and bad, right and wrong. He writes of his best remembered recent dream:

> I was in control of an orchestra in a red concert hall, and I had a baton, and all the usual stuff, but the players kept getting the music wrong, and the more I tried to correct them, the more they got it wrong, and the audience kept walking out of the room until the only man left was a Greek Orthodox monk who kept clapping loudly and saying encouraging things.

Another 17-year-old recalls in swooning terms the comfort of an idolised rock star's empathy and understanding:

The most memorable dream I can think of involved meeting my favourite rock band at school and talking to the lead singer. I remember not being able to say much at first, and that he seemed to understand. It was almost overwhelming, and I recall that there was a lot of emotion in that dream.

This teenager's dream and men's above-quoted teenage memories involve them remembering or imagining looking idolisingly to others as gods. But men, and to a lesser extent women, also remember idolising themselves as gods, as I will now illustrate.

Self-idolisation

Asked to name the person they most idolised or admired, the majority of secondary school and university students I studied, if they named anyone at all, named a man, not a woman.[40] The girls more often named a man they knew personally – a relative, friend, or even, in several instances, an ex-boyfriend. The boys more often named someone they did not know personally – someone rendered an idol by public acclaim.

Sometimes, consistent with the psychoanalytic tenet that young people idolise and model themselves not so much on their fathers as on their fathers' superego gods,[41] students said they most admired a man deified or idolised by their fathers' generation – Karl Marx, Martin Luther King, Che Guevarra, and Donald Bradman. More often they named a man lauded by their own generation: footballers Pele, Eric Cantona, Roberto Baggio, Ian Rush, and Neville Southall; cricketers Mike Atherton, David Gower, Darren Gough, and Geoff Boycott; film stars Dieter Brummer and Leonardo DiCaprio; rock stars Kurt Hammett and Bruce Springsteen. Many named men idolised by virtue of dying young – Jimi Hendrix, John Lennon, Jim Morrison, Freddy Mercury, Ayrton Senna, and Kurt Cobain.

Researchers find that young men often idolise themselves, and grandiosely identify with the superlatives such figures represent. Asked to describe their 'actual' and 'ideal' self, men are more likely than women students to conflate the two. They grandly describe themselves as though they were already their ideal selves.[42] They are more likely to describe themselves in self-inflating terms.[43] They reckon themselves to be more attractive than young women reckon themselves to be.[44]

Teenage boys also idealise and idolise themselves in their dreams. They describe dreams of equalling or bettering today's rock music and sports idols.[45] This often contrasts starkly with their earlier dreams of being self-divided and alone. Examples include a 14-year-old in my secondary school study who, after writing a recurring childhood dream of being isolated in a desert, far from family and friends, went on to say of his best remembered recent dream:

There was crowds and crowds of people. I was playing tennis against Andre Agassi and Pete Sampras at the same time. They didn't win a point. And I won. The grass tennis court was bright green and the crowd cheered me.[46]

Others similarly find that young men more often than young women recount what the Freudian analyst Michael Balint called 'philobatic', or bombastic, dreams of phallic grandiosity.[47] Men remember teenage fantasies of themselves as heroic saviours. Recalling himself in his teens at the beginning of this century, the French film-maker, Marcel Pagnol, described in his autobiography, *The Time of Secrets and the Time of Lies*, repeated self-idolising dreams of rescuing the girls he then longed for:

> the nocturnal rescue of grateful young ladies has always heralded the birth of a *grande* passion. Up to my *baccalaureat* I rescued a good dozen of them. I wrested them from cruel kidnappers, from raging storms at sea, from volcanic eruptions and even from earthquakes. These imaginary exploits proved the virile generosity of my feelings: their frequent change of object, however, seemed to show that my passions were neither eternal nor fatal, since the heroic rescuer would fairly soon take refuge in the next life-saving.[48]

Today's teenagers similarly cultivate self-idolising dreams of heroism inspired by passion and rewarded with desire requited. A 14-year-old writes:

> My most recent memorable dream is me being in the army. And for some reason I had to rescue my girlfriend. I vividally [sic] remember getting shot, but it did not really harm me. I managed to rescue my girlfriend and get out of the war zone by a Jeep. And then having sex.

Another 14-year-old remembers a dream of sports heroism winning him an *ersatz* princess as his bride: 'I dreamt that I was playing cricket for England and got 600 runs and 19 wickets in the match and we won and I became world famous and married Michelle Pfeiffer'. Still another 14-year-old, after recalling a recurring nightmare of losing his mother, remembers a recent dream of scoring the winning goal in the Wembley Cup Final.

Some idolise themselves as sexual giants. They remember, or invent with their friends, crude dreams – modelled perhaps on the images purveyed by TV, video, or magazine pornography – in which they feature as sexually magnetic. A 14-year-old, after remembering a recurring nightmare of himself alone 'in the middle of nowhere' threatened by 'a massive army' about to kill him, imagines himself surrounded by adoring women. He writes:

> My most recent memorable dream, which occurs over and over again, is where I start at a party, with lots of really nice girls, and they all really

fancy me and aren't afraid to show it. . . . Then two of them follow me home, and I shag them out and they give me a blow job.

Earlier in this chapter I indicated that Freudian and Jungian theorists recommend young men to resolve isolation, individuation, and separation from their mothers in adolescence, and the fears and inner divisions to which this gives rise, through self-idealising and self-idolising identification with their fathers and with other men as though they were gods or heroes. I pointed out that these theorists argue that this enables boys to acquire the 'phallic prowess', which they claim is needed for sex, including presumably the sexual success the above-quoted 14-year-old dreams is already his.

To the extent that teenage boys succeed in escaping the divisions unleashed by divorcing themselves from an inner containing and controlling image of the mother through fleeing into self-idolising idealisation of themselves as phallic conquistadors, they often forget the divisions impelling their flight. Women, by contrast, often remember. Remaining aware of their continuing closeness with their mothers through adolescence and beyond, the minority of women who remember idealising themselves as gods or heroes in their teens often also remember its origin as escape from divided closeness with their mothers as comforting and confining, loved and hated, oppressive and oppressed.

Judy, in her early sixties, is a case in point. Just as, in their published autobiographies, some women remember imagining themselves as men,[49] Judy remembers dreaming, when she was 15, that she was a man. She remembers likening herself, in her dream, to the midshipman hero of C. S. Forrester's novel, *Captain Hornblower*, which a boy she then knew lent her to read. She tells me that in her dream:

I'm standing on a ship's deck. I'm a man in uniform, a naval officer. . . . I've asked a young girl, or two young girls, to swim out to the ship in the evening from the harbour where we're anchored. It feels like some South American place. . . . I am a man, anything goes, the world is mine. The women/girls have not arrived. But . . . I know they'll come.

Her dream reminds her of the grand men that the boys with whom she went to prep school went on to become after leaving Eton and Oxford. I asked her about her father – a world famous physicist. But she does not want to talk about him. She wants to talk about her mother. She talks of being convinced, as a teenager, that her mother was plotting to poison her. She talks of her teenage dread of becoming 'a slavish mirror image' of her mother. Despite her mother having died many years ago, Judy still experiences her as an 'incubus' weighing her down. She still thinks of her mother, as she remembers thinking of her in her teens, as overburdening and overburdened both with Judy and with Judy's brothers and sisters.

She recalls dreading becoming as sexually repressed as her mother. She was so repressed, Judy says, she never allowed herself to consummate an extra-marital affair with a man with whom she fell in love when Judy was a teenager. 'All she ever did,' Judy complains, 'is write letters to him.' In her teens Judy dreaded she too would become a woman too inhibited to act on, and realise what she wanted sexually. Fleeing this fate, she distanced herself from her mother with daydreams of herself as completely uninhibited. She imagined herself as a whore with 'lots of strange men adoring me, wanting to have me'. Looking back, she likens her imagined teenage self to the prostitute housewife in Bunuel's film, *Belle de Jour*. But, above all, it is her self-idolising escape, aged 15, into a dream of being a magnificent sea captain – the longed for, and idolised male object of others' desire – that she most wants to talk to me about from her teens.

More often, doubtless by virtue of being women not men and therefore not well-equipped biologically or socially for male-centred self-idolisation, women talk of teenage memories and dreams of looking to others, not them-selves, as idolised gods and heroes. They remember idolising men as saving them from divided adolescent love and hate of their mothers. It is this escape from the divisions of adolescence that I will consider next.

9 Saviours

Fiction and folklore are full of tales of young women looking to men to save them from divided love and hate of those assigned to mother them as children. It is the theme of many of the Brothers Grimm stories, for instance, on which American and European children are still often brought up. Again and again these stories depict young girls saved by princes from being imprisoned or even dying at the hands of hateful wise women, stepmothers and witches replacing mothers who might have loved them.[1]

Fictional saviours

The story of Rapunzel, as many will remember, begins with a sorceress punishing a childless couple for stealing her vegetables by making them promise that, as soon as the wife has a baby, she will give it to her. True to their promise the mother gives up her child – a little girl. The sorceress brings her up as though she were her own. She calls her Rapunzel. When Rapunzel is 12 she becomes the most beautiful girl in the world, to which the sorceress reacts by imprisoning her high up in a tower, in the middle of a forest, from which Rapunzel only escapes after a passing prince, hearing her singing, falls in love with her, climbs up, declares his love, and asks her to marry him.

Even more familiar perhaps is the story of the princess, in *The Sleeping Beauty*, wished all manner of good magic by the wise women invited to her christening. But a thirteenth wise woman, embittered at not having been invited to the feast, curses her with dying on her fifteenth birthday. Her curse is commuted, and the princess is doomed to fall into a coma for a hundred years, from which she is only revived when the thorn thicket surrounding the castle in which she is immured is parted to let in a passing prince who, finding her, kisses her awake.

Snow White is similarly rescued. She too is victim of an older woman's malicious spite – her stepmother's envy. Bereaved of her mother, Snow White might have looked to her stepmother for love, but the latter, hating her for her good looks, sends her into the forest to be killed. And, when Snow White survives, she pursues and tricks her into eating a poisonous apple, and leaves her for dead. Snow White is only saved by a prince, travelling through the forest, seeing and falling in love with her through the glass coffin in which she lies. He commands her coffin to be raised and taken to his castle, whereupon the apple falls out of her mouth, she comes back to life, and he declares his love.[2]

Young girls being saved by princes and other high-born strangers from good mothers replaced by cruel stepmothers and witches is not only the stuff of fairy tales. It is also the stuff of comics. The feminist psychologist, Valerie Walkerdine,[3] draws attention to stories, in *Bounty* and *Tracy*, of girls as endlessly forebearing victims of horrid stepmothers and vicious foster mothers. These stories, Walkderdine claims, pave the way for the teenage romance, 'Some day my prince will come'.

This scenario, of course, is again and again depicted in teen romance.[4] It is also a repeated scene in the classics studied in secondary school. These include Charlotte Brontë's novel, *Jane Eyre*, about young Jane, starved of the love of her foster mother in favour of the latter's love for her son, John. Sent to boarding school Jane is similarly starved of affection from the schoolmistresses supposed to take care of her there. Far from looking after their charges they viciously beat them for sins that are more their own than their pupils' doing. Jane is only rescued from these nightmare women of her teens by the love of the man for whom she works on leaving school – the wealthy and imposing, aloof and distant Mr Rochester.

Young women themselves often tell similar tales. They tell stories of hero-ines looking to men to save them from the frustrated love of the women deputed to love and look after them as children. In her 1883 novel, *The Story of an African Farm*, begun when she was 20, the South African socialist and feminist, Olive Schreiner, tells the story of two orphan girls – Lyndall and Em – consigned to the care of a heavy, self-serving, gullible, sex-starved, widowed Boer-woman, 'Tant Sannie'. Neglected, left by Sannie to fend for themselves on the dreary and desolate farmstead where they live, Lyndall escapes, as a young woman, for a passionate affair with a handsome stranger whom she in turn longs to quit for a yet stronger, nobler man or ideal to whom to kneel down, honour, and obey.

Schreiner depicts the young Lyndall being saved by men from her step-mother's ridiculous and obscene-seeming craving for sex. More often teenage novels depict maternal figures as sexless, ill, or as ruthlessly punishing their charges' sexuality. This is particularly evident in girls' school stories.[5] An example is Antonia White's 1933 novel, *Frost in May*, the first and often reis-sued book in Virago's reprint series. It tells the tale of Nanda who, in the absence of her sickly and hospitalised mother, is sent to a convent boarding school where the nuns frustrate any wish Nanda might have to be mothered by them. One nun falls ill and dies. Another terrifies her pupils with horror stories about sex, including a gruesome tale of a bride getting lost in a dungeon and mysteriously dying there on the day of her marriage. Meanwhile, other nuns viciously set themselves against the life and vivacity of their teenage pupils' friendships and crushes, including Nanda's crush on a boy-like fellow-pupil, Rosario. The nuns' death-dealing, oppressive, and anti-libidinal regime only ends for Nanda when she is expelled, aged 14, for writing a novel in which she models the characters on her imprisoned and imprisoning school mistress nuns from whom her novel's heroine is saved by an exotic stranger and, before him, by an admirer who 'having 'swooned with her in the languid ecstasies of a waltz' took her out on the balcony and 'pressed a kiss of burning passion on her scarlet mouth, a kiss which had some of the reckless intoxication of the music that throbbed out from the Hungarian band they could hear in the distance'.[6]

It is, of course, pure *schmalz*. Nevertheless, the romantic image of young girls saved by men from hateful maternal figures lives on despite the contrary anti-romantic image forwarded by punk rock, Madonna, and their successors. What are we to make of the fantasies involved? True to their general neglect of fantasy, non-analytic psychologists are generally silent on the subject. Meanwhile, although a few psychoanalysts write about the fantasies and myths, and about the images of men as gods and heroes inspiring teenage boys (as illustrated in Chapter 8), psychoanalysts are generally silent about young women's fantasies – including their fantasies of being saved by men from neglectful, cruel, and hateful mothers. A notable exception is Karen Horney, the first and perhaps only psychoanalyst to talk explicitly of what she termed women's 'boy craziness'.

Karen Horney

Horney was one of the first psychoanalysts to take issue in the 1920s with Freud's notorious penis envy theory of women's psychology. Ten years later she went on to take issue with the reiteration by Freudian psychoanalysis of the ideology that women should centre their lives on finding a man to love them. Quoting Marlene Dietrich's song, 'I know only love, and nothing else', Horney drew attention to the way psychoanalysts often, in effect, reiterate Dietrich's refrain and what Horney termed its 'patriarchal ideal . . . of woman as one whose only longing is to love a man and be loved by him'.[7]

Horney deplored the damage done women by this ideal. Driven by the single thought 'I must have a man',[8] she wrote, women often sacrifice every-thing – including all interest in school, college, and work – only to make themselves all the more beholden to, and dependent on, pursuing and securing a man to look after them financially as well as emotionally. Yet many analysts, Horney observed, overlook the ill-effects of this pursuit because it accords with patriarchy and its ideology of women as essentially beholden to men.

Opposing this ideology, and its reiteration by psychoanalysis, Horney drew attention to the untoward currents in what she called women's 'boy craziness'. She noted that her boy crazy women patients evinced three character trends. First, she wrote, they dreaded becoming dependent on her, as they also dreaded remaining dependent on their mothers, from whom they looked to men to save them. Second, they sought to counter their dependency on Horney – as on their mothers – by making her dependent on, and jealous of them. Third, they experienced Horney's attempt to understand and analyse their boy craziness as an attempt by her to put obstacles in the way of their pursuing men, just as their mothers had seemingly sought to put obstacles in their way when they were teenagers, making them react by becoming more intent than ever on getting a man. Horney attributed the hatred dividing her women patients from their mothers – as it also divided them from her – to their blaming their mothers for their having been loved less than other members of their families as children. Fearing lest their mothers retaliate against their blaming and hating them by attacking them, Horney concluded, is a major trend impelling women's boy craziness.

Although the conflicts causing boy crazy and other neurotic symptoms often begin in childhood, Horney emphasised that the personality changes involved often begin in adolescence.[9] These changes, she wrote, include sexual inhibition and frigidity, compulsively sublimating desire for sex into doing well at school, devil-may-care detachment, and lesbianism. Horney hypothesised that these personality changes, together with women's boy craziness, are in large part a reaction to the exacerbation of the adolescent girl's divided love for her mother, by her construing her first periods as signifying that her mother, through her hatred of her, has retaliated by making her bleed.

Through frigidity, Horney wrote, young women seek to avert further damage by abdicating from sexual rivalry with their mothers. Through emotional detachment they seek to protect themselves from their mothers upsetting them any further. Through lesbianism they convert hatred and fear of their mothers into love and desire for other women. And through boy craziness they remain sexually rivalrous with their mothers whilst also looking to men to save them from any wrath that their rivalry with their mothers might incur.

Generalising from her claims about women's boy craziness, Horney maintained that neurosis in both sexes is due to the souring of love by hate. Neurosis, she wrote, is due to 'persistent longing for the love of a mother, which was not freely given in early life'.[10] Fearful of expressing their resulting anger lest this yet further alienate their mothers, Horney maintained, neurotics as children deny their anger by experiencing not themselves but others – and the world generally – as hostile and angry. They seek to allay their resulting anxiety through craving affection, submission, or power, or through withdrawing from others. They assume that if others are affectionate to them, or if they submit to, dominate over, or withdraw from others, they can thereby protect themselves from being hurt by them.

As girls, Horney claimed, women often adopt the first two tactics. They crave affection or submission to others because these are the traits men most want of them.[11] This, she maintained, is yet another cause of women's boy craziness, the general character of which she based both on her patients' experience as indicated above and on her own teenage boy craziness.

Horney's own boy craziness

Born in Eilbek near Hamburg in the 1890s, the daughter of a sailor father who was often away at sea, and of a dominating mother who favoured Karen's older brother Berndt at Karen's expense, Horney described her teenage boy craziness as though it were that of a patient she called Clare,[12] of whom she wrote:

> There was a strong, though for a child intangible, community between the mother and brother from which she was excluded. The father was no help. He was absent most of the time, being a country doctor. Clare made some pathetic attempts to get close to him but he was not interested in either of the children. His affection was entirely focused on the mother in a kind of helpless admiration. Finally, he was no help because he was openly despised by the mother, who was sophisticated and attractive and beyond doubt the dominating spirit in the family. The undisguised hatred and contempt the mother felt for the father, including open death wishes against him, contributed much to Clare's feeling that it was much safer to be on the powerful side.[13]

Disappointed in her mother preferring her brother, Clare clung for affection both to him and to her mother. Then when her brother abandoned her in his early teens for other interests, Clare threw herself into her schoolwork. And, when she too became a teenager, she threw herself into a succession of affairs.

The same was true of Horney. Her teenage boy craziness involved a succession of crushes and liaisons, beginning with her and her friends' shared passion for their schoolmaster, Herr Schulze, and for another teacher, Fraulein Banning. This was followed by her becoming infatuated with an actor teacher from Stuttgart – 'handsome, big, very bright'.[14] Next she had a whirlwind Christmas romance with Schorschi, a friend of her brother. This was succeeded by a longer affair with Rolf, a music student whom she happened to meet on the train taking her to school. Then, no sooner did Rolf leave town to pursue his studies elsewhere, than she pursued Ernst, a man her mother took in as a lodger after she left Karen's father and set up home with Karen and her brother, Berndt, in Hamburg.

What emerges from Karen's account of these affairs is that they were driven by longing to escape from, and to be saved from, crippling conflicts and divisions between her parents, and most of all from intensely divided love and hate between her mother and herself. She writes passionately of her love and adoration of her mother, Sonni. She refers to Sonni as 'My Beloved Mother', as her 'dearest in the whole world', and as her and her brother's 'greatest happiness, our one and all'.[15]

But she also writes in her teenage diaries of bitter, hate-filled tension between her mother and father. She writes of both wanting to get away, and of wanting to stay and look after her mother. When she is 15 she writes:

I've just been on the Heideberg alone, for Mutti is awfully down again . . . it was so lovely up there . . . it brings peace to my heart. . . . For things are bad at home, and Mutti, my all, is so ill and unhappy. Oh, how I would love to help her and cheer her up.[16]

Unable to make her mother happy, Karen's worries about her turn to resentment. She begins to deplore her mother stopping her getting away. She grumbles about her mother's small-mindedness. She grumbles about her mother's snobbery. She despises her mother for obstructing and opposing, out of anti-semitic prejudice, her affair with the Jewish Rolf.

On the one hand she writes of the 'fluid atmosphere of coziness' spread by her mother in the 'tantalizing little idyll' and 'doll's house' her mother makes for Karen on moving to live with her in Freiburg where she studied medicine. On the other hand she writes of her hatred of her mother for keeping her close. She complains of her mother sulking, and of her mother's readiness to take offence, as ploys to secure and maintain Karen close to her. She describes her mother as 'extravagant', 'cold-hearted', and as lacking 'self-control'. She loathes her mother's neediness. She writes of her mother having 'to be first everywhere . . . hence her having managed to make me, even up to my eighteenth or nineteenth year, look upon her as perfection herself'.[17]

She resents her mother's unquenchable craving for Karen to be with her. She dwells on her mother 'morbidly seeking for expressions of affection from those nearest to her – insatiably', and deplores the way her mother thereby 'becomes an almost intolerable burden to everybody'.[18] In her early twenties she remembers the extremes of her earlier love and hatred for her mother. She writes of her as her 'greatest childhood love', and of the loathing and detestation to which her mother drove her.

Writing about her boy craziness, she describes her teenage obsession with getting and thinking about her man as a means of fleeing, and escaping the tension and muddle of love and hatred between her parents, and between her mother and herself. Thinking about the current man in her life enables her to escape the confusion, since, as she puts it 'if "he is my thought day and night", how then should other thoughts have room?'.[19]

She pleads her 'longing to get out of the atmosphere of our house' as cause of her schoolgirl passion for Rolf.[20] At medical school, she writes to her fellow-student, Oskar Horney, of intolerable 'tension between Mother and me', of depressing disharmony between them, of wanting her mother dead or far away, and of looking to thoughts of Oskar and Rolf to save her. She writes to Oskar: 'I am so drowned by all these exasperations that I have to think steadily about you and Rolf, not to drown in my own anger and not to lose all joy in life'.[21]

Perhaps it was her also wanting to be saved from her divided love of her mother that impelled Horney's self-confessed attraction, as Oskar's young wife, to 'brutal and rather forceful men'. Perhaps this also contributed to her impulse 'to blend in with the will of a man' – to get away.[22] Arguably it was the fixation of her teenage obsession with boys and men as escape from divided love and hatred of her mother that led to her continuing boy craziness – which she referred to as her endless 'crushes' and 'vagabonding' as a 'strumpet' – through her marriage to Oskar Horney, and, following their divorce, in a succession of affairs – with acquaintances, friends, colleagues, patients, and students – to the end of her life.[23]

Horney died in 1952. What have others made since of women's boy craziness and its teenage origins? Precious little. True to their general neglect of fantasy, non-analytic psychologists have written little about the fantasies involved. Nor have psychoanalysts. The literary theorist and psychoanalyst, Julia Kristeva, has however written on a related subject in discussing Marguerite Duras's novel, *The Lover*.

Julia Kristeva

Kristeva's account of Duras's *The Lover* is influenced by the work of the French psychoanalyst, Jacques Lacan. Although Lacan's followers are often hostile to Horney's development of psychoanalysis,[24] Lacan in effect advocated what Horney described. Whereas Horney analysed women's tendency to look to men to save them from divided love of their mothers, Lacan not only analysed but in effect also recommended men as well as women to look to men to save them from their mothers. He recommended both sexes to look to men to save them from the grandiose, psychotic-making delusion of being everything the mother desires. Both sexes' salvation from this fate depends, Lacan claimed, on the intervention of the father. Their salvation depends on recognition by the mother of the law against the child's incestuous union with her, this law being represented, according to Lacan, in the patriarchal societies, in which he maintained we all live, by the father.[25]

While Lacan focused on the risks of becoming crazily grandiose about ourselves, from which he claimed the child is only saved by the intervention of the father, Kristeva focuses on what she calls the horror of 'abjection'.[26] She focuses on the child's fear of being engulfed by, and disappearing back into the mother. The child, Kristeva claims, is only saved from this fear by the mother having an interest beyond her child and herself, this interest being represented by what she terms, following Freud, the father of our individual pre-history. His intervention is crucial, she claims, if the child is to be saved and freed from abjection and disappearance into the mother, and from the mother being nothing but his 'paranoid-schizoid' fantasies about her.[27]

Only through the intervention of the father, Kristeva maintains, can children recognise their mothers to be separate from their fantasies about them. Recognising their separateness is the motive, according to Kristeva, impelling children to use language to bridge the separation between them. In the first instance this involves using what Kristeva terms the 'semiotic' precursors of language, namely 'drives and their articulation' as distinct from 'signification' involving 'identification of the subject and its object'.[28]

Boys, as men, Kristeva claims, recognise and bridge separation from the mother both through language and through taking a lover in her place. Not so women. They are less able to recognise, countenance, or put something – represented by a lover – as stand-in for their separateness from their mothers. Kristeva explains the greater frequency of depression in women in these terms, in terms of their being more wedded and addicted to what she calls 'the maternal Thing'.[29] This returns me to Duras's novel, *The Lover*, in terms of which Kristeva seeks to illustrate women's lack of separation from their mothers.

The Lover

In *The Lover* Duras writes, as though the narrator were herself, of an affair in her mid-teens with a wealthy stranger from Fushun in Manchuria, whom she meets by chance on a ferry taking her from her mother's home in Sadec to her boarding school in neighbouring Saigon. Duras dwells not so much on the affair as on its impetus, the narrator's teenage feeling of being divided between being hemmed in by her mother's depression – 'the way she'd suddenly be unable to wash us, dress us, or sometimes even feed us'[30] – and wanting to escape and get away.

The narrator attributes her mother's depression to her father, 'the only man she had ever loved',[31] dying thirteen years before. She also attributes her mother's misery to her having been taken advantage of, and ruined – as a lone, widowed woman – by the French officials at the Land Registry in Cambodia cheating her of the compensation due to her when the estates she bought in South Indo-China were flooded and destroyed. Another cause of her mother's unhappiness, she says, is her being yet further exploited, impoverished, and drained by her older son, Pierre, by his drug addiction and tyranny over her. The latter includes Pierre making her beat the narrator, out of jealousy of her closeness with their younger brother, Paulo.

Duras's narrator recounts her teenage hatred of her mother and their common family fate of 'ruin and death which was ours whatever happened, in love or in hate'.[32] She writes of her teenage embarrassment and shame at her mother's visible dejection – the poverty of her clothes, her clumsy bearing, her 'incredible ungainliness, with her cotton stockings darned . . . her dreadful shapeless dresses mended', her down-at-heel shoes, her awkward, painful walking.[33] She portrays her own depression at not being able to restore or make her mother better:

> the loathing of life that sometimes seizes her, when she thinks of her mother and suddenly cries out and weeps with rage at the thought of not being able to change things, not being able to make her mother happy before she dies, not being able to kill those responsible.[34]

She fears being invaded by her mother's depression. She likens this fear to her terror of a mad woman (who lived near her teenage home) clutching at her in the street. She writes of her teenage 'certainty that if the woman touches me, even lightly, with her hand, I too will enter into a state much worse than death, the state of madness'.[35]

Recalling her dread of drowning in the same sea of madness and depression as her mother, however, she also luxuriates in memories of her teenage immersion in, and closeness with her mother. She remembers lying in bed with her mother – 'she nestles up against her in tears'[36] – crying that her mother loves her brother Pierre so much more than her. She remembers hugging her mother – 'The mother doesn't cry – a corpse'.[37] She remembers her mother and herself hugging each other, her 'mother still without a single tear. Killed by life'.[38]

She remembers lying together in bed with her schoolfriend, Hélène Lagonelle. She remembers adoring Hélène's breasts and naked body. She describes their shared sexual confidences – these include Hélène telling her that some of their fellow-boarders earn money as prostitutes. She recalls being wary of sharing with Hélène, still a virgin at 17, the fact that she has begun having an affair. Learning about prostitutes from Hélène, she determines to become one herself. She determines to get her lover to treat her as a whore. She already wears a man's hat – her brother's flat-brimmed, brownish-pink fedora. To this she adds – cannibalising her mother as it were – her mother's discarded, flashy, garish, gold lamé shoes. She recasts her attire as that of a prostitute. She whores herself to her lover. Repeatedly lying to him about her age, she seduces him, when she is still not yet 15, into having sex with her in his apartment in Cholon, a Chinese enclave of Saigon.

Whoring herself to him, she identifies with her mother's shamefulness – her poverty, her ruined lands, her discarded garishness, her loathesome son, Pierre. But she thereby also distances herself from her mother in courting a man who, unlike her mother, is not French but Chinese, not poor but rich. His father's wealth and influence also enables her literally to get away from her mother's depression which she equates with 'the horror of Sadec'.[39] Using his father's money and status, her lover negotiates for her brother's debts to be settled, for her mother to be refunded the money owed her for her ruined lands, and for her mother to thus have the means to fund the still teenage narrator's escape to France from Sadec, which she equates with her mother.

Duras's narrator represents her North China lover as her saviour, as enabling her to escape from her teenage divided love of her mother. But does his intervention do the trick? Not according to Kristeva. Far from her lover saving her, Kristeva argues, her affair with him keeps her immersed in identification with her mother. Just as her mother is lifeless with her, Duras's narrator is lifeless with her lover. Faced with his passion – with him telling her he loves her wildly – she remains silent. 'She could say she doesn't love him,' Duras writes. 'She says nothing'.[40] She tells him that her 'mother's misfortune took up the space of dreams'.[41]

Necromantically falling in love with her mother's deadly dejection, writes Kristeva, Duras's narrator is as dead to her lover as her mother is to her. She seeks to do away with her closeness with her mother as quasi-corpse by looking to her lover. But she is as inanimate with him as her mother is with her. Or as Kristeva puts it 'Destroy, the narrating daughter in *The Lover* seems to say, but in erasing the mother's image she simultaneously takes her place'.[42]

Kristeva quotes Duras's novel as evidence that looking to men to save her from abject oneness with her mother does not serve to separate or individuate Duras's narrator from her mother. Ironically, however, Kristeva thereby contradicts her own and Lacan's claim that fathers and lovers save both women and men from abject or grandiose fusion with their mothers. Whatever the function of the father in saving and individuating the child from the mother, men do not necessarily serve to individuate girls from their mothers, at least not according to Kristeva's analysis of the tale Duras tells in *The Lover*.[43]

But this is no surprise. Looking to a man to individuate and save her from her mother involves Duras's teenage narrator fleeing from, rather than confronting and working to integrate her divided love and fusion with her mother. No wonder, therefore, that it continues and recurs with her lover. Nevertheless, although looking to a lover to save her is not in itself a solution, many women in adolescence continue to look to men to save them from divided and fraught fusion with their mothers, just as Duras describes the teenage narrator doing in *The Lover*. An example comes from a woman, whom I will call Cathy. In a sense, as I will explain, her story can be understood as an instance of what has sometimes been referred to – by Jungians but not by Freudian psychoanalysts – as women's Elektra complex.[44]

Elektra

Cathy describes herself as a teenager as 'man mad'. Writing about both sexes' madness about men, the US psychologist Dorothy Dinnerstein claims it, or at least both sexes' false idealisation of men, is an effect of men's relative absence from our early lives in so far as we are mainly looked after as children by women, not men.[45] Men therefore constitute a readily idealisable escape, writes Dinnerstein, from the far from idealising fantasies with which we imbue the women who first mother us. Hence our looking to men to save us.

Analytically-minded psychologists write that we not only look to men to save us from our mothers. They claim that we also look to men, and in the first place to the father, to save our mothers from us – from our divided feelings and fantasies. Putting this aspect of child development in theoretical terms, the psychoanalyst Hanna Segal writes that the father can be seen

> as protecting the mother and the child from a stream of mutual projective identifications, in phantasy and in reality. It is an important factor in establishing the mother's right to separateness. He can also be perceived

as a provider of goodness for mother, of the kind that the infant cannot provide.[46]

Others point out that looking to men as providers, protectors, and saviours, and seeking to escape fearful love- and hate-filled fantasies about the mother through idealising the father, can flounder due to girls experiencing their fathers to be just as much victims of their mothers as they are.[47] Like Elektra, in Sophocles' classic drama, women often become preoccupied with the idea that their mothers have emasculated and psychically, if not physically, murdered their fathers, just as, in Greek mythology, Elektra's mother, Clytemnestra, murders Elektra's father, Agammemnon. Women as adolescents often become preoccupied with looking to men – as the young Elektra looks to Orestes – to save them.[48]

This returns me to Cathy. She is a successful doctor in her late fifties who, in telling me about herself as a teenager, dwells at length on her teenage hatred of her mother's savage attacks on her father. She also tells me how, as a teenager, she looked to men to save her from her horrid, murderous-seeming mother. In keeping with theories which claim that girls deal with divided love of their mothers by attributing everything good to the father and everything bad to the mother,[49] Cathy describes her mother as utterly beastly and her father as wonderfully caring when she was a teenager.

Yet she also remembers her father's bad side – the way he disparaged her mother for submitting to, and serving him. It was so confusing, Cathy says. How could one want to grow up to become a woman when, like her mother, women were so often mocked by their men? It was all the more confusing, Cathy says, because, as a teenager, she felt it was not so much her father who mocked her mother, as her mother who mocked him. She was horribly cruel both to her father and to her, while he was so 'sweet, and kind, and nice'. When she was 16 she wrote bitterly in her diary:

> I do wish Mummy wasn't so *horrible*, spiteful. She's always making out she's so much better than Daddy, so much more cultured, so much nicer, more amusing. It makes me furious . . . I know it's terrible but I *hate* her, I *hate* her. Arguing – as always . . . getting at Daddy.

Years later, the first images Cathy recalls from her teens include one of herself as an ideal mother – as the Madonna – followed by an image of her mother's loathesome 'getting at' and quarrelling with her father. 'I used to be the Virgin Mary in the play at school,' she tells me. Then she adds:

> But the memory that's the most powerful is going upstairs and writing 'I hate my mother' hundreds of times in my diary. My most vivid memories are of my parents quarrelling. There was one – I can't remember what the quarrel was about – I know it was at breakfast time. I jumped on my bike – we were in the depths of the countryside, there was a hill that rose up

behind the house – I bicycled up, crying up to the top of this hill. I just cried, and cried, and cried on top of this hill. . . . After a bit, I calmed down, went back, and everybody was as if nothing had happened.

That was the worst of it, she remembers, nobody talking about what was going on. And not being able to talk to anybody about how much she hated her mother. She dreaded her friends finding out, just as years later, when things went wrong between her husband and herself, she dreaded his finding out how much she hated him.

Recalling herself as a child, she remembers hating her mother for loving her brother so much more than her. She remembers hating her mother for treating her, unlike her brother, Tony, with such coldness and lack of warmth. She longed for her mother to love her as much as she loved Tony. Perhaps that was why she rigged herself up in boys' clothes – to win her mother's love by dressing like him. Whatever the cause she says:

I insisted on wearing boys' clothes from about 8 till about 13. I wore boys' shorts with proper button-up flies, and boys' jerseys and things. And I was really angry when it turned out I was a girl after all, and that there was no getting round the fact that I was a girl.

She wanted her mother to love and be as close to her as she seemed to be to her brother. Yet she also could not bear to be close to her mother. She could not bear the idea of becoming physically the same. She hated her mother using the fact of her approaching adolescence to remind her that she was becoming a woman like her:

My mother one day said, 'I think you'd better start wearing a top'. She didn't say very much. She just said, 'I think you've got to start wearing a top'. And I realised it was because my breasts were developing. And I was really angry about that, and upset.

She remembers that when she began menstruating she could not abide her mother being close to her, or knowing anything about it. When she had her periods, she says, she would wait for her mother to go out and then rush downstairs to put her used towels on the fire before her mother came home. Or she would take them back to boarding school and dispose of them there. Anything to avoid the cloying intimacy of her mother knowing about her being a woman like herself.

Like many young women today, Cathy both wanted and could not bear to be physically or emotionally close to her mother when she was a teenager. She and her mother could not share with each other their divided feelings about each other. Instead Cathy shared what she felt with her friends. This included sharing similarities and differences between them regarding the bodily changes involved in their becoming women. She remembers a friend telling her, when she was 9, about using sanitary towels. She remembers retorting, 'I'm not going to do that'. And she remembers her friend's rejoinder, 'You'll have to. You wouldn't want blood running down your legs, would you?'. Cathy also remembers being upset some years later at her friends sharing with each other the fact that, unlike Cathy, they had already started having periods.

She recalls other occasions when, far from feeling left out by the other girls' togetherness with each other, she got together physically as well as emotionally with her fellow-boarders at school. She remembers an occasion when another girl:

> took me into bed and kissed and cuddled me. I would have been 12. I can still remember the smell of the talcum powder she used. It was like someone mothering me. She would have been a lot older – 17. It was one of these schools where everyone had pashes. I shared a bedroom with her. She said 'You're so sweet'. So all that, those were probably good experiences, looking back.

Most of all, however, Cathy tells me about herself and her friends sharing with each other their teenage 'man madness'. Her 15- to 17-year-old diaries are full of entries recording her and her friends' preoccupation with 'boy-hunting', with finding and getting boys from a neighbouring school to notice and smile at them. Again and again she records their shared delight at the boys acknowledging them. The following example is one of many similar entries in her teenage diary:

> We passed lots and lots of boys going to or returning from games, none of whom we knew, but going along to the show we saw Tom looking out of one of the downstairs windows of New House. He gave us a wonderful smile and we were much cheered.

But, just as Cathy as a teenager hated her mother for despising her father, and just as she remembers her father and his friends despising and mocking their wives for serving and looking after them, she felt that her fellow-schoolgirls despised and mocked her. Identifying with them, she despised and mocked herself. When she was 15, she wrote, '[We] all went out for a walk with the intention of picking up new boys (what flirts!)'.

But where did her despised flirtation and madness about men come from? As a child, disappointment in her mother's coldness towards her and preference for her brother drove her to dress as a boy like him. She also learnt early to masturbate to comfort herself. Then, in her teens, she traded dressing in boys' clothes and identifying with them for longing to be loved by them. Identification gave way to desire. Masturbation gave way to romance. She told herself stories of wonderful men saving her from her mother's petty-mindedness and hateful lack of warmth and generosity. Her father, murderously destroyed and emasculated in her eyes by her mother – just as

Elektra's father is murdered by her mother – hardly seemed to be the heroic saviour – the Orestes – she needed. She imagined other men saving her:

> I used to tell myself long, long stories. I did this throughout my teenage years, *Woman's Own* fantasies, unbelievable. There would be this boy called Dion or Mark. It would go on night after night. Each night it would advance a little bit. So the first few nights would be spent in setting the scene. I remember one. There were lots. In this, it was about going skiing, because my mother took us skiing when we were about 14. The culminating point in this fantasy, because my mother didn't take us out in sleighs, you saw other people going out in sleighs, and in this fur-lined sled, this boy would declare his love. It took months from meeting this boy on the slopes, ending up with my being completely loved, and doted on by this boy. . . . Sex wasn't the point of it. The point of it was being loved.

Now Cathy scorns her teenage addiction to girl-meets-boy love stories. Others similarly scorn their adolescent obsession with *Woman's Own* stories and other pulp romance as absurd, male-inflating trash. A journalist, following the recent death of Mr Boon of Mills and Boon, Harlequin-style, romance fiction fame, writes:

> I was an addict from the age of 12 to 17. I sacrificed my O-levels to Mr Boon's books, and even my piano Grade Six. While practising scales, I read Mills & Boons at the music stand. I even made a tape of *arpeggios* to foil my mother while I walked among men with V-shaped torsos and powerful thighs. I couldn't get enough of these tales of devastating attraction, terrible misunderstandings, heart-wrenching partings and, in the end, sweet reunion.[50]

She scorns her teenage obsession with men as giants and saviours. So too does Cathy. So too do countless other women. Nevertheless, today's teenagers continue to aggrandise and idealise men. Like Karen Horney and Marguerite Duras in their diaries and novels about adolescence, they too idealise men as saviours, and as means of escaping from divided and fraught love of their mothers, as I will end this chapter by illustrating.

Today's saviours

Interviewing teenagers, feminist researchers conclude that girls often look to their fathers to save them from lack of affirmation from their mothers. The US feminist and psychoanalyst, Jessica Benjamin, writes of young women fleeing un-affirming and crippling identification with their mother's oppression and lack of self-esteem for 'ideal love in relationship to their fathers in order to get vicarious access to subjectivity'.[51] In keeping with Benjamin's claim, a teenage girl lauds her father as inspiring whereas she describes her mother as grumblingly down to earth. She says:

> My dad is such a sweetie. Umm, he works a lot, obviously, because he's a doctor, when he's home... But he, I swear he knows everything. Like whenever I have like math problems or science problems, I can go to him and if he doesn't know it he can figure it out . . . and now we're thinking, he has his pilot license, and we're gonna go out to lunch and fly to Small Sun Bay. We get along great. I used to have problems with my mom but it was about stuff like cleaning your room which isn't stuff dad really cares about. So, we get along.[52]

Working-class girls, by contrast, often experience their fathers as being as lack-lustre and powerless as their mothers. As a result they often turn earlier than middle-class girls from idealising their fathers to idealising other men as saving them from their mothers. Hence, writes US psychologist Karin Martin, the early adolescent preoccupation of working-class girls – particularly white working-class girls – with teen idols, teen romance, and pop and rock love ballads. Hence too the idealising terms in which they describe the boys and men of their memories and dreams. One girl tells Martin:

> I always think about this guy I met this summer. I wicked fell in love, wicked bad. I didn't just love him, but I wicked fell-in-love. You know, swept me off my feet. I just think about his face, the way he used to sing to me. He was wicked awesome. He used to like sing reggae to me. He was awesome. He was just one of a kind.[53]

Young women in England similarly romanticise their men. A student in her twenties writes of herself, aged 14, pleading for men to save her from mirrored sameness with her mother:

> Oh no, let me out. Which one am I? Why can't she leave me alone? Claws, hate, loathing, pills, <u>bathroom</u>, mirror. . . . Look at your eyes. They're filled with tears and hurt. Look at your face. It's so unfair. Unfair. Unfair. Why does she have to do it to me? What's wrong with me? She's jealous, she hates me, she wants to <u>be</u> me. She wants my life. She wants to eat me. Get away. Leave me alone. . . . Dream about love. Men love me. <u>He's</u> always there. And so is he. And also him. I must keep them close. I must always keep them. Who cares if she hates me? I've always got him. I'll take him and I'll get him . . . MINE.[54]

Today's teenagers still dream of men rescuing them from hatred and danger. Secondary school students imagine TV characters, celebrities, and rock stars saving them. A 12-year-old writes a dream of 'Our house burning down and me getting stung by a bee. And being rescued by Dr Who!' A 14-year-old dreams: 'waves were engulfing me . . . Tom would be standing there. Then I would turn again but see nothing. Other times Kurt Cobain would be there'.

They recall dreams of men and boys saving them from internecine feuds with their mothers, women, and friends. A 17-year-old remembers the following dream:

> Everyone is playing with their friends except for me who is being bullied. Suddenly this boy (like Peter Pan) comes out of the sky and gives me magic flying dust. I tie all of the bullies to the goalposts and fly off to the clouds.

A 13-year-old – after writing a repeated dream of her schoolmistress tying her to a chair, sellotaping her mouth, and all the other children laughing at her and calling her names – writes a recent dream of being threatened with imprisonment, being granted temporary reprieve, and going off 'hand in hand' with a boy 'I fancy in real life'. Another girl remembers a nightmare of herself, in the kitchen of the house where she lives alone with her mother, 'feeling something crawl over my foot . . . a massive spider, its eyes are like this: ☉ ☉'. Then she gets away. She tells a dream of being outside, hailed by her schoolmaster as a quasi-regal figure:

> I am sitting on the roadside and a car keeps driving past me. I look into the window and see Mr Jenkins, my history teacher. He sees me and grins and waves slowly, like the Queen. This continues for a long time.

Others share with interviewers waking fantasies, often modelled on magazine stories analogous to those fuelling the romantic fantasies remembered by Cathy from her teens. Twelve-year-old Victoria tells an interviewer about her mounting unhappiness at her mother betraying her closeness to her by siding with her father when he is there, while deploring her misery with him to Victoria when he is out of the house. Divided between her mother both confiding in and betraying her, Victoria seeks refuge in the following daydream:

> I'm hoping some day I will fall in love with a man and we will be happy and live happily ever after. . . . He is going to be at least six foot and have a beard and a mustache and he's going to be really nice and gentle and . . . the perfect prince.[55]

Yet it was this self-same fantasy, Victoria admits – her mother's wishful-thinking image of her father as a prince – that drove her mother into marriage with him that had now gone disastrously wrong.

Other researchers similarly find that acting on their yearning for their men to be princes often causes more problems than it solves. They find that idealising men as saving them from conflicts and divisions between their parents and themselves often leads to the problems posed women by marrying and becoming mothers in their teens.[56] Researchers find that the greater the divisions and conflicts teenage girls suffer, and the greater the insecurity in their attachment to their families, the more they idealise men,[57] and look for romance with powerful and dominating men to save them.[58]

Boys sometimes do the same. Twelve-year-old Benjamin tells his New York analyst, Rick Berenstein, that he dreads being no more able to stand up to his drunken and brutal father than his mother in the fights he overhears them having every night.[59] He goes on to indicate that he hopes to escape being as weak as his mother through the strength afforded by having sex with an enormously well-endowed man. He tells Berenstein:

> he 'crotch gazed' at men all the time, especially on the bus and the subway when they were in one place long enough to be stared at. He would wonder how big their penises were, wonder if he could guess by the size of the bulge in their pants. And then he went on, 'Sometimes I imagine that the man notices me staring at him, and he takes me back to his apartment. We get undressed and he has a very big penis and he fucks me'.[60]

But were Benjamin to act on this fantasy, were he to conclude that because one man did not save him by giving him the masculine strength he wanted, he must find another man, he would, says Berenstein, become launched on 'a constant search for a bigger penis, a more powerful phallus, a more genuine man'.[61] It would prove an endless quest. For no man can equal or match the phallic giants of Benjamin's fantasies and dreams. They can never equal either sexes' aggrandised and idealised images of them as gods, heroes, or saviours as escape from their divided teenage selves and loves. What then is to be done?

10 Fallen idols

Before answering the question raised at the end of Chapter 9, a reminder of some of the problems posed both sexes by their idealising – grandiose and romantic – teenage fantasies about men and masculinity.

Problematic grandiosity and romance

One problem is the illusion of teenage boys that, simply by virtue of being men, they are already the grand figures their sex is often depicted as being. The psychoanalyst, Wilfred Bion, put this in terms of 'the schoolboy belief in the hero who never does any work and yet is always top of the form – the opposite of the "swot"'.[1] This belief leads many men as teenagers not to do the work necessary to achieving their aspirations. This undoubtedly contributes to their doing so much worse than girls in secondary school league tables, and attributed by some to our currently widespread 'laddish anti-learning culture'.[2]

Imagining themselves to be heroic lads as answer to any upset, separation, and division they might otherwise experience in themselves and in relation to others also undoubtedly contributes to the problems posed both sexes by men's delinquency in acting on their pre-teen and teenage macho fantasies,[3] like that of an 11-year-old who dreams:

> we had been playing football all day and then we went to Pete's. We raided the fridge and freezer and got legless. Then we all went up to John's house but on the way we met the unfriendly dog. We started to annoy it. So it chased us. We all turned around and kicked it until it was unconscious and didn't move.

Both sexes suffer from being victims, like the dog in this boy's dream, of men seeking to avert vulnerability to others' unfriendliness by making much of themselves through savagery and attack. Paradoxically, however, grandiosely glorifying their masculinity risks increasing men's vulnerability. Many fear the toll exacted by their grandiosity.

Teenage boys tell stories of grandiosity turning to disaster, or even into global catastrophe. A 14-year-old writes:

> I dreamt I had become a member of a really big rock/grunge band and that I was really rich and all our records had gone platinum. I was in the middle of singing the song called the '4th of July' by Soundgarden which is about the end of the world when everything in the song came true. The floor opened and engulfed everything and everyone except me and I was left alone on a completely deserted Earth.

His nightmare is akin to the disaster befalling young Frankenstein, in Mary Shelley's novel, begun when she was 19, for seeking to equal God by creating life.[4]

Others tell nightmares of glory turned to failure. Another teenager in my secondary school study dreamt of 'missing an open goal in Holland against Germany in the European Cup'. They remembered nightmares of success arousing others' envious attack. A 12-year-old dreamt of winning Wimbledon and collecting the trophy only to be rewarded by a man machine-gunning down both him and the admiring crowd. A 14-year-old dreamt he was in a rock group when the screaming girls' adulation of him turned into them beating him up. Another boy dreamt adulation was an illusion – that he was playing for Liverpool at Wembley for the FA Cup and then discovered that the applause came from tape recorders, not people, in the stands.

Grown men tell stories of their self-idolising hopes and illusions being similarly dashed. They also talk of their anxieties and fears about their masculinity. They worry about doing damage to themselves or others in aggrandising themselves at home and at work in pursuing the achievement and prowess valorised for their sex. More often they suffer anxiety lest their pursuit of macho success proves futile. They suffer from not being the gods, heroes, and saviours they and others, including their lovers, expect and want them to be.[5]

Many men project their disillusion into others. They blame their colleagues, friends, and lovers for stopping them achieve the glory they feel should be theirs. They become tetchy, peevish, paranoid even, at others not recognising them to be the great guys they believe themselves to be. Alternatively, like Willy Loman in Arthur Miller's play, *Death of a Salesman*, they tell stories to themselves and others of being the most successful chaps ever, only to collapse into suicidal dejection at being nothing of the kind.

Frequently men suffer the ignominy of their inflated image of themselves proving hollow and absurd. The feminist literary critic, Jacqueline Rose, reiterates Virginia Woolf's account of men's emptiness in this respect:

> her view of men as 'cripples in a cave' buckling under the crushing weight of what is required of them; her picture of Hitler as no more or less than a

terrifying void: 'that ridiculous little man, why ridiculous? Because no one of it fits. Encloses no reality'.[6]

Rose concludes that 'Seen in this light, feminism . . . is the answer . . . to patriarchy as a form of lunacy, known only too well by the men who are meant to embody its bravura on the verge of collapse'.[7]

Men's madness – their 'lunacy' – is also often fuelled by dread of homosexuality, including dread of the shame involved in homosexuality being equated with not being a man but a wimp, a woman, or a queen. Women too suffer from our society's stereotypes of men and masculinity. Lesbians suffer from the denigration of their desire as male not female. Lesbian and heterosexual women – as well as gay and straight men – also suffer from trying to embody the ideals they learn as children, but above all as adolescents, to equate with men.

Women make men suffer for male-dominated society's ideals of their sex. They punish men for not being the ideal figures they imagine and want them to be. This has perhaps never been more eloquently expressed than by Ibsen in his turn-of-the-century depiction of the leading women in his plays – notably in *The Doll's House* and *Hedda Gabler* – leaving or decrying their men for disillusioning them of their romantic aspirations for them.[8]

Girls and women today express similar disillusion. A 13-year-old recalls dreams of being kept in by her mother, of drowning, and of looking in vain to a lifeguard to save her. Another 13-year-old, after writing a nightmare of being buried alive with her mother, writes a dream of looking to a boy, sanctified in the distance as someone who might save her from being trapped with her friend turned tormentor, only to be disappointed in him being nothing but a pictorial image. She writes that in her dream:

> I can see a huge puddle of ice with a boy I know sitting in the yoga position on the ice. We run towards him. But I slip and break my ankle. My friend picks me up, but as we reach the ice she throws me across the ice and I skid towards him and knock him over. But he's only a cardboard picture.

Women often punish men for proving to be nothing but an empty 'cardboard picture' cut-out. In her autobiography, *Love's Work*, Jacqueline Rose's sister, the political theorist, Gillian Rose, describes both her own and other women's anger at their fortuitous or calculated disappointment in their men:

> behind my early idealisation of men and dependence on them, there lurked a rage at having been deserted by my fathers, and at their having allowed my mother to dispose of them. Then I discovered the even more deep-seated corollary in the lack of independence of my carefully chosen current lover. I have observed in some of my women friends that their principled anger arising from the history of their oppression by father,

husband, lover, covers up the deeper but unknown rage at the carefully chosen impotence of the current partner.[9]

Better then to rework the divided selves and loves which (as explained in previous chapters) often impel women's and men's escapist, male-centred grandiosity and romance. Otherwise both sexes will continue to be at risk of the problems posed by such escapism, and by 'rage' at others and themselves for not realising the illusions involved. This returns me again to Freud. For he and his followers have addressed precisely this issue.

Freudian solutions

In the first place they note the ills caused their patients by their idealising illusions. Freud noted the harm done both sexes by quitting divisions within themselves and in relation to others for illusory, but deadly, self-isolating, and self-idealising preoccupation with themselves. He likened the effect to the fate of Narcissus, son of the Greek river-god Cephissus, who became so enamoured with his reflection in a pool, and so wanted to embrace himself, he fell in and drowned.[10] Freud also drew attention to the harm done women and men by seeking to escape the self-dividing division between wanting and dreading incest by identifying with an inflated 'superego' version of the father forbidding it.[11] By identifying with this inflated figure, Freud pointed out, women and men inflate their self-importance at the cost of remaining in thrall to this god-like figure's forbidding and guilt-inducing effects. This is a major cause, Freud claimed, of the ills bringing both women and men into therapy.[12]

A recent example of the anxiety caused by our superego gods comes from a 19-year-old who, elaborating on a dream of being pursued by threatening men, tells me about a holiday she has just taken with her father. She talks of nightmares she had while they were away. She talks of nightmares made all the more threatening by her waking up from them with the sense that the God of her family's Catholic religion was there with her. It was reassuring, she says. But, she adds, it was also frightening. She remembers dreaming about the engine of an aeroplane, and waking up and thinking, 'God exists. He must exist for us to be able to go so high and invent things'. She remembers waking up from another dream of being attacked, and again thinking 'God exists'. Again she found the thought of God comforting. Again she found the thought of Him frightening and intimidating. 'It was too big maybe,' she says. Trying to figure it out, she goes on, 'I also remember looking at the stars in my dream. But it too was scary, frightening'.

As for Freud, as well as writing about the 'scary' making effects of idealising men as superego gods, he also wrote of the ills resulting from making those we love into gods as defence against being disillusioned in them. He pointed out that this runs the risk of depressingly hating ourselves, not those in whom we fear being disappointed, for not living up to the god-like ideals we foist on them.[13] Freud went on to write of the harm done women by fleeing divided love and hate of their mothers for deification and idealisation of their fathers and the men they marry, only to find their idealisation of their men becoming mired in the same hatred of the mother that impelled them to idealise their fathers as children.[14]

Freud accordingly made it his business to seek to expose, so as to rework, the divisions of love and hate, but above all the division of the conscious and unconscious mind, so as to reverse his patients' otherwise damaging escape into idealising and deifying their fathers. He thereby sought to reduce the harshly guilt-inducing inner superego image of the father that is the counterpart of deifying him. Freud's follower, Jacques Lacan, adopted a somewhat similar programme.

He argued that the task of psychoanalysis is to expose the harm – the self-alienation – involved in identifying with the imaginary ideal of ourselves which, he said, we entertain as toddlers in idolising our reflection in the mirror and in others' imagined, idolising desire for us.[15] He wrote of the need to undo the paralysing effect of imagining ourselves to be one with these idealised, reflected images, and of imagining our ideals and desires to be already fulfilled so there is no need to do anything to begin to fulfil them for real.[16] He claimed that, within patriarchal society, desire and its idealisation is symbolised by the idea of having or being the phallus.[17]

Lacan, like Freud, was arguably involved in exposing, diagnosing and treating the ills done to both women and men as individuals by the phallic and other illusions bred by patriarchy. Feminists, by contrast, are concerned with collectively exposing and combatting its social ills. Nevertheless, some feminists argue that Freudian psychoanalysis is relevant to this project. A recent example comes from the work of the US feminist philosopher, Judith Butler. She urges women to don what she calls 'the lesbian phallus' so as to disrupt and explode the occlusion by, and conflation of, sexed identity with heterosexual desire which, following Lacan, she says is represented by the phallus. This includes disrupting the phallic conflation of identity and desire evident, she says, in the time-honoured story of the midwife announcing, 'It's a girl!', thereby anticipating, Butler claims, the happy-ever-after ending – namely, the registrar doing things with words with his announcement, 'I pronounce you man and wife'.[18] Others, however, deplore the focus of Judith Butler and other Lacanian feminists on the phallus.

Luce Irigaray

Deploring the phallocentrism of psychoanalysis, beginning with Freud's notorious penis-envy theory of women's psychology, some argue that the solution to the problems posed women, at least, by idealising, and envying men as phallus, lies in developing an alternative, non-phallocentric, woman-centred theory. This is the stance adopted by the French psychoanalyst and feminist, Luce Irigaray.

Irigaray rejects the focus of Lacanian and other Freudians on the father and on the phallus. Instead she focuses on mothers and on women's divided love of their mothers in both wanting and not wanting to be the same. As a daughter she pleads with her mother:

> Keep yourself/me outside, too. Don't engulf yourself or me in what flows from you into me. I would like both of us to be present. So that the one doesn't disappear in the other, or the other in the one.[19]

She threatens that, if she and her mother cannot become separate in being together, she will look to a man to save her. She tells her mother 'if you lead me back again and again to this blind assimilation of you . . . I'll turn to my father. I'll leave you for someone who seems more alive than you'.[20]

But Irigaray rejects this patriarchal solution to women's divided love. She insists that mothers and daughters can face and resolve their divided love and recognise that they are two, not one, without looking to the father or other men to save them. She tells women:

> We are not voids, lacks which wait for sustenance, fulfillment, or pleni-tude from an other . . . No event that makes us women. Long before your birth, you touched yourself, innocently. Your/my body does not acquire a sex by some operation, by the act of some power, function or organ. You are already a woman; you don't need any special modification or interven-tion. . . . No need to fashion a mirror image to be 'a pair', or to repeat ourselves a second time. We are two, long before any representation of us exist.[21]

Irigaray symbolises women's already existing recognition of their separateness from each other, and of their divided loves in terms of the two lips of the labia.[22] She counters in terms of this gynocentric image, derived from women's biology, Lacan's phallocentric 'master discourse'. Others, by contrast, counter prevalent discourses idealising men and masculinity not in terms of biology but by urging women to return to now often forgotten women-centred myths and legends. The feminist and Jungian therapist, Clarissa Pinkola Estes, opts for this solution in her recent US best-seller, *Women who Run with the Wolves*, in which she answers, by implication, the stories of men as heroes recently popularised and promulgated by the US poet and Jungian, Robert Bly.

Jungian alternatives

Bly draws on Jungian theory to oppose men's current emasculation. He blames it on our having dethroned men as fathers. Men's fall from grace, Bly says, has left us, like the fatherless Jack in the story, *Jack and the Beanstalk*, 'stuck in the frightful scene in which the Giant [representing "adolescent envy and greed"] is eating and Jack is watching from his hiding place'.[23]

He argues that men should counter the strength acquired by women through feminism by strengthening themselves through being initiated into manhood like the prince in the Brothers Grimm story, *Iron John*.[24] The story tells how a prince takes a key from under his mother's pillow, unlocks and frees a Wild Man from a cage in which he is imprisoned, and leaves with him for the forest where the Wild Man initiates him into the skills he needs to become a hero in battle, for which he is rewarded with a princess as his bride.

Bly argues that today's men, and that today's boys on the verge of manhood, like the prince in the Brothers Grimm story, should similarly take and repossess the key symbolically kept from them by the mother, and needed by them to liberate their inner Wild Man. He urges young men to leave the hearth and home of their mothers and to be initiated and inducted by older men – in men's groups, for instance – into acquiring the strength they need to become men for real.

Following Bly, Estes[25] argues that, just as men need to reconnect with their inner Wild Man, women need to find and pursue the promptings of their inner Wild Woman. She maintains, however, that women cannot look for guidance to the same stories that Bly recommends since these often recast folklore in woman-hating terms. Instead she recommends more woman-friendly stories, including a Russian version of the story more usually known in England and America as *Cinderella*.

The Russian story is called *Vasalisa*. It begins with Vasalisa's mother dying. Just before she dies, she gives Vasalisa a doll, which she bids her always to keep with her, to feed and nourish when it is hungry, and to consult whenever she needs help. After the mother dies, her widowed husband remarries. Vasalisa's stepmother and newly acquired stepsisters proceed to mistreat Vasalisa cruelly. They make her into their household drudge.

Cinderella is saved from a similar fate by Prince Charming.[26] Not so Vasalisa. According to Estes' account, Vasalisa is saved through recognising and working to resolve her otherwise divided love and hate of the mothers in her life. They are represented, says Estes, by the doll bequeathed her by her mother, and by her mother's counterpart, a murdering, forest-dwelling witch, called Baba Yaga, to whom Vasalisa's cruel stepmother and stepsisters send her on the pretext that they need fire from Baba Yaga so that Vasalisa can go on cooking their food, and heating their home. Paradoxically, however, writes Estes, in sending her into the forest, her stepmother also saves Vasalisa by preventing her from remaining a victimised, abjectly downtrodden, stay-at-home, too-good little girl. Furthermore, by sending her into the forest, Vasalisa's stepmother makes her confront another aspect of her mother in herself – in Baba Yaga.

Through the help of the doll bequeathed Vasalisa by what Estes (following the psychoanalyst Donald Winnicott) calls her 'good-enough' mother, Vasalisa passes all the trials imposed on her by Baba Yaga. These include cleaning, cooking, and sorting poppy seed from dirt, representing love and hate, good and bad, life and death. Having faced and sorted out these divided aspects of herself in relation to others, Vasalisa is then urged and enabled by the doll to assume, rather than refuse, the strength symbolised in the story by a fiery skull on a stick. The skull, Estes claims, represents the 'ancestral knower' Vasalisa needs to confront so as finally to resolve her divided love and hate of her stepmother and stepsisters.

Estes tells *Vasalisa*, and other similar, female-centred stories to draw attention to the strength and independence women can secure through confronting and working to resolve the divisions and mixed feelings of love and hate between themselves and their mothers in becoming separate whilst also remaining close. In this, Estes' message is not unlike that of the psychoanalyst, Melanie Klein, and her followers.[27]

Kleinian answers

Klein claimed that children, fearful of losing the mother they love through hating and attacking her, defend against this fear by loudly and vehemently declaring that they can get on perfectly well without her.[28] Hence the toddler's omnipotent brag: 'I'm the King of the Castle'. Hence too his tantrums protesting his independence faced with his mother putting limits on him having or doing whatever he wants.

The child's brag, however, fails to do the trick. It falls short of its promise of enabling him to get on perfectly well without his mother. This is charmingly illustrated by a 12-year-old who, after writing and drawing a picture to illustrate a gruesome dream of disposing of his mother and father as 'cut in half at the top of their legs', writes a dream of the damage to his parents – at least to his mother's car – being no obstacle to his doing without them. In his dream he says:

> Me and my friend were in a football team and we had to get to London to play in a game. We had to use my Mum's car (which is not very relyable [sic], and had just broken down the day before this dream) and we couldn't get it to start so, we cut holes in the floor and we used our feet to move the car along by running and also someone (my friend) pushed, (I steered), and it took us ages to get to London.

The Kleinian analyst, Henri Rey,[29] and his followers,[30] recount similar examples. They tell of the 'ages' long effort and frequent futility of women's and men's bombast in seeking to escape the damage done by attacking – 'cutting holes in' – and hating those they love by proclaiming that they have no need of them. Rey illustrates the futility of this stance with a patient's dream of reaching god-like to the heavens. In his dream

> he was balancing a long pole on his nose; it reached right to the sky and had a baby balanced on the end. As he awoke he said to himself, 'This fucking penis is good for nothing, it is so big that it is useless'.[31]

The answer to such penis-based brag and its uselessness, Kleinian analysts claim, is to enable women and men to recover and again know about the divided love and hate, and division and separation from their parents as a couple, impelling them to escape into male-centred, 'phallic' self-idolisation. This also entails enabling women and men to become conscious of, and take back into themselves, feelings of love and hate that they otherwise fail to integrate and instead divide, disown, and project into others.[32] This process of integration, which Kleinians advocate, is helped in therapy, they say, by the therapist sharing and containing the patient's divided feelings, as the psychoanalyst Wilfred Bion claimed the mother contains her child's split-off feelings so that he can take them back into himself as integrated, containable, and contained by her (see Chapter 2). To illustrate this process I will describe two final examples from my work as a therapist, this time examples bearing on problematic adult repercussions of teenage fantasies of male-centred, 'boy crazy' grandiosity and romance. I will call the patients involved Len and Lisa.

Boy crazy grandiosity

Len is an architect. He first came for therapy when he was in his mid-thirties. An architect colleague had suggested he might find therapy helpful in enabling him to get out of the rut in which he felt he was stagnating both at work and at home. At least that was what Len initially told me.

Like many men, he went on to tell a story of himself that began with early separation from his mother. In his case the separation had been total. His mother died when he was 13. Her loss reminded him of other losses: the death of his older sister in childbirth when Len was 9; and the loss of his father when his father remarried a year after his wife, Len's mother, died.

At some level Len worried that he might have contributed to the loss of his mother and sister. He worried that, like the damage he felt his architecture clients inflicted on him in intruding into his personal life, he might damage his wife in having sex with her when she was pregnant. He remembered dreading he might cause her to die, like his sister, in childbirth. He was horrified at the sight of his wife giving birth – her flesh putrid and disgusting like that of his dying mother.

More often, however, his divided feelings of depression and guilt at the thought of damaging and contributing to the loss of those he both loved and was horrified and disgusted by were obscured by another story he told about himself. He described how, following his mother's death, he became the supremo in his family. Just as he told me he allayed vulnerability to attack by his peers by patronising them as 'disadvantaged' and giving them cigarettes, he allayed vulnerability to his mother's loss by patronising his father as more bereaved than he was by her death.

Meanwhile at school he triumphed over any upset he might have felt by becoming a 'big deal' artist. He also became a Don Juan. Seducing women into crediting him with being the perfect lover kept at bay the discreditable hatred as well as love of his mother and others which he might otherwise have felt at losing them through their dying. Sex, he told me, is a 'fuck off' to death.

It was the same with his politics. He recalled a dream of his car being boxed in when he was visiting a friend, and of his saving the day by giving the lads a loudspeaker. It was his solution to being 'boxed in' by closeness with, dependence on, and fear of losing those he loved. Rise above it all. Speechify. That was the motto impelling him to become a demogogue student activist. It had similarly impelled him to become a 'wild cannon' and 'maverick' at work. He kept the firm together. Without him, he said, the business would collapse.

It was the same with his wife. Just as he had grandly taken his father under his wing when he was a teenager, he had grandly taken his wife under his wing in marrying her. Just as he derided his father's dependence on him, and his mother's nervous debility following the death of her daughter and father, and just as he derided his mother's fat and sweaty body before she died, he derided the dependence of his wife that led him to marry and save her from the misery and abjection of growing up an unwanted foster child.

It was the same with me. He derided me. He had no respect for my trade. He bad-mouthed psychoanalysis as endless talk of 'murderousness and death'. He dismissed therapy with a two-finger gesture of contempt. He called it 'furtive'. He likened me to the fool who, going to the theatre, hangs up what little intellect he has along with his hat in the cloakroom outside. He short-changed me. He told me it was my fault, that I must have made a mistake in calculating his bill. He resented paying. Anyway why should he? He was 'a special case', too important to be bothered with such financial trivialities. He had no need of me. Rather I needed him. He spoke of my being lost without him when his work stopped him attending one of his appointments.

Slowly, however, his attitude changed. Cracks began to become apparent in his grandiosity. So too did the separation and loss of his mother and others that he had long sought to escape by imagining himself (like the above-mentioned psychoanalyst, Henri Rey's patient) God-like above any such humdrum contingencies. Faced with the prospect of losing me over the Christmas break, he recalled a dream:

> Mr Bouverie [a senior partner in his architecture firm] and I were having Christmas lunch. But there was only very measly turkey legs. We asked for some more and got some wine. But I lost the turkey leg. I woke up looking for it.

The loss of his 'measly turkey leg' was a striking contrast to his previous inflated image of himself as having the phallus, as the Freudian analyst Jacques Lacan might have put it. His dream reminded him of his car. Like the broken down car in the dream of the 12-year-old (also described earlier in this chapter), Len's car was a crock. But he could not bear to lose it. He assumed he could magically fix it, just as he imagined he could fix everything and everyone when his mother died. Thinking of her loss reminded him of one of his customers who, when Len's job for him ended, could not bear to say 'Goodbye'. He talked of those who, rather than face loss of those they love, escape into suicide. Along with his dawning recognition of his and others' difficulties in facing separation and loss came increasing recognition of the divided feelings involved. Now, as well as remembering his mother as someone he hated and was horrified by, he also remembered loving her. He remembered her goodness. He wished she had lived to see his achievements so he could stop driving himself to ever more superlative feats.

He began to acknowledge his initial fear of depending on and of losing his identity were he to become dependent on and involved in therapy with me. Having begun therapy by idealising himself, he now idealised me as 'an omniscient therapist' whom he also hated and wanted enviously to spoil and depose. Anxious about our work together, he recalled a recurring dream of being chased by a clown, and of tearing off the clown's mask not so much to expose him as a fraud but out of 'livid' hatred of the clown, now equated with me, for making him feel so beholden to others helping him.

Following the next holiday break, he told me he had realised he valued and missed therapy when it was not there. He confessed to having begun therapy in 'grandiose' fashion, and to now feeling quite the reverse – that he was not very 'adept' at it. He despaired of taking in anything good. All he took in, he said, was bad – cigarettes and beer. He was preoccupied with bad people, with the killers of 2-year-old Jamie Bulger, for instance. He became depressed lest, contrary to his former grand image of himself, of ensuring his teenage daughter's success at school where her teachers had failed, he could not get her through her exams.

He was laid low with flu. He worried lest his debility lose him his wife. He worried that she might heartlessly 'dethrone' and 'dispense' with him, as he had dispensed with his mother and others rather than countenance their loss. Having previously dispensed with his wife as useless compared to him, he now acknowledged that she also helped him. It was because she had suggested he might find therapy helpful, he now told me, that he had first asked me to take him on as a patient.

He began to value not only his wife's help, but also his father's ability to use help, so unlike his own inability to use others' help when his mother died. A memory came back to him of himself, aged 8, miserable at losing his father one day in a crowded supermarket. Facing his unhappiness at these and other separations and losses, he acknowledged wanting therapy. He wanted its 'containment', he said. He wanted me to keep an eye on him, as he kept an eye on his teenage daughter, so as to work to resolve, rather than flee into self-glorification from his divided feelings about being with others and fearing their loss. He asked me to help him with his job. He also increasingly faced the fact of his poverty, which he had previously indicated and brushed aside, leaving me, not him, to worry about it. Beyond therapy, he set about remedying his lack of money. He set about furthering the skills he needed to become the good son, husband, father, worker, and friend he had previously

imagined he already was in the self-aggrandising story of saving everybody at
home and at work with which he had begun.

Boy crazy romance

Whereas Len began therapy making much of himself as the best-of-the-best,
symbolised according to Lacanians by the idea of 'having the phallus', others,
like Lisa, whose therapy I will recount in a moment, entertain the illusion in
Lacanian terms of 'being the phallus', of being the ideal object of others'
desire. Or, to put it in more common sense terms, they are driven by the boy
crazy romance of imagining themselves to be the ideal others most crave and
want them to be.

Anna Freud recounted just this romance.[33] She described how – divided
within themselves by puberty reviving their childhood rivalries with, and
desire for, their parents – teenagers often turn from their parents to others
whom they idealise, and with whom they seek to identify instead (see p.110).
She also described teenagers acting 'as if', as the psychoanalyst Helene
Deutsch once put it,[34] they were those whom they idealise. In the case of girls,
Anna Freud added, teenagers often act as if they were the ideal figure the boys
and men they fall in love with want them to be. She illustrated this outcome
with the example of a 15-year-old who, with the onset of puberty, gave up all
her former interests in favour of the sole desire of being whatever the man she
currently idolised most wanted of her. The only respite, she dreamt, was for
the world to end. Only then would she be relieved of the burden and strain of
trying to be what her man of the moment most wanted her to be.

Recently the feminist philosopher, Elizabeth Grosz, has recounted a similar
story. She describes how, within Lacanian terms, the vainglorious, narcissistic
woman spends hours primping, titivating, and beautifying herself. Grosz
writes of such a woman:

> She devotes loving time and energy to the image she has for others, her
> representation in the world. She paints/shaves/plucks/diets/exercises her
> body, and clearly derives pleasure from compliments about her looks.
> Her whole body becomes the phallus to compensate for a genital 'defi-
> ciency', which she is able to disavow through her narcissism. The art of
> illusion and semblance become her greatest assets. She can utilize these
> techniques to mask, or cover over this 'secret' insufficiency.[35]

This brings me to Lisa. She was a jazz musician in her late forties when I saw
her in therapy some years ago. Her doctor referred her because of her
complete loss of confidence following the failure of her marriage. Lisa began
by telling me of the teenage origin of her symptoms. She told me how, as a
teenager, she experienced her mother as 'blank', 'stupid', and 'dumb'. She
remembered her father deriding her mother as 'useless' and as 'a nervous

wreck'. She talked of her mother's depression when she, Lisa, was 17. She remembered nightmares of witches, shopping, and cooking. She told me:

> There was a dream I used to have as a child – witches holding a market in the back garden. I knew something bad would happen . . . I have anxiety dreams now about cooking – about the shops shutting – and I haven't got the things I need.

More often, however, she said nothing of cooking, witches, and mothering. Instead she talked about her father – over and over again. She idolised him. She told me how she had always sought to please him. She recalled her teenage excitement at his adventure stories of saving her from damning closeness with her mother through the two of them running away to become free-as-air buskers.

Years later, in therapy with me, she still wore the motley garb of the wandering minstrel. To this she had added the accretions of whatever else her father and the men who took his place, including the boyfriend for whom she had left her husband, seemingly most wanted her to be as the price of saving her from her mother. She had taught herself chess to be the sparring partner her father wanted to prove himself 'champion of the world . . . of the universe even', as Lisa put it. She had learnt Latin and Greek to become the classical scholar one of her boyfriends seemingly most wanted her to be. She became a financial wizard to better another lover's previous girlfriend's City prowess. She pretended to the passionate feelings her present lover apparently most longed for her to feel.

She told her story in terms of a folk tale, recounted by Boccaccio and others, of a downtrodden peasant woman who is saved from abjection by passing each of a succession of tests a king sets her to ensure she meets the standard he requires to make her his queen. Lisa said her lack of confidence was chiefly due to her dread lest she fail the tests her current boyfriend set her as the cost of saving her from her fraught life with her husband which had replaced her fraught and divided love of her mother as a teenager.

Just as she was divided in her teenage love and hate of her mother, she was divided in her feelings about me. On the one hand she treated me, as she treated her mother, as a drudge with whom closeness was only bearable provided she enliven our togetherness with talk of her boy crazy affairs. Otherwise she hated being with me. She hated confiding her menopausal symptoms that made her so like her middle-aged mother when she, Lisa, was a teenager, and so unlike the ideal she wanted her succession of boyfriends to credit her with being. She recounted an image of hearing her father returning from the dead, dismissing her, as he had dismissed her mother when Lisa was in her teens, saying, 'So that's what it's come to. You never did do anything. Just ordinary and middle-aged.' She hated confessing this image, just as she hated sharing with me the fact that, far from being the wonderfully kind woman she wanted to be in her boyfriends' eyes, she wanted cruelly to hurt and crush them in revenge for all the energy she expended in striving to be the princess of their dreams.

She also hated admitting the ordinariness of her problems, including the ordinariness of her preoccupation with, and unhappiness at feeling left out. This feeling had been horribly borne in on her, she said, when she was 13 and her father got together with her mother and, without any regard for her, uprooted and moved her and the rest of the family to the other end of the country to get himself out of a financial scrape. She hated confessing to me that, contrary to her earlier story of her father promising to save her from her mother by the two of them running away together, he and her mother had always been very much wedded to each other – to the exclusion of Lisa.

She hated being with me and confiding to me her unhappiness about being excluded. But she also loved seeing me. She valued our togetherness. It would be paradise, she told me, were I to include her among my friends. She wanted to charm me just as she felt driven to charm her men. She read my books to make herself the patient I might most want her to be. But then she hated me for seemingly squeezing this confession out of her, for having 'the last laugh' as she felt her father had had over her. She sobbed that whatever she did would be done to please me, that nothing felt real, that she was just a hollow 'sham', an empty shell.

Just as she felt divided between love and hate of me, she made me feel divided. I felt divided between feeling full of her boy crazy stories, and as empty as she often felt herself to be. Perhaps that was why, alongside the warmth and brilliance of her talk, I often felt inwardly shivery and cold as though it were I, not her, who, with her thin clothes and play-acted veneer, had no warming substance inside.

Perhaps it was my containing these divided feelings – including feeling both her coldness and warmth – that enabled her to take them back into herself as containable and contained. Perhaps it was her sharing her divided feelings as they arose in therapy with me that contributed to her retelling her story to include her mother. Now she included her not only as a hated incompetent from whom she had wanted to be saved in her teens by her father and then by a succession of boyfriends and lovers, but as someone she loved and remembered, unlike her men, as always reliably there for her.

She began to fashion a new story for herself of becoming closer to her mother and to others rather than fleeing her divided love of them for romance with distant and elusive men. She represented this development in terms of a jazz improvisation on which she now worked. It was on the theme of 'London Bridge is falling down'. It was a fitting epitaph to the monument she had previously sought to make of herself as phallus – as Lacan might have put it – as the ideal the men saviours in her life seemingly most wanted her to be. The crumbling of this monument resulted in her no longer being so troubled by the lack of confidence which first brought her to therapy. Her present to me of her resulting jazz composition marked the end of her therapy. It also brings me to the end of this book. What, to conclude, has it all been about?

Part V

Conclusion

11   Beyond memories and dreams

I began with the phrase 'boy crazy'. I also began with the prevalent amnesia of psychologists, psychiatrists, and psychoanalysts regarding the transforming impact of adolescence in shaping our adult lives and loves. I described many women's and men's resistance to remembering their teens, and to finding out, or reading about the experience of teenagers themselves. Hopefully, my referring to adolescence in the title of this book will not result in it suffering the fate of being consigned to virtual oblivion like Stanley Hall's classic tome on the subject.

I have every reason to worry on this account. For both women and men are resistant to knowing, reading, and thinking about adolescence. So too are teenagers. This resistance is particularly marked in teenage boys. They often refuse absolutely to talk about or share their experiences of being teenagers with others, especially with their parents, teachers, and other adults. Warning me off studying adolescence, a mother of four grown sons insisted, 'You can't do research on adolescents. They are too inarticulate.'

Whether or not they are inarticulate, adolescents and adults are bound to be relatively inarticulate, monosyllabic even, in replying to closed-ended, 'yes–no' questionnaires about their teenage years. They are also likely to be inhibited about saying much about their experiences of adolescence in so far as what they most remember and want to talk about is what they feel most diffident and inhibited about, namely love and sex. And this inhibition is fuelled, in England at least, by the embargo on adults inviting under-age students in school to talk about their feelings about and experiences of sex.

Nevertheless, despite this embargo, and despite the inarticulate-making inhibition and resistance of women and men, young and old alike, to talking, thinking, and writing about their experiences, and deepest longings and fears as teenagers regarding sex and love, these obstacles can be overcome. They can be overcome, as I hope I have demonstrated, by replacing closed-ended, 'yes–no' interview questions and questionnaires with the invitation to women and men to write down or say whatever comes to mind in association to their pre-teen and teenage years.

This, of course, is very much akin to the method adopted by Freud in founding psychoanalysis. He encouraged his patients to say whatever came to mind and occurred to them in association to their symptoms. In doing so (as I pointed out in Chapter 1), his patients often found themselves recalling trivial and not so trivial incidents from their teens. In being pressed, in turn, to say whatever came to mind in association to these incidents, and in association to the trivial and not so trivial bits and pieces of their dreams, Freud's patients found themselves undoing the memories and dreams with which they had begun their treatment with him. In the process they often found themselves revealing, filling in, and ironing out incongruities and gaps in their account of their pre-teen, teenage, and adult lives. Pressing himself and his patients to pursue their associations to their memories and dreams, Freud discovered that, as he put it, 'every dream reveals itself as a psychical structure which has a meaning and which can be inserted at an assignable point in the mental activities of waking life'.[1]

I discovered much the same in interviewing women and men for this book. Many were fellow-students in an extra-mural class devoted to studying James Joyce's account, in his novel *Ulysses*, of the fictional, middle-aged Leopold Bloom looking back on his own youth and on that of Stephen Dedalus (see p.39). Having volunteered – sometimes after initial reluctance – to talk with me about their teens, the students found themselves recalling incidents which, like dreams, at first often seemed trivial, nonsensical, and absurd. Their free associations, however, often revealed the teenage incidents they remembered to be not at all trivial, but to symbolise eloquently and represent what was most important from their teens in determining the rest of their lives.

The same was true of the students I asked to write down, anonymously, their adolescent memories and dreams. Some told me their names, and volunteered to talk further with me about what they had written. Their associations to the teenage facts and fantasies they had written down revealed them to represent transforming moments in their life's 'storyline', as the narrative therapist Roy Schaffer might put it.[2] This was often due to their lives being fundamentally altered and transformed by their acting on the longings and fears expressed in their teenage memories and dreams.

For our memories and dreams are not only stories we tell ourselves. They also impel us to act. This is particularly evident in adolescence when the pressure to become grown up makes both sexes, more than ever, seek to act on their memories and dreams to realise or assuage the fears and desires impelling them.[3] Dissociating from our agency in this matter, however, we often experience the fears and desires expressed in our memories and dreams as telling us, rather than us as telling them.[4]

Freudian and Jungian therapy involves reversing this process. It involves exposing our agency in constructing the memories and dreams of our waking and sleeping lives. Freudian and Jungian therapy also involves exposing our agency in acting on the longings and anxieties involved. In acting on our memories and dreams, including those bequeathed us from our teens, our memories and dreams come to rule us, as I have sought to illustrate through recounting examples from my work as a therapist.

If the patients whose stories I have told were helped by therapy, this was, arguably, largely due to their knowing that, whatever their memories and dreams revealed about their divided adolescent selves and loves, both in relation to others and to me, I would still be there, session after session, to go on talking about, experiencing, and piecing together with them the bits and pieces, fragments and divisions involved. They could be confident that I would go on working with them in the hope of arriving at a more secure integration of, and solution to, these divisions than afforded by the symptoms with which they began therapy.[5]

The work of therapists and their patients is akin, in this respect, to the work mothers, daughters and their friends do together in resolving divisions between them in adolescence. Adolescent girls and their mothers (as described in Chapters 5 and 6) are often particularly adept at facing with each other their divided loves and hates so as to further their continuing togetherness, development, and change. Therapy also seeks to bring about change. Through exploring divisions within their patients, and in their patients' relationships with others, therapists seek to bring about change in their patients' attachment to, and detachment from, others in their immediate inner and outer world.

Feminism, about which I have talked throughout this book, goes further. It seeks to bring about improvement and change in women's and men's social as well as personal experience. It seeks to bring about a world in which both sexes might more readily act on and realise what is best in their dreams without being beguiled by false promises. This includes exposing, challenging, and overturning the male dominance of our society which often drives men in early childhood, and women in adolescence, to divide themselves from their mothers, and to escape these divisions through falsely aggrandising and romantically idealising men as gods, heroes, and saviours.

The struggle to bring about a society more committed to recognising and meeting our need not to divide ourselves from our mothers and others, and committed instead to fostering our continuing closeness and community with each other – the latter often equated with women and femininity[6] – is now more urgent than ever. In recent years we have seen the escalating destruction of state- and community-run services in the name of macho individualism, free market enterprise and competition. The mutual commitment to each other of the state and its citizens, of employers and their employees, of families and their members, has increasingly been eroded, done away with, and destroyed.[7] Whatever recent moves to reverse this process – sometimes, it seems, more a matter of window-dressing propaganda than of substantive reconstruction – it is crucial that we go on exposing as illusion what is false in the often male-centred myths of individualism driving us apart. It is also crucial because these myths are a major source of the pain – as well as pleasure – involved in the 'boy crazy' story with which I began, and through which I have sought to highlight the importance of analysing adolescence – its memories and dreams.

Notes

Abbreviation

SE   The Standard Edition of the Complete Psychological Works of Sigmund Freud translated and edited by James Strachey, London: Hogarth Press, 1953–74.

1 Remembering adolescence

1 D. Orr (1995) 'Mea pulpa', *The Guardian Weekend*, 21 October, pp. 13–16.
2 R. Boycott (1996) 'Scenes from a jolly awkward life', *Independent on Sunday*, 17 November, pp. 4–7: 4.
3 For a résumé, see G. D. Painter (1959, 1965) *Marcel Proust*, London: Penguin Books, p. 449.
4 A. Beckett (1996) 'Mother of invention', *Independent on Sunday*, 5 May, pp. 32–33: 32. Jenny Diski recounts her childhood and teenage memories of her mother at greater length in J. Diski (1997) 'A feeling for ice', *London Review of Books*, 2 January, pp. 13–22. Another British novelist, Rose Tremain, tells a similar story of starting writing to fill the vacuum left by her father leaving her, her mother, sister, and Nan; by the family home being sold; and being sent to boarding school 'all in the same year' when she was '10 coming on 11'. R. Tremain (1997) *Desert Island Discs*, BBC Radio 4, 12 October.
5 Spring 1993 Directive, Mass Observation Archive, Brighton: University of Sussex.
6 Examples of the current focus of developmental psychology on the early infant determinants of adult psychology include D. L. Newman, A. Caspi, T. E. Moffitt and P. A. Silva (1997) 'Antecedents of adult interpersonal functioning: effects of individual differences in age 3 temperament', *Developmental Psychology*, vol. 33(2), pp. 206–17.
7 P. van Heeswyk (1997) *Analysing Adolescence*, London: Sheldon Press.
8 *A Winter's Tale*, Act III, Scene iii.
9 C. Dickens (1859) *A Tale of Two Cities*, Harmondsworth: Penguin Books, 1970, p. 35. Recent quotations of this passage with reference to adolescence include M. Freely (1996) 'The horrors of unlucky 13', *The Guardian*, 31 January, pp. 6–7.
10 M. Rutter and D. J. Smith (1995) *Psychosocial Disorders in Young People*, Chichester: Wiley.
11 S. Moore (1995) 'Stressed out on life', *The Guardian*, 1 June, pp. 2–3.
12 D. Malcolm (1996) 'Suffer the little children', *The Guardian*, 16 May, pp. 8–9.
13 My finding in this respect is similar to the finding that men students less often recall their dreams than women. See R. F. Martinetti (1989) 'Sex differences in dream recall and components of imaginal life', *Perceptual and Motor Skills*, vol. 69(2), pp. 643–49.

14 A. Green (1992) 'A psychoanalyst's point of view concerning psychosis at adolescence' in A. Z. Schwartzberg (ed.) *International Annals of Adolescent Psychiatry*, Chicago: University of Chicago Press.

15 This is noted, for example, by K. K. Novick and J. Novick (1994) 'Postoedipal transformations: latency, adolescence, and pathogenesis', *Journal of the American Psychoanalytical Association*, vol. 42(1), pp. 143–69, and by M.-J. Gerson (1994) 'Standing at the threshold', *Psychoanalytic Psychology*, vol. 11(4), pp. 491–508. For the opposite claim – that adolescence is very much a matter of current psychoanalytic research – see J. Cohen (1997) 'Child and adolescent psychoanalysis', *International Journal of Psycho-Analysis*, vol. 78(3), pp. 499–520.

16 See, for example, A. Green (1996) 'Has sexuality anything to do with psychoanalysis?', *International Journal of Psycho-Analysis*, vol. 76, pp. 871–83; J. Mitchell (1996) 'Sexuality and psychoanalysis: hysteria', *British Journal of Psychotherapy*, vol. 12(4), pp. 473–79.

17 Particularly important in this respect was the study by G. S. Hall (1904) *Adolescence: Its Psychology, and its Relations to Physiology, Anthropology, Sociology, Sex, Crime, Religion and Education*, New York: Appleton. Or, as feminist psychologist, Chris Griffin, puts it, 'adolescence first emerged as an ideological construct in the late nineteenth century. . . . G. Stanley Hall's two-volume text *On Adolescence* is generally taken as the key moment of "discovery"'. C. Griffin (1997) 'Troubled teens', *Feminist Review*, vol. 55 (Spring), pp. 4–21: 8.

18 See, for example, J. Neubauer (1992) *The Fin-de-Siècle Culture of Adolescence*, New Haven: Yale University Press.

19 See, for example, M. Foucault (1976) *A History of Sexuality*, London: Penguin Books; J. Weeks (1979) *Sex, Politics and Society*, London: Longman.

20 Perhaps this explains why popular culture and academic journals began to become concerned with male adolescence at the beginning of this century, whereas female adolescence had already emerged as an issue in the late 1880s, according to C. A. Nathanson (1991) *Dangerous Passage: The Social Control of Sexuality in Women's Adolescence*, Philadelphia: Temple University Press, 1991.

21 See, for example, R. Williams (1973) *The Country and the City*, London: Chatto and Windus.

22 S. Freud (1899) 'Screen memories', *SE3*, p. 311.

23 ibid., p. 316.

24 S. Freud (1896) 'The aetiology of hysteria', *SE3*, pp. 200 1.

25 S. Freud (1895) A project for a scientific psychology, *SE1*, pp. 353–56. See also L. Appignanesi and J. Forrester (1992) *Freud's Women*, London: Weidenfeld and Nicolson, p. 136. For recent evidence that it is often at adolescence that the impact of earlier sexual abuse first manifests itself, see S. B. Gordon (1990) 'Adolescent sexuality: treatment of the sleeper effects of sexual abuse' in E. L. Feindler and R. K. Grace (eds) *Adolescent Behaviour Therapy Handbook*, vol. 2, pp. 233–52.

26 Freud wrote that Dora was aged 14 and 16 at the time. Recent evidence, however, indicates that Freud mistook her age by a year in both instances. See Appignanesi and Forrester, op. cit.

27 S. Freud (1905) 'Fragment of an analysis of a case of hysteria', *SE7*, p. 64.

28 ibid., p. 94.

29 S. Freud (1939) *Moses and Monotheism*, *SE23*, p. 79.

30 S. Freud (1918) 'From the history of an infantile neurosis', *SE17*, p. 29.

31 ibid., p. 41.

32 See S. Freud (1907) 'Delusions and dreams in Jensen's "Gradiva"', *SE9*; S. Freud (1916) 'Some character-types met with in psycho-analytic work', *SE14*; S. Freud (1928) 'Dostoevsky and parricide', *SE21*; S. Freud (1919) 'The "uncanny"', *SE7*.

33 Respondents were asked to circle which of the following they lived with: mother, father, sister/s, brother/s, other/s.

2 Detached sons

1 D. H. Skuse *et al.* (1997) 'Evidence from Turner's syndrome of an imprinted X-linked locus affecting cognitive function', *Nature*, vol. 387 (12 June), pp. 706–8.

2 S. Orbach (1994) 'Emotional illiteracy' in *What's Really Going on Here?*, London: Virago, p. 5. Another therapist, Roger Horrocks, similarly writes of 'a male malaise – what I would loosely call male autism – a state of being cut off from natural feelings and expressiveness and contact with others'. R. Horrocks (1994) *Masculinity in Crisis*, London: Macmillan.

3 R. Picardie (1996) 'The myth about men', *Independent on Sunday – Real Life*, 19 May, p. 3.

4 S. Moore (1996) 'Men behaving sadly', *The Guardian*, 25 April, p. 5.

5 S. Freud (1909) 'Analysis of a phobia in a five-year-old boy', *SE10*, pp. 7–8.

6 See, for example, S. Freud (1924) 'The dissolution of the Oedipus complex', and S. Freud (1925) 'Some psychical consequences of the anatomical distinction between the sexes', *SE19*.

7 Although I deplore the generic use of male pronouns to refer to children whatever their sex, I will follow this practice to distinguish children from their primary carers who, because of continuing sexual inequalities in childcare, are almost always women.

8 R. Greenson (1968) 'Dis-identifying from mothers', *International Journal of Psycho-Analysis*, vol. 49, pp. 370–74: 370.

9 N. Chodorow (1978) *The Reproduction of Mothering*, Berkeley: University of California Press. For more recent examples see A. Phillips (1993) *The Trouble with Boys*, London: HarperCollins; and E. Jordan (1995) 'Fighting boys and fantasy play: the construction of masculinity in the early years of school', *Gender and Education*, vol. 7(1), pp. 69–86.

10 W. R. Bion (1986) *The Long Week-End*, London: Free Association Books, p. 34.

11 P. Vallely (1996) 'When Jon Snow told his family secrets', *The Independent*, 2 November, p. 21. From V. and M. Glendinning (eds) *Sons and Mothers*, London: Virago, 1996.

12 Tony Kildwick, born 1919, Yorkshire, in Testimony Films (1996) *A Man's World: l. The Boy*, BBC2, 9. 50–10. 30 p.m., Thursday, 6 March.

13 Geordie Todd, born 1912, North Shields, in Testimony Films, op. cit.

14 See, for example, Andrews, G., Morris-Yates, A., Howie, P. and Martin, N. (1991) 'Genetic factors in stuttering confirmed', *Archives of General Psychiatry*, vol. 49(11), pp. 1034–35.

15 One study, for instance, finds stammering begins in boys, on average, at 32.76 months, with girls who stutter beginning stuttering significantly earlier than boys who stutter. See E. Yairi and N. Ambrose (1992) 'Onset of stuttering in preschool children', *Journal of Speech and Hearing Research*, vol. 35(4), pp. 782–88. Surprisingly, however, in over 400 references to stuttering in *Psychological Abstracts* for the last five years – several of which indicated its greater frequency in men, and many of which advanced sophisticated genetic and neurological explanations – no researcher suggested that this sex difference might be due to boys being taught to gag on their feelings. Nevertheless, boys are significantly more likely than girls not only to stammer but also to suffer other speech and language-processing disorders. See, for example, J. S. Hyde and M. C. Lin (1988) 'Gender differences in verbal ability: a meta-analysis', *Psychological Bulletin*, vol. 104, pp. 53–69.

16 W. H. R. Rivers (1920, p. 209) quoted by A. Young (1995) *The Harmony of Illusions: Inventing Post-Traumatic Stress Disorder*, New Jersey: Princeton University Press, p. 65.

17 My thanks to Andy Duggan for drawing my attention to this finding.

18 W. H. R. Rivers (1917) quoted by Young, op. cit., p. 67.
19 P. Barker (1995) *The Ghost Road*, London: Viking, p. 96.
20 A. Stevens (1995) *Private Myths: Dreams and Dreaming*, London: Hamish Hamilton, p. 97.
21 S. Freud (1920) *Beyond the Pleasure Principle, SE18*. For a recent account of recurring dreams, see G. W. Dornhoff (1996) *Finding Meaning in Dreams*, New York: Plenum.
22 S. Freud (1900) *The Interpretation of Dreams, SE5*.
23 S. Freud (1916–17) *Introductory Lectures on Psycho-Analysis, SE16*, p. 314.
24 D. W. Winnicott (1953) 'Transitional objects and transitional phenomena' in *Playing and Reality*, London: Penguin Books, 1971, p. 19.
25 *City Lives*, National Sound Archive, London.
26 My thanks to Peter Wollen for reminding me of this example in a lecture drawing on his worldwide web article about *Bambi*.
27 Other researchers similarly find that the recurrent dreams recalled from childhood by students are more likely than their recent recurring dreams to involve threatening folklore or fictional characters, see P. R. Robbins and R. H. Tanck (1992) 'A comparison of recurrent dreams reported from childhood and recent recurrent dreams', *Imagination, Cognition and Personality*, vol. 11(3), pp. 259–62.
28 C. G. Jung (1961) *Memories, Dreams, Reflections*, London: Fontana, 1967, pp. 107–8.
29 Bowlby based his conclusion on the finding that all fourteen children (eleven boys and three girls, average age 9.5 years) diagnosed as 'affectionless characters' from a group of forty-four children referred for child guidance with symptoms involving stealing, had suffered prolonged separation in early childhood from their mothers, or mother-substitutes. J. Bowlby (1944) 'Forty-four juvenile thieves', *International Journal of Psycho-Analysis*, vol. 25, pp. 1–57, 207–28.
30 J. Bowlby (1965) *Child Care and the Growth of Love*, London: Penguin Books, p. 13.
31 D. W. Winnicott (1938) 'Skin Changes in relation to emotional disorder', *St John's Hospital Dermatological Society Report*, quoted by A. Phillips (1988) *Winnicott*, London: Fontana, p. 48.
32 See, for example, D. W. Winnicott (1960) 'The theory of the parent–infant relationship', *International Journal of Psycho-Analysis*, vol. 41, pp. 585–95.
33 See, for example, D. W. Winnicott (1969) 'The use of an object' in *Playing and Reality*, op. cit.
34 W. R. Bion (1962) 'A theory of thinking' in *Second Thoughts*, London: Karnac, 1984, pp. 114–15.
35 F. MacCarthy (1994) *William Morris*, London: Faber, p. 11.

3 Divided adolescents

1 S. Townsend (1982) *The Secret Diary of Adrian Mole aged 13³ᐟ⁴*, London: Methuen, p. 28.
2 A. C. Kinsey *et al.* (1948) *Sexual Behavior in the Human Male*, Philadelphia: W. B. Saunders.
3 A. Adegoke (1992) 'Relationship between parental socio-economic status, sex, and initial pubertal problems among school-going adolescents in Nigeria, *Journal of Adolescence*, vol. 15, pp. 323–26.
4 One reference was to bed wetting in Vietnam veterans, the other to a 31-year-old man treated electrically for nocturnal emissions and for being unable to ejaculate when he was awake. See respectively T. A. Mellman *et al.* (1995) 'Nocturnal/daytime urine noradrenergic measures and sleep in combat-related PTSD (post-traumatic stress disorder)', *Biological Psychiatry*, vol. 38(3), pp.

174–79; and D. E. Stewart and D. A. Ohl (1989) 'Idiopathic anejaculation treated by electroejaculation', *International Journal of Psychiatry in Medicine*, vol. 19(3), pp. 263–68.

5 R. von-Krafft-Ebing (1991) 'Ueber pollutionsartige Vorgange beim Weibe (On pollution-like phenomena in the female)', *Zeitschrift-fur-Sexualforschung*, vol. 4(1), pp. 67–72. In his article Krafft-Ebing equates women's dreams about sex with men's wet dreams, and women's vaginal lubrication with men's ejaculation.

6 J. H. Stein and L. W. Reiser (1994) 'A study of white middle-class adolescent boys' response to "semenarche" (the first ejaculation)', *Journal of Youth and Adolescence*, vol. 23(3), pp. 373–84.

7 A. Gaddis and J. Brooks-Gunn (1985) 'The male experience of pubertal change', *Journal of Youth and Adolescence*, vol. 14, pp. 61–69. There is also the occasional reference to helping prepare boys for wet dreams, see C. Paddack (1987) 'Preparing a boy for nocturnal emissions', *Medical Aspects of Human Sexuality*, vol. 21, pp. 15, 16. See also A. Adegoke (1993) 'The experience of spermarche among selected adolescent boys in Nigeria', *Journal of Youth and Adolescence*, vol. 22, pp. 201–9; C. Downs and M. J. Fuller (1991) 'Recollections of spermarche', *Current Psychology*, vol. 10, pp. 93–102.

8 J. Garbarino (1985) *Adolescent Development* cited by S. Moore and D. Rosenthal (1993) *Sexuality in Adolescence*, London: Routledge.

9 This aspect of teenage boys' response to puberty is discussed in general terms by D. Flaming and J. Morse (1991) 'Minimizing embarrassment', *Issues in Comprehensive Pediatric Nursing*, vol. 14(4), pp. 211–30.

10 S. Thompson (1984) 'Search for tomorrow: feminism and the reconstruction of teen romance' in C. Vance (ed.) *Pleasure and Danger*, London: Virago, p. 351.

11 G. Grass (1961) *Cat and Mouse*, London: Penguin Books, 1963, p. 32.

12 One survey, for instance, finds that by age 21, 83 per cent of men and 77 per cent of women say they have masturbated. See M. Janus (1993) *The Janus Report on Sexual Behavior*, Chichester: Wiley. For a recent review of 177 such studies, see M. B. Oliver and J. S. Hyde (1993) 'Gender differences in sexuality: a meta-analysis', *Psychological Bulletin*, vol. 114(1), pp. 29–51.

13 M. D. Story (1982) 'A comparison of university student experience with various sexual outlets in 1974 and 1980', *Adolescence*, Winter, pp. 737–47.

14 H. Leitenberg, M. J. Detzer and D. Srebnik (1993) 'Gender differences in masturbation', *Archives of Sexual Behavior*, vol. 22(2), pp. 87–98.

15 J. C. Jones and D. H. Barlow (1990) 'Self-reported frequency of sexual urges, fantasies, and masturbatory fantasies in heterosexual males and females', *Archives of Sexual Behavior*, vol. 19, pp. 269–79.

16 C. LoPresto, M. Sherman and N. Sherman (1985) 'The effects of a masturbation seminar on high school males' attitudes, false beliefs, guilt, and behavior', *Journal of Sex Research*, vol. 21, pp. 142–56.

17 A. Brown (1996) 'It was the sex and drugs that did it', *Independent on Sunday – Real Life*, 19 May, p. 10.

18 J. C. Jones and D. H. Barlow (1990) 'Self-reported frequency of sexual urges, fantasies and masturbatory fantasies in heterosexual males and females', *Archives of Sexual Behavior*, vol. 19(3), pp. 269–79.

19 J. Pallavicini (1984) 'La sexualidad en adolescentes normales universitarios (Sexuality in normal adolescent university students)', *Revista de Psichiatria Clinica*, vol. 21(1), pp. 47–56.

20 In one US study only 25 per cent of men, compared to 50 per cent of women attributed their first sexual intercourse to affection for the person with whom they had sex, see R. T. Michael, J. H. Gagnon, E. O. Laufman and G. Kolata (1994) *Sex in America* in F. P. Rice (1996) *The Adolescent*, Boston: Allyn and Bacon. Similarly a study of students' sexual fantasies indicated that men less often mentioned

romance and commitment. See K. N. Hardin and S. R. Gold (1989) 'Relationship of sex, sex guilt, and experience to written sexual fantasies', *Imagination, Cognition and Personality*, vol. 8(2), pp. 155–63. Others find that among 12- to 18-year-olds, while girls report being aroused by their romantic involvement with others, boys more often report being aroused by visual stimuli. See R. Knoth *et al.* (1988) 'Empirical tests of sexual selection theory', *Journal of Sex Research*, vol. 24, pp. 73–89.

21 See, for example, J. R. Faulkenberry, M. Vincent, A. James and W. Johnson (1987) 'Coital behaviors, attitudes and knowledge of students who experience early coitus', *Adolescence*, vol. 22, pp. 321–32; S. Moore and D. Rosenthal (1993) *Sexuality in Adolescence*, London: Routledge; J. Dusek (1996) *Adolescent Development and Behavior*, New Jersey: Prentice Hall.

22 D. A. Rosenthal, S. M. Moore and I. Brumen (1990) 'Ethnic group differences in adolescents' responses to AIDS', *Australian Journal of Social Issues*, vol. 25, pp. 220–39.

23 S. R. Leiblum, R. C. Rosen, M. Platt, R. J. Cross *et al.* (1993) 'Sexual attitudes and behavior of a cross-sectional sample of United States medical students', *Journal of Sex Education and Therapy*, vol. 19(4), pp. 235–45.

24 See, for example, E. Ostrov *et al.* (1985) 'Adolescent sexual behaviour', *Medical Aspects of Human Sexuality*, vol. 19(5), pp. 28–36.

25 See, for example, D. Aaronvitch (1996) 'Don't you know that it's different for girls?', *Independent on Sunday*, 11 February, p. 3.

26 D. Glaser and S. Frosh (1993) *Child Sexual Abuse*, London: Macmillan, p. 31–32.

27 D. Wight (1994) 'Boys' thoughts and talk about sex in a working class locality in Glasgow', *Sociological Review*, vol. 42(4), pp. 703–37.

28 D. Wight (1995/96) 'Beyond the predatory male' in L. Adkins and V. Merchant (eds) *Sexualising the Social*, London: Macmillan.

29 ibid., p. 14.

30 Wight (1994) op. cit., p. 723.

31 N. Way (1996) 'Experiences of desire, betrayal, and intimacy', *New Psychologies Conference*, Tarbert, 28 June–1 July, pp. 5–6. For a somewhat different image of urban teenage boys as loyal and close to each other, see the 1995 film, *La Haine*, directed by Maltieu Kassovitz.

32 E. White (1982) *A Boy's Own Story*, London: Picador, pp. 15–16.

33 ibid., p. 25.

34 Wight (1995/96) op. cit., p. 13.

35 See, for example, C. Muehlenhard and S. W. Cook (1988) 'Men's self-reports of unwanted sexual activity', *Journal of Sex Research*, vol. 24, pp. 58–72.

36 See, for example, S. Freud (1914) 'On the history of the psycho-analytic movement', *SE14*, pp. 17–18.

37 For an account of this pressure see, for example, M. Foucault (1976) *The History of Sexuality*, London: Penguin, 1978. The feminist psychologist, Chris Griffin, puts this pressure in terms of a contradictory discourse of sexual freedom and control, advanced most notably by Stanley Hall in his 1904 textbook on adolescence. See C. Griffin (1997) 'Troubled teens', *Feminist Review*, vol. 55, pp. 4–21.

38 F. Wedekind (1891) *Spring Awakening*, tr. Ted Hughes, London: Faber, 1995, pp. 6–7: 8.

39 R. Musil (1906) *Young Thouless*, London: Panther Books, pp. 23–24.

40 ibid., p. 34.

41 J. W. Jackson and P. Costello (1997) *John Stanislaus Joyce*, London: Fourth Estate.

42 J. Joyce (1916) *A Portrait of the Artist as a Young Man*, London: Penguin Books, 1960, p. 14.

43 Joyce, ibid., pp. 90, 91.

44 Alain-Fournier (1913) *Le Grand Meaulnes*, London: Penguin, 1966, p. 148. See also S. A. Leavy (1990) 'Alain-Fournier: memory, youth, and longing', *Psychoanalytic Study of the Child*, vol. 45, pp. 495–531.
45 E. Hoffman (1989) *Lost in Translation*, London: Heinemann, p. 5.
46 ibid., p. 119.
47 D. W. Winnicott (1960) 'Ego distortion in terms of true and false self' in *Maturational Processes and the Facilitating Environment*, London: Hogarth, 1965. For recent evidence see L. Murray, A. Fiori-Cowley, R. Hooper, and P. Cooper (1996) 'The impact of postnatal depression and associated adversity on early mother–infant interactions and later infant outcome', *Child Development*, vol. 67, pp. 2512–26.
48 P. van Heeswyk (1997) *Analysing Adolescence*, London: Sheldon Press, p. 44.
49 Transcript from archive of *City Lives*, London: National Sound Archive.
50 ibid.
51 For an account of this process see J. Kovel (1995) 'On racism and psychoanalysis' in A. Elliott and S. Frosh (eds) *Psychoanalysis in Contexts*, London: Routledge.
52 For a useful account of this argument see C. Norris (1987) *Derrida*, London: Fontana.
53 R. M. Rilke (1910) *The Notebooks of Malte Laurids Brigge*, New York: Norton, 1949, p. 66.
54 R. Hughes (1929) *A High Wind in Jamaica*, London: Chatto and Windus, pp. 134–35.
55 M. M. Gergen and K. J. Gergen (1993) 'Narratives of the gendered body in popular autobiography' in R. Josselson and A. Lieblich (eds) *The Narrative Study of Lives*, London: Sage.
56 M. Bragg (1996) 'Out of my mind with terror', *The Times*, 15 January, p. 15.
57 A moving fictional account of this effect of sexual enlightenment is provided by A. Moravia (1944) *Two Adolescents*, New York: Signet, 1950.
58 S. Freud (1909) 'Family romances', *SE9*.
59 S. Freud (1912) 'On the universal tendency to debasement in the sphere of love', *SE11*, p. 181.
60 See, for example, S. Freud (1916–17) *Introductory Lectures on Psycho-Analysis*, SE15–16; S. Freud (1927) 'Fetishism', *SE21*; S. Freud (1940) 'Splitting of the ego in the process of defence', *SE23*.
61 S. Freud (1910) *Leonardo da Vinci and a Memory of his Childhood*, *SE11*, p. 96.
62 S. Freud (1922) 'Some neurotic mechanisms in jealousy, paranoia and homosexuality', *SE18*, p. 230.
63 S. Freud (1912) op. cit., p. 183.
64 See, for example, S. Freud (1910) 'A special type of choice of object made by men', *SE11*; and S. Freud (1920) 'The psychogenesis of a case of female homosexuality', *SE18*.
65 S. Freud (1928) 'Dostoevsky and parricide', *SE21*, pp. 192–93.
66 A. Freud (1936) *The Ego and the Mechanisms of Defence*, London: Hogarth, 1968, p. 162.
67 ibid., p. 153.
68 A. Freud (1958) 'Adolescence', *Psychoanalytic Study of the Child*, vol. 13, pp. 255–78.
69 M. Laufer and E. Laufer (1989) *Developmental Breakdown and Psychoanalytic Treatment in Adolescence*, New Haven: Yale University Press, p. 12.
70 F. Ladame (1995) 'The importance of dreams and action in the adolescent process', *International Journal of Psycho-Analysis*, vol. 76, pp. 1143–53.
71 Laufer maintains that, although many of his clinical examples involve adolescent boys, his thesis is also relevant to girls. See M. Laufer (1976) 'The central masturbation fantasy, the final sexual organization, and adolescence', *Psychoanalytic*

Study of the Child, vol. 31, pp. 297–316. More recently, however, Laufer admits that girls might resort less often than boys to masturbation as means of resolving the sexual conflicts of adolescence: see M. Laufer (1995) 'Psychological development in adolescence' in M. Laufer (ed.) *The Suicidal Adolescent*, London: Karnac Books.

72 Laufer (1976) op. cit., p. 302.

73 ibid. For a critique of the limited clinical usefulness of this concept see P. Sullivan (1992) 'Fantasme masturbatoire radieux (Radiant masturbatory fantasy)', *Psychiatrie de l'Enfant*, vol. 3 5(1), pp. 33–42.

74 See, for example, E. Laufer (1992) 'Outcome of psychotic breakdown in adolescence: the perverse solution' in A. Z. Schwarzberg (ed.) *International Annals of Adolescent Psychiatry*, Chicago: Chicago University Press.

75 M. Glasser (1979) 'Some aspects of the role of aggression in the perversions' in I. Rosen (ed.) *Sexual Deviation*, Oxford: Oxford University Press; M. Glasser (1986) 'Identification and its vicissitudes as observed in the perversions', *International Journal of Psycho-Analysis*, vol. 67, pp. 9–17; M. Glasser (unpublished) 'The weak spot – Some observations on male sexuality'.

76 M. Laufer (1989) 'Adolescent sexuality: a body/mind continuum', *Psychoanalytic Study of the Child*, vol. 44, pp. 281–94, 293–94.

77 Laufer writes that the body image only becomes integrated to form the basis of the person's sexual and gender identity at the end of adolescence, and that when the body image is distorted it remains to form a psychotic core of the adult personality. See M. Laufer (1991) 'Body image, sexuality, and the psychotic core', *International Journal of Psycho-Analysis*, vol. 72(1), pp. 63–71.

78 Laufer (1989) op. cit., p. 289.

79 See, for example, J. D. Cordeiro (1992) 'The adolescent individuation process' in A. Z. Schwartzberg (ed.) *International Annals of Adolescent Psychiatry*, Chicago: University of Chicago Press. E. Laufer (1987) 'Suicide in adolescence', *Psychoanalytic Psychotherapy*, vol. 3(1), pp. 1–10; Laufer and Laufer, op. cit. See also F. Ladame (1992) 'Suicide prevention in adolescence', *Journal of Adolescent Health*, vol. 13(5), pp. 406–8.

80 K. Mehra (1997) 'Interferences in the move from adolescence to adulthood: the development of the male' in M. Laufer (ed.) *Adolescent Breakdown and Beyond*, London: Karnac.

81 For an account of this fascination, see R. Horrocks (1995) *Male Myths and Icons: Masculinity in Popular Culture*, London: Macmillan.

82 D. Campbell (1995) 'Discovering, explaining and confronting the monster', Freud Museum Spring Conference, London: National Film Theatre, 18 March; also discussed by I. Ward (1996) 'Adolescent phantasies and the horror film', *British Journal of Psychotherapy*, vol. 13(2), pp. 267–76.

4 Schizoid and suicidal splitting

1 P. van Heeswyk (1997) *Analysing Adolescence*, London: Sheldon Press, p. 35.

2 ibid., p. 38.

3 A. Jablensky *et al.* (1992) 'Schizophrenia: manifestations, incidence and causes in different countries', *Psychological Medicine: Monograph Supplement 20*, Cambridge: Cambridge University Press.

4 P. Galdos and J. van-Os (1995) 'Gender, psychopathology, and development: from puberty to early adulthood', *Schizophrenia Research*, vol. 14(2), pp. 105–12.

5 See R. F. W. Diekstra, C. W. M. Kienhorst and E. J. de Wilde (1995) 'Suicide and suicidal behaviour among adolescents' in M. Rutter and D. J. Smith (eds) *Psychological Disorders in Young People*, Chichester: Wiley.

6 See, for example, D. R. Heacock (1990) 'Suicidal behavior in Black and Hispanic youth', *Psychiatric Annals*, vol. 20(3), pp. 134–42; P. L. McCall (1991) 'Adolescent and elderly white male suicide trends', *Journal of Gerontology*, vol. 46(1), pp. S43–S51; P. A. May and N. Van-Winkle (1994) 'Indian adolescent suicide', *American Indian and Alaska Native Mental Health Research*, vol. 4, pp. 5–34; C. Pritchard (1995) *Suicide – the Ultimate Rejection?* Milton Keynes: Open University Press; L. A. Pagliaro (1995) 'Adolescent depression and suicide', *Canadian Journal of School Psychology*, vol. 11(2), pp.191–201; D. T. L. Shek (1995) 'Adolescent suicide in Hong Kong: 1980–1991, *International Journal of Adolescent Medicine and Health*, vol. 8(1), pp. 65–86.

7 See, for example, G. P. Amminger, R. Mutschlechner and F. Resch (1994) 'Social competence and adolescent psychosis', *British Journal of Psychiatry*, vol. 165(2), pp. 273.

8 D. Offer, E. Ostrow, K. K. Howard and R. Atkinson (1992) 'A study of quietly disturbed and normal adolescents in ten countries' in A. Z. Schwarberg (ed.) *International Annals of Adolescent Psychiatry*, Chicago: University of Chicago Press.

9 See, for example, D. Raymond (1994) 'Homophobia, identity, and the meaning of desire' in J. Irvine (ed.) *Sexual Cultures and the Construction of Adolescent Identities*, Philadelphia: Temple University Press. A 1997 report from the UK Sex Education Forum similarly speculates that, due to the outlawing by British Clause 28 legislation of education about homosexuality, 'considerable numbers of male teenage suicides may be homosexual boys who interpreted the classroom silence as prohibition'. L. Grant (1997) 'How do boys turn into men?', *The Guardian*, 25 March, p. 8.

10 W. Farrell (1994) *The Myth of Male Power*, London: Fourth Estate, p. 13. See also M. Wilson (1981) 'Suicidal behaviour: toward an explanation of differences in female and male rates', *Suicide and Life-Threatening Behaviour*, vol. 11(3), pp.131–39; J. Salisbury and D. Jackson (1996) *Challenging Macho Values*, Brighton: Falmer Press.

11 E. Durkheim (1888) *Suicide: A Study in Sociology*, London: Routledge, 1952.

12 M. Laufer (1995) 'Understanding suicide' in M. Laufer (ed.) *The Suicidal Adolescent*, London: Karnac, p. 75–76.

13 ibid., p. 75.

14 R. Cahn (1992) 'The theory of psychosis at adolescence' in A. Z. Schwartzberg *et al.* (eds) *International Annals of Adolescent Psychiatry*, Chicago: University of Chicago.

15 M. Laufer (1992) 'Adolescent psychosis, fact or fiction? A psychoanalytic view of adolescent assessment and treatment' in A. Z. Schwarzberg, ibid.

16 ibid., p. 153–54. Others recount cases of adolescent paedophile fantasies linked to longing to be loved as a girl. See A. Hurry (1990) 'Bisexual conflict and paedophilic fantasies in the analysis of a late adolescent', *Journal of Child Psychotherapy*, vol. 16(1), pp. 5–28.

17 Laufer (1992) op. cit., p. 154.

18 M. Laufer (1976) 'The central masturbation fantasy, the final sexual organization, and adolescence', *Psychoanalytic Study of the Child*, vol. 31, pp. 297–316: 311.

19 ibid., p. 310.

20 ibid., pp. 311–12.

21 Laufer (1995) op. cit., p. 81. See also A. Hurry (1978) 'My ambition is to be dead', *Journal of Child Psychotherapy*, vol. 4(4), pp. 69–83.

22 Laufer (1976) op. cit., p. 310, 311.

23 The psychologist, Colwyn Trevarthen, puts this in terms of the mother being 'live company' to her child. See C. Trevarthen (1978) 'Modes of perceiving and codes of acting' in H. J. Pick (ed.) *Psychological Modes of Perceiving and Processing*

Information, Hillsdale: Lawrence Erlbaum; quoted by A. Alvarez (1992) *Live Company*, London: Routledge.

24 R. D. Laing (1959) *The Divided Self*, London: Penguin, 1965, pp. 116, 118.

25 D. Burston (1996) *The Wing of Madness: The Life and Work of R. D. Laing*, Cambridge, Mass.: Harvard University Press.

26 For a recently published account of the possible contribution of this defence in the genesis of childhood autism see D. W. Winnicott (1967) *Thinking about Children*, New York: Addison-Wesley.

27 Laing, op. cit., p. 95, emphasis as in original.

28 H. Guntrip (1968) *Schizoid Phenomena, Object-Relations and the Self*, London: Hogarth.

29 Laing, op. cit., p. 106.

30 ibid., p. 120.

31 ibid., p. 122.

32 ibid., p. 124.

33 ibid., p. 130.

34 ibid., p. 71.

35 ibid., p. 70.

36 ibid., p. 73.

37 I have changed all identifying details of patients referred to in this and other chapters in the continuing absence of clear guidelines regarding patient anonymity. See A. Goldberg (1997) 'Writing case histories', *International Journal of Psycho-Analysis*, vol. 78(3), pp. 435–38.

5 Attached daughters

1 For a recent argument to this effect see D. H. Skuse *et al.* (1997) 'Evidence from Turner's syndrome of an imprinted X-linked locus affecting cognitive function', *Nature*, vol. 387(12 June), pp. 705–8.

2 E. Z. Tronick and J. F. Cohn (1989) 'Infant–mother face-to-face interaction', *Child Development*, vol. 60, pp. 85–92.

3 For a review of the data see J. S. Hyde and M. C. Linn (1988) 'Gender differences in verbal ability: a meta-analysis', *Psychological Bulletin*, vol. 104, pp. 53–69.

4 See, for example, K. S. Berger and R. A. Thompson (1995) *The Developing Person*, New York: Worth Publishers.

5 J. D. Wine (1981) 'From defect to competence models' in J. D. Wine and M. D. Smye (eds) *Social Competence*, New York: Guilford Press; and J. A. Hall (1984) *Nonverbal Sex Differences: Communication Accuracy and Expressive Skill*, Baltimore: Johns Hopkins.

6 D. Oppenheim, A. Nir, S. Warren and R. Emde (1997) 'Emotion regulation in mother–child narrative co-construction', *Developmental Psychology*, vol. 33(2), pp. 284–94; C. A. Haden, R. A. Haine and R. Firush (1997) 'Developing narrative structure in parent–child reminiscences across the preschool years', *Developmental Psychology*, vol. 33(2), pp. 295–307.

7 S. Freud (1933) *New Introductory Lectures on Psycho-Analysis*, SE22, p. 133.

8 Freud (1933) op. cit.

9 See, for example, S. Freud (1916) 'Some character-types met with in psychoanalytic work', *SE14*.

10 S. Freud (1905) 'Transformations of puberty' in *Three Essays on the Theory of Sexuality*, *SE7*, pp. 227–28.

11 N. Chodorow (1978) *The Reproduction of Mothering*, Berkeley: University of California Press.

12 Carol Gilligan, personal communication.

13 I document this point further in J. Sayers (1991) *Mothering Psychoanalysis*, London: Penguin.
14 S. Isaacs (1943) 'The nature and function of phantasy' in J. Riviere (ed.) *Developments in Psycho-Analysis*, London: Hogarth, 1952, p. 83.
15 See, for example, M. Klein (1952) 'On observing the behaviour of young infants' in *Envy and Gratitude and Other Works 1946–1963*, London: Hogarth, 1975.
16 See, for example, M. Klein (1937) 'Love, guilt and reparation' in *Love, Guilt, and Reparation and Other Works 1921–1945*, London: Hogarth, 1975.
17 See, for example, M. Klein (1957) 'Envy and Gratitude' in *Envy and Gratitude*, op. cit.
18 See, for example, M. Klein (1928) 'Early stages of the Oedipus complex' in *Love, Guilt and Reparation*, op. cit.; and M. Klein (1932) *The Psycho-Analysis of Children*, London: Hogarth, 1975.
19 My thanks to Alison Barr for this example.
20 See, for example, B. Zani (1991) 'Male and female patterns in the discovery of sexuality during adolescence', *Journal of Adolescence*, vol. 14(2), pp. 163–78.
21 C. Gallagher (1997) 'Despair, despair, despair . . . spare', Paper given to the *Fourth Annual Conference of the Universities Association for Psychoanalytic Studies*, Canterbury, 17–18 May.
22 S. Orbach (1996) 'Teen effort', *The Guardian Weekend*, 1 June, p. 6.
23 H. Mantel (1995) *An Experiment in Love*, London: Viking, p. 114.
24 T. Apter (1995) *Secret Paths*, New York; Norton, p. 58.
25 J. Frame (1982) *To the Island*, London: Paladin, 1987, p. 146.
26 E. K. Dahl (1995) 'Daughters and mothers: aspects of the representational world during adolescence', *Psychoanalytic Study of the Child*, vol. 50, pp. 187–204, 191.
27 One study finds that within two or three months of their first period only 20 per cent of girls reported positive responses, 20 per cent reported negative responses, while the remainder – the majority – felt unsure or reported mixed feelings. See D. Ruble and J. Brooks-Gunn (1982) 'The experience of menarche', *Child Development*, vol. 53, pp. 1557–66. See also S. Moore (1995) 'Girls' understanding and social construction of menarche', *Journal of Adolescence*, vol. 18, pp. 87–104.
28 For further examples see S. Phillips (1996) *Beyond the Myths: Mother–Daughter Relationships in Psychology, History, Literature and Everyday Life*, London: Penguin Books.
29 E. A. Kissling (1996) 'Bleeding out loud: communication about menstruation', *Feminism and Psychology*, vol. 6(4), pp. 481–504, 494.
30 ibid., p. 499.
31 K. Martin (1996) *Puberty, Sexuality, and the Self*, London: Routledge, p. 30.
32 ibid., p. 103.
33 E. Wurtzel (1994) *Prozac Nation: Young and Depressed in America – A Memoir*, pp. 19–20.
34 See, for example, S. Freud (1918) 'The taboo of virginity', *SE11*; S. Freud (1924) 'The economic problem of mascochism', *SE19*.
35 For an update on the subsequent lives of both teenagers see A. Daniels (1997) 'The secret history', *The Guardian*, 9 January, pp. 4–5.
36 H. Deutsch (1944) *The Psychology of Women: Vol. 1 – Girlhood*, New York: Bantam, 1973; H. Deutsch (1973) *Confrontations with Myself*, New York: Norton.
37 I describe this and other aspects of Deutsch's life and work in greater detail in Sayers, op. cit.
38 Martin, *op. cit.*, p. 102
39 P. Noller and V. Callan (1991) *The Adolescent in the Family*, London: Routledge.
40 L. B. Hendry *et al.* (1992) 'Adolescents' perceptions of significant individuals in their lives', *Journal of Adolescence*, vol. 15, pp. 255–70.
41 T. Apter (1990) *Altered Loves*, Brighton: Harvester Wheatsheaf.

42 One study of US families reports that, compared to fathers, mothers become increasingly negative towards their daughters as they physically mature. See R. Montemagor *et al.* (1993) 'Effects of pubertal status and conversation topic on parent and adolescent affective expression', *Journal of Early Adolescence*, vol. 13(4), pp. 131–47.

43 T. Apter (1993) 'Altered views: fathers' closeness to teenage daughters' in R. Josselson and A. Lieblich (eds) *The Narrative Study of Lives*, London: Sage, p. 185.

44 ibid., p. 174.

45 C. McCullers (1946) *The Member of the Wedding*, London: Penguin, 1962, p. 32.

46 Some argue that men's inhibition in this respect is a major factor contributing to their daughters' eating disorders in adolescence. See M. Maine (1991) *Father Hunger*, Carlsbad CA: Gurze Books.

47 Apter (1993) op. cit., p. 169.

48 ibid., p. 186.

49 M. P. McCabe and J. K. Collins (1990) *Dating, Relating and Sex*, Sydney: Horowitz Grahame.

6 Divided friends

1 M. Rutter and M. Rutter (1992) *Developing Minds*, London: Penguin. See also L. Zarbatany, M. Van Brunschot, and S. Pepper (1996) 'Effects of friendship and gender on peer group entry', *Child Development*, vol. 67, pp. 2287–2300.

2 S. Moore and J. Boldero (1991) 'Psychosocial development and friendship function in young Australian adults', *Sex Roles*, vol. 25, pp. 521–36. See also V. Griffiths (1995) *Adolescent Girls and their Friends*, Aldershot: Avebury.

3 M. Atwood (1988) *Cat's Eye*, London: Virago, 1990, p. 213.

4 ibid., p. 98.

5 ibid., p. 93.

6 ibid., p. 4.

7 ibid., p. 78.

8 ibid., p. 81.

9 ibid., pp. 57–58.

10 ibid., p. 48.

11 ibid., p. 62.

12 ibid., p. 155.

13 ibid., p. 189.

14 E. Winkler (1996) 'That little bully – was that you?', *Independent on Sunday*, 20 October, p. 6. For other first-hand accounts see J. Gordon and G. Grant (1997) *How We Feel: An Insight into the Emotional World of Teenagers*, London: Jessica Kingsley.

15 L. Brown and C. Gilligan (1992) *Meeting at the Crossroads: Women's Psychology and Girls' Development*, Cambridge, Mass.: Harvard University Press, p. 50.

16 ibid., p. 54.

17 ibid., p. 59.

18 ibid., pp. 59–60.

19 See, for example, R. Montemayor, M. Eberly and D. J. Flannery (1993) 'Effects of pubertal status and conversation topic on parent and adolescent affective expression', *Journal of Early Adolescence*, vol. 13(4), pp. 431–47.

20 L. B. Hendry, W. Roberts, A. Glendinning and J. C. Coleman (1992) 'Adolescents' perceptions of significant individuals in their lives', *Journal of Adolescence*, vol. 15, pp. 255–70.

21 P. Noller and V. Callan (1991) *The Adolescent in the Family*, London: Routledge.

22 For evidence that young women more often share their dreams than young men see P. R. Robbins and R. H. Tanck (1988) 'Interest in dreams and dream recall', *Perceptual and Motor Skills*, vol. 66(1), pp. 291–94.

23 E. A. Kissling (1996) 'Bleeding out loud: communication about menstruation', *Feminism and Psychology*, vol. 6(4), pp. 481–504, 492

24 Others likewise report that, following first menstruation, girls describe learning most about sex from their peers. See, for example, T. V. Mayehiso and N. Twaise (1993) 'Assessment of parental involvement in imparting sexual knowledge to adolescents', *South African Journal of Psychology*, vol. 23(1), pp. 21–23.

25 J. Brooks-Gunn (1992) 'The impact of puberty and sexual activity upon the health and education of adolescent girls and boys' in S. S. Klein (ed.) *Sex Equity and Sexuality in Education*, Albany: State University of New York Press.

26 Diary entry for 5 January 1944 in A. Frank (1953) *The Diary of Anne Frank*, London: Pan Books, pp. 114–15.

27 T. Apter (1990) *Altered Loves*, Hemel Hempstead: Harvester Wheatsheaf, p. 161.

28 Atwood, op. cit., p. 158.

29 S. de Beauvoir (1949) *The Second Sex*, London: Penguin Books, 1953, p. 380.

30 J. Berger (1973) *Ways of Seeing*, New York: Viking, p. 46.

31 See, for example, V. Hey (1997) *The Company She Keeps*, Milton Keynes: Open University Press.

32 K. Martin (1996) *Puberty, Sexuality, and the Self*, London: Routledge, p. 66. Sharon Thompson records similar rivalries. See S. Thompson (1994) 'What friends are for' in J. M. Irvine (ed.) *Sexual Cultures and the Construction of Adolescent Identities*, Philadelphia: Temple University Press.

33 M. P. McCabe and J. K. Collins (1990) *Dating, Relating and Sex*, Sydney: Horowitz Grahame.

34 M. Fine (1988) 'Sexuality, schooling, and adolescent females: the missing discourse of desire', *Harvard Educational Review*, vol. 58, pp. 59–53.

35 S. Thompson (1990) 'Putting a big thing into a little hole: teenage girls' accounts of sexual initiation', *Journal of Sex Research*, vol. 27, pp. 341–61. Another study of questionnaire responses of 87 college men and 122 college women found the women were significantly more likely to report that their first sexual experience left them feeling less pleasure, satisfaction, and excitement, and more sadness, guilt, nervousness, tension and embarrassment. J. M. Guggino and J. J. Ponzetti (1997) 'Gender differences in affective reactions to first coitus', *Journal of Adolescence*, vol. 20, pp. 189–200.

36 For interview examples see D. Tolman (1994) 'Doing desire: Adolescent girls' struggles for/with sexuality', *Gender and Society*, vol. 8, pp. 324–42, and Martin, op. cit.

37 For evidence of young women ridiculing, exposing, and resisting men's phallic brag in its terms see B. Skeggs (1991) 'Challenging masculinity and using sexuality', *British Journal of the Sociology of Education*, vol. 12(2), pp. 127–39; J. Kitzinger (1995) 'I'm sexually attractive but I'm powerful', *Women's Studies International Forum*, vol. 18(2), pp. 187–96; J. Ussher (1997) *Fantasies of Femininity*, London: Penguin.

7 Depressed and eating disordered ambivalence

1 See, for example, C. Eiser *et al.* (1995) 'The emergence during adolescence of gender differences in symptom reporting', *Journal of Adolescence*, vol. 18(3), pp. 307–16.

2 A. Angold and C. W. Worthman (1993) 'Puberty onset of gender differences in rates of depression', *Journal of Affective Disorders*, vol. 29(2–3), pp. 145–58.

3 For examples see A. C. Petersen *et al.* (1991) 'Adolescent depression: Why more girls?', *Journal of Youth and Adolescence*, vol. 20(2), pp. 247–71; T. L. Campbell, B. M. Byrne and P. Baron (1992) 'Gender differences in the expression of depressive symptoms in early adolescents', *Journal of Early Adolescence*, vol. 12(3), pp. 326–38; P. Baron and T. L. Campbell (1993) 'Gender differences in the expression of depressive symptoms in middle adolescents', *Adolescence*, vol. 28(112), pp. 903–11; M. Phipher (1994) *Reviving Ophelia*, London: HarperCollins; E. Fambonne (1995) 'Depressive disorders' in M. Rutter and D. J. Smith (eds) *Psychosocial Disorders in Young People*, Chichester: Wiley; E. Frydenberg (1996) *Adolescent Coping*, London: Routledge.

4 See, for example, P. Cohen *et al.* (1993) 'An epidemiological study of disorders in late childhood and adolescence', *Journal of Child Psychology and Psychiatry*, vol. 34(6), pp. 851–67, 769–77.

5 K. Martin (1996) *Puberty, Sexuality, and the Self*, London: Routledge, p. 116ff.

6 A. Angold and M. Rutter (1992) 'Effects of age and pubertal status on depression in a large clinical sample', *Development and Psychopathology*, vol. 4(1), pp. 5–28.

7 B. Allgood-Merten, P. M. Lewinsohn and H. Hops (1990) 'Sex differences in adolescent depression', *Journal of Abnormal Psychology*, vol. 99(1), pp. 55–63.

8 P. Baron and R. C. MacGillivray (1989) 'Depressive symptoms in adolescents as a function of perceived parental behaviour', *Journal of Adolescent Research*, vol. 4(1), pp. 50–62.

9 G. Lackovic, M. Dekovic and G. Opacic (1994) 'Pubertal status, interaction with significant others, and self-esteem of adolescent girls', *Adolescence*, vol. 29(115), pp. 691–700.

10 A. K. Boggiano and M. Barrett (1991) 'Gender differences in depression in college students', *Sex Roles*, vol. 25(11/12), pp. 595–605.

11 See, for example, K. Hawton and J. Fagg (1992) 'Deliberate self-poisoning and self-injury in adolescents', *British Journal of Psychiatry*, vol. 161, pp. 816–23; M. Wilson (1981) 'Suicidal behavior: toward an explanation of differences in female and male rates', *Suicide and Life-Threatening Behavior*, vol. 11(3), pp. 131–39; Y. Solomon and J. Farrand (1996) '"Why don't you do it properly?" Young women who self-injure', *Journal of Adolescence*, vol. 19, pp. 111–19.

12 This example, and the examples of Mandy and Jennifer also described in this chapter, in which I have again changed all identifying details, come from a survey I conducted of all 1992 referrals to one area health authority's child and adult psychiatric clinics.

13 S. Freud (1926) *Inhibitions, Symptoms and Anxiety*, SE20, p. 143.

14 I give further details of Ann's story in J. Sayers (1995) *Freudian Tales*, London: Vintage, 1997.

15 Martin, op. cit.

16 P. J. Adams, *et al.* (1993) 'Body dissatisfaction, eating disorders and depression', *Journal of Child and Family Studies*, vol. 2(1), pp. 37–46.

17 See, for example, M. M. Tobin-Richards, A. M. Boxer and A. C. Petersen (1983) 'The psychological significance of pubertal change' in J. Brooks-Gunn and A. C. Petersen (eds) *Girls at Puberty*, New York: Plenum; L. D. Dorn, L. J. Crockett, and A. C. Petersen (1988) 'The relation of pubertal status to intrapersonal changes in young adolescents', *Journal of Early Adolescence*, vol. 8(4), pp. 405–19.

18 P. Duncan, P. Ritter, S. Dornbush, R. Gross and J. Carlsmith (1985) 'The effects of pubertal timing on body image, school behavior and deviance', *Journal of Youth and Adolescence*, vol. 14, pp. 227–36.

19 E. Fombonne (1995) 'Eating disorders' in Rutter and Smith, op. cit.

20 J. Brooks-Gunn and M. P. Warren (1985) 'Measuring physical status and timing in early adolescence', *Journal of Youth and Adolescence*, vol. 14, pp. 163–89; E. Koff and J. Rierdan (1993) 'Advanced pubertal development and eating disturbances in

early adolescent girls', *Journal of Adolescent Health*, vol. 14(6), pp. 433–39; G. R. Leon, J. A. Fulkerson, C. L. Perry and R. Cudeck (1993) 'Personality and behavioural vulnerabilities associated with risk status for eating disorders in adolescent girls', *Journal of Abnormal Psychology*, vol. 102(3), pp. 438–44.

21 See, for example, L. Smolak, M. P. Levine and S. Gralen (1993) 'The impact of puberty and dating on eating problems among middle school girls', *Journal of Youth and Adolescence*, vol. 22(4), pp. 355–68.

22 E. Diebel-Braune (1991) 'Einige kritische Überlegungen zum Stand der psychoanalytischen Blumie-Diskussion (Some critical reflections on the status of the psychoanalytic discussion of bulimia)', *Zeitschrift-fur-Psychosomatische-Medizin-und-Psychoanalyse*, vol. 37(3), pp. 292–304; E. Cauffman and L. Steinberg (1996) 'Interactive effects of menarcheal status and dating on dieting and disordered eating among adolescent girls', *Developmental Psychology*, vol. 32(4), pp. 631–35.

23 See, for example, E. A. Plaut and F. Hutchinson (1986) 'The role of puberty in female psychosexual development', *International Review of Psycho-Analysis*, vol. 13(4), pp. 417–32.

24 R. Joffe (1989) 'Mary: attempted suicide' in M. Laufer and M. E. Laufer (1989) *Developmental Breakdown and Psychoanalytic Treatment in Adolescence*, New Haven: Yale University Press.

25 I explain this further in J. Sayers (1988) 'Anorexia, psychoanalysis, and feminism: fantasy and reality', *Journal of Adolescence*, vol. 11, pp. 361–71.

26 For examples see M. Laufer (1997) *Adolescent Breakdown and Beyond*, London: Karnac.

27 S. Bordo (1993) *Unbearable Weight*, Berkeley: University of California Press.

28 Silberstein *et al.* (1987), quoted by Martin, op. cit., p. 37.

29 K. Chernin (1985) *The Hungry Self*, London: Virago.

30 S. Orbach (1986) *Hunger Strike*, London: Faber. See also C. Bloom *et al.* (1995) *Eating Problems: A Feminist Psychoanalytic Treatment Model*, London: HarperCollins.

31 M. Dana (1987) 'Boundaries' in M. Lawrence (ed.) *Fed Up and Hungry*, London: Women's Press.

32 See evidence from E. Belotti (1975) *Little Girls*, quoted in S. Orbach (1978) *Fat is a Feminist Issue*, New York: Paddington Press.

33 For evidence on this point see E. Z. Tronick and J. F. Cohn (1989) 'Infant–mother face-to-face interaction', *Child Development*, vol. 60, pp. 85–92. Summarising the evidence, Orbach and Schwarz write: 'We hold baby boys for longer periods of time than baby girls. We breast feed boys for longer, wean them later and each feeding period is longer than it is for girls'. S. Orbach and J. Schwarz (1997) 'Playing the gender game', *The Guardian*, 14 June, pp. 1–2: 2.

34 D. W. Winnicott (1960) 'Ego distortion in terms of true and false self' in *The Maturational Processes and the Facilitating Environment*, London: Hogarth, 1972.

35 This often involves ignoring other interpersonal (e.g. paternal) and social factors, indicated, for instance, by A. E. Swarr and M. H. Richards (1996) 'Longitudinal effects of adolescent girls' pubertal development, perceptions of pubertal timing, and parental relations in eating problems', *Developmental Psychology*, vol. 32(4), pp. 636–46.

36 For evidence see S. Wooley (1994) 'Sexual abuse and eating disorders' in M. Fallon, S. Katzman and S. Wooley (eds) *Feminist Perspectives on Eating Disorders*, New York: Guilford Press. Others, by contrast, report that sexual abuse is no more frequent in eating disordered than in other young women. See Fombonne, op. cit.

37 S. Freud (1905) 'Fragment of an analysis of a case of hysteria', *SE7*.

38 For further examples of loved and hated anorexic maternal identification see H. Malson and J. Ussher (1997) 'Femininity, death and the anorexic body', *Mortality*, vol. 2(1), pp. 43–61.

8 Gods and heroes

1 N. L. Galambos, D. M. Almeida and A. C. Petersen (1990) 'Masculinity, femininity, and sex role attitudes in early adolescence: explaining gender intensification', *Child Development*, vol. 61, pp. 1905–14. Other related examples include T. Alfieri, D. N. Ruble, and E. T. Higgins (1996) 'Gender stereotypes during adolescence: developmental changes and the transition to Junior High School', *Developmental Psychology*, vol. 32(6), pp. 112 9–37; N. Edley and M. Wetherell (1997) 'Jockeying for position: the construction of masculine identities', *Discourse and Society*, vol. 8(2), pp. 203–17.

2 W. James (1901–2) *The Varieties of Religious Experience*, London: Fontana, 1960, p. 177.

3 ibid., p. 173.

4 ibid., p. 180.

5 ibid., p. 220.

6 ibid., pp. 243–44.

7 E. D. Starbuck (1899) *The Psychology of Religion: An Empirical Study of the Growth of Religious Consciousness*, London: W. Scott, 1911.

8 Recently a few psychologists have applied his theories to adolescence. See D. Offer, E. Ostrov, K. K. Howard and R. Atkinson (1988) 'William James: The "I" and the "Me"' in *The Teenage World*, New York: Plenum.

9 A. Freud (1922) 'Beating fantasies and daydreams' in *Writings of Anna Freud*, Vol. I, London: Hogarth, 1974. For evidence that Anna Freud was describing herself in this essay see E. Young-Bruehl (1988) *Anna Freud*, New York; Summit Books.

10 A. Freud (1936) *The Ego and the Mechanisms of Defence*, London: Hogarth, 1968, p. 168.

11 F. Mauriac (1935) 'The End of the Night' in *Thérèse Desqueyreux*, London: Penguin, 1972, p. 227.

12 A. Freud (1958) 'Adolescence', *Psychoanalytic Study of the Child*, vol. 13, pp. 255–78: 272.

13 ibid., p. 272.

14 E. Erikson (1968) *Identity: Youth and Crisis*, New York: Norton, p. 132. For examples of recent applications of Erikson's theory see A. J. Stewart, C. Franz and L. Layton (1988) 'The changing self: using personal documents to study lives', *Journal of Personality*, vol. 56(1), pp. 41–74; E. S. Adler and R. Clark (1991) 'Adolescence: a literary passage', *Adolescence*, vol. 26(10 4), pp. 757–68.

15 Erikson (1968) op. cit., p. 128.

16 This ideology, of course, is not a US monopoly. Many in England similarly recount themselves as transformed in adolescence from poor children into self-made heroes. See J. Peneff (1990) 'Myths in life stories' in R. Samuel and P. Thompson (eds) *The Myths We Live By*, London: Routledge.

17 Erikson symbolised the self-realising US ideals he so much admired in his own case by changing his name, on acquiring US citizenship, from that of his German paediatrician stepfather, Theodor Homburger, to 'Erikson', literally 'son of Erik', as though he had fathered himself. See P. Roazen (1976) *Erik Erikson*, New York, Macmillan; D. Burston (1996) *The Wing of Madness*, Cambridge, Mass.: Harvard University Press. Details of his subsequent life and work can be found in R. S. Wallerstein (1995) 'Obituary: Erik Erikson (1902–1994)', *International Journal of Psycho-Analysis*, vol. 76(1), pp. 173–75.

18 See, for example, M. Mahler, E. Pines and A. Bergman (1975) *The Psychological Birth of the Child*, New York: Basic Books.
19 P. Blos (1967) 'The second individuation process of adolescence', *Psychoanalytic Study of the Child*, vol. 22, pp. 162–86. Ironically, and contrary to Blos's thesis, psychologists find that while 'emotional detachment' from parents, including presumably the mother, can be adaptive in stressful family situations, when 'the affective nature of the parent–adolescent relationship is positive (e.g. maternal warmth is high or intensity of parent–adolescent conflict is low) . . . positive adolescent adjustment is more likely when adolescents report less emotional autonomy'. T. Fuhrman and G. N. Holmbeck (1995) 'A contextual-moderator analysis of emotional autonomy and adjustment in adolescence', *Child Development*, vol. 66: 793–811: 793.
20 P. Blos (1984) 'Son and father', *Journal of the American Psychoanalytic Association*, vol. 24(5), pp. 301–24, reprinted in D. Breen (1993) *The Gender Conundrum*, London: Routledge. See also P. Blos (1985) *Sons and Fathers* referred to in A. H. Esman (1997) 'Obituary: Peter Blos (1903–1997)', *International Journal of Psycho-Analysis*, vol. 78(4), pp. 813–14. Other Freudians, by contrast, argue that young people need to de-idealise their fathers. See R. N. Atkins (1989) 'The fate of the father representation in adolescent sons', *Journal of the American Academy of Psychoanalysis*, vol. 17(2), pp. 271–91.
21 Blos (1984) op. cit., p. 63.
22 M. Kundera (1995) *Slowness*, London: Faber, 1996, pp. 43, 44.
23 See, for example, C. Gilligan (1987) 'Adolescent development reconsidered' in C. E. Irwin (ed.) *Adolescent Social Behavior and Health*, vol. 37, pp. 63–92, San Francisco, Jossey-Bass; and M. Levene (1990) 'Female adolescent development', *Melanie Klein and Object Relations*, vol. 8(1), pp. 31–42. For defences of Blos and Erikson against his feminist critics see respectively J. E. Marcia (1993) 'The relational roots of identity' in J. Kroger (ed.) *Discussions on Ego Identity*, Hillsdale, NJ: Erlbaum; and J. Streitmatter (1993) 'Gender differences in identity development', *Adolescence*, vol. 28(109), pp. 55–66.
24 Levene, op. cit., for example, maintains that the emphasis of Erikson and Blos on emotional disengagement promotes individualism, separation and isolation, which are all inimical to the adolescent girls' need for a sense of continuity, connection and care in relationships.
25 P. Tyson and R. L. Tyson (1990) *Psychoanalytic Theories of Development*, New Haven: Yale University Press, p. 291. Others similarly recommend 'idealizing transference' of adolescents to 'new heroes' to increase 'the balance of integration of the drives'. J. Cordeiro (1992) 'The adolescent individuation process' in A. Z. Schwartzberg (ed.) *International Annals of Adolescent Psychiatry*, Chicago: University of Chicago Press.
26 C. G. Jung (1961) *Memories, Dreams, Reflections*, London: Fontana, 1993, p. 50.
27 ibid., pp. 61–62.
28 ibid., pp. 62, 72.
29 ibid., pp. 91, 94, 107, 108.
30 ibid., pp. 110–11.
31 J. Kerr (1995) 'Madness', *London Review of Books*, 23 March, pp. 3–6: 3.
32 ibid.
33 C. G. Jung (1912) *Symbols of Transformation, The Collected Works of C. G. Jung*, Vol. 5, London: Routledge, 1956, p. 258.
34 M.-L. von Franz (1981) *The Problem of the Puer Aeternus*, Boston: Sigo Press, p. 16.
35 ibid., p. 59.
36 Jung (1912) op. cit., p. 259.

37 C. G. Jung (1940) *The Archetypes of the Collective Unconscious, Collected Works,* Vol. 9, London: Routledge, p. 167.
38 Jung (1961). For further details of this aspect of Jung's theory see L. Hinton (1979) 'Jung's approach to therapy with mid-life patients', *Journal of the American Academy of Psychoanalysis,* vol. 7(4), pp. 525–41; A. Samuels, B. Shorter and F. Plant (1986) *A Critical Dictionary of Jungian Analysis,* London: Routledge; B. Mandl (1986) 'Images of transformation: Joyce's *Ulysses* in mid-life', *Journal of Mental Imagery,* vol. 10(2), pp. 79–86; J. Satinover (1986) 'The myth of the death of the hero: a Jungian view of masculine psychology', *Psycho-Analytic Review,* vol. 73(4), pp. 553–65.
39 A. Stevens (1990) *On Jung,* London: Penguin Books, p. 125.
40 Similar studies include A. L. Greene and C. Adams-Price (1990) 'Adolescents' secondary attachments to celebrity figures', *Sex Roles,* vol. 23(7–8), pp. 335–47.
41 J. Chasseguet-Smirgel (1975) *The Ego-Ideal,* London: Free Association Books, 1985.
42 A. K. Boggiano and M. Barrett (1991) 'Gender differences in depression in college students', *Sex Roles,* vol. 25(11/12), pp. 595–605. Another study similarly finds that children and adolescents 'rely on feelings of omnipotence to close the gap between the ideal self and the actual self'. See E. Bleiberg (1987) 'Adolescence, sense of self, and narcissistic vulnerability', *Bulletin of the Menninger Clinic,* vol. 52(3), pp. 211–28. Another study reports that men students show greater positive illusions about themselves than women students. See M. T. Gabriel, J. W. Critelli and J. S. Ee (1994) 'Narcissistic illusions in self-evaluations of intelligence and attractiveness', *Journal of Personality,* vol. 62(1), pp. 143–55.
43 See, for example, J. O'Leary and F. Wright (1986) 'Shame and gender issues in pathological narcissism', *Psychoanalytic Psychology,* vol. 3(4), pp. 327–39.
44 H. Rodriguez-Tomé *et al.* (1993) 'The effects of pubertal changes on body image and relations with peers of the opposite sex in adolescence', *Journal of Adolescence,* vol. 16(4) pp. 421–38.
45 The only 14-year-old girl to recall a dream approaching the 14-year-old boys' dreams of heroic sports success wrote that in her most memorable recent dream, 'I was hurdeling [sic] with all these top athletes and I won'.
46 A recent questionnaire study similarly finds that boys (more often than girls) turn to sport as a coping mechanism. See E. Frydenberg and R. Lewis (1993) 'Boys play sport and girls turn to others', *Journal of Adolescence,* vol. 16, pp. 253–66.
47 H. H. Hopf (1992) 'Geschlechtsunterschiede in Traumen (Differences of sex in dreams)', *Praxis der Kinder psychologie under Kinderpsychiatrie,* vol. 41(5), pp. 176–84.
48 M. Pagnol (1960) *The Time of Secrets and the Time of Lies,* London: Picador, 1994, p. 97.
49 In a novel, begun when she was 18, the South African socialist and feminist Olive Schreiner depicts a young woman yearning: 'How nice it would be to be a man. She fancied she was one till she felt her very body grow strong and hard and shaped like a man's'. O. Schreiner (1926) *From Man to Man,* London: Virago, 1982, p. 226. Similarly the Black American activist, Maya Angelou, recalls that, when she was growing up, she 'wished my soul that I had been born a boy', M. Angelou (1969) *I Know why the Caged Bird Sings,* London: Virago, 1984, p. 74. Psychologists similarly find that Black American teenagers, for instance, dream of being White. See, for example, B. E. Williams (1987) 'Looking for Linda: identity in Black and White', *Child Welfare,* vol. 66(3), pp. 207–16.

9 Saviours

1 Versions vary. The stories recounted below are all taken from J. and W. Grimm (1812) *Selected Tales*, London: Penguin Books, 1982.
2 For an alternative, Oedipal, self-psychology interpretation see R. Schafer (1992) *Retelling a Life: Narrative and Dialogue in Psychoanalysis*, New York: Basic Books, pp. 167–69.
3 V. Walkerdine (1985) 'Some day my prince will come' in *Schoolgirl Fictions*, London: Verso, 1990; and V. Walkerdine (1997) *Daddy's Girl*, London: Macmillan.
4 For examples see L. K. Christian-Smith (1994) 'Young women and their dream lovers' in J. M. Irvine (ed.) *Sexual Cultures and the Construction of Adolescent Identities*, Philadelphia: Temple University Press; See also, L. K. Christian-Smith (ed.) *Texts of Desire: Essays on Fiction, Femininity, and Schooling*, London: Falmer Press, 1993.
5 For an account of their appeal see R. Auchmuty (1992) *A World of Girls: The Appeal of the Girls' School Story*, London: Women's Press.
6 A. White (1933) *Frost in May*, London: Virago, 1978, p. 202.
7 K. Horney (1935) 'The overvaluation of love' in *Feminine Psychology*, New York: Norton, 1967, p. 182.
8 ibid., p. 185.
9 K. Horney (1935) 'Personality changes in female adolescents', ibid.
10 K. Horney (1937) 'The neurotic need for love', ibid., p. 254.
11 K. Horney (1935) 'The problem of feminine masochism', ibid.
12 For evidence that Horney based Clare on herself see B. Paris (1994) *Karen Horney*, New Haven: Yale University Press.
13 K. Horney (1942) *Self Analysis*, London: Routledge, p. 49.
14 K. Horney (1899–1911) *The Adolescent Diaries of Karen Horney*, New York: Basic Books, 1980, p. 49.
15 ibid., pp. 17,19, 36.
16 ibid., p. 45.
17 ibid., p. 251.
18 ibid., p. 260.
19 ibid., p. 71.
20 ibid., p. 127.
21 ibid., p. 224.
22 ibid., p. 238.
23 For details see Paris, op. cit.
24 See, for example, J. Mitchell and J. Rose (1982) *Feminine Sexuality*, London: Macmillan.
25 See, for example, J. Lacan (1955–56) 'On a question preliminary to any possible treatment of psychosis' in *Ecrits*, London: Tavistock, 1977.
26 J. Kristeva (1980) *The Powers of Horror*, New York: Columbia University Press, 1982.
27 J. Kristeva (1983) *Tales of Love*, New York: Columbia University Press, 1987.
28 J. Kristeva (1987) *Black Sun*, New York: Columbia University Press, 1989, pp. 264–65.
29 ibid., p. 71.
30 M. Duras (1984) *The Lover*, London: HarperCollins, 1986, p. 17.
31 M. Duras (1991) *The North China Lover*, London: HarperCollins, 1994, p. 23.
32 Duras (1984), p. 29.
33 ibid., p. 6.
34 ibid.
35 ibid., p. 89.
36 Duras (1991), p. 15.

37 ibid., p. 16.
38 ibid., p. 17.
39 From the soundtrack to the 1992 film, *The Lover*, by Jean-Jacques Annaud.
40 Duras (1984), p. 40.
41 ibid., p. 50.
42 Kristeva (1987), op. cit., p. 243.
43 A further twist is added by those who argue that *The Lover* is an account of an actual or imagined teenage affair of Duras's mother, as though it were her own. See, for example, Michel Tournier (1985) 'The faces of Marguerite Duras', *Vanity Fair*, July, pp. 64–67. Duras, however, later wrote that the 14-year-old in *The Lover* was herself. See, for example, M. Duras (1987) *Practicalities*, London: HarperCollins, 1990; and M. Duras (1992) *Yann Andrea Steiner*, London: Hodder & Stoughton, 1994. Duras also generalised the experience she described in *The Lover*. She said that 'always, or almost always,... the mother represents madness', and that one of the discoveries of teenagers is the lack of a god to fill the resulting void (Duras 1987, op. cit., p. 49).
44 For an example of Freud's rejection of the notion of an Elektra complex, see S. Freud (1931) 'Female sexuality', *SE21*.
45 D. Dinnerstein (1976) *The Mermaid and the Minotaur*, New York: Harper & Row.
46 H. Segal (1997) 'The Oedipus complex today' in *Psychoanalysis, Literature and War*, London: Routledge, p. 88.
47 J. Chasseguet-Smirgel (1964) 'Feminine guilt and the Oedipus complex' in *Female Sexuality*, London: Virago, 1981.
48 This dynamic is particularly well brought out by Hugo von Hofmannsthal in the libretto he wrote for Strauss's opera, *Elektra*, after reading Freud's *Studies on Hysteria*. See S. Goldhill (1997) 'Hofmannsthal and the Greeks' in programme notes for *Elektra*, London: The Royal Opera.
49 See, for example, Chasseguet-Smirgel, op. cit.
50 O. Stewart-Liberty (1996) 'i lost my heart to mills & boon', *Independent on Sunday – Real Life*, 21 July, p. 10.
51 J. Benjamin (1988) *Bonds of Love*, quoted by K. Martin (1996) *Puberty, Sexuality, and the Self*, London: Routledge, p. 61.
52 Martin, op. cit., pp. 99–100.
53 ibid., p. 63.
54 A similar idea is evoked in S. Plath (1957) 'Mad girl's love song', *Granta*, 4 May, p.19.
55 L. Brown and C. Gilligan (1992) *Meeting at the Crossroads*, Cambridge, Mass.: Harvard University Press, p. 151.
56 See, for example, S. Sharpe (1987) *Falling for Love: Teenage Mothers Talk*, London: Virago; L. Robins and M. Rutter (1990) *Straight and Devious Pathways from Childhood to Adulthood*, New York: Cambridge University Press; E. Griffin-Shelley (1994) *Adolescent Sex and Love Addicts*, Westport, Conn.: Praeger D. L. McDonald and J. P. McKinney (1994) 'Steady dating and self-esteem in high school students', *Journal of Adolescence*, vol. 17, pp. 557–64.
57 J. A. Feeney and P. Noller (1991) 'Attachment style and verbal descriptions of romantic partners', *Journal of Social and Personal Relations*, vol. 8(2), pp. 187–215.
58 D. H. Felmlee (1994) 'Who's on top? Power in romantic relationships', *Sex Roles*, vol. 31(5/6), pp. 275–95.
59 For further evidence of adolescent preoccupation with their parents' fighting, see G. T. Harold, F. D. Fincham, L. N. Osborne, and R. D. Conger (1997) 'Mom and Dad are at it again: adolescent perceptions of marital conflict and adolescent psychological distress', *Developmental Psychology*, vol. 33(2), pp. 333–50.
60 R. Berenstein (1995) *Lost Boys*, New York: Norton, p. 53.
61 ibid., p. 58.

10 Fallen idols

1 W. R. Bion (1948–51) *Experiences in Groups*, New York: Ballantine, 1974, p. 78.
2 S. Byers quoted by J. Carvel (1998) 'Help for boys lagging behind at school', *The Guardian*, 5 January, p. 4. See also A. Phillips (1993) *The Trouble with Boys*, London: Pandora.
3 See, for example, J. H. Pleck, F. L. Sonenstein and L. C. Ku (1994) 'Problem behaviors and masculinity ideology in adolescent males' in R. D. Ketterlinas and M. E. Lamb (eds) *Adolescent Problem Behaviors*, Hillsdale NJ: Erlbaum.
4 See also H. Keyishian (1989) 'Vindictiveness and the search for glory in Mary Shelley's *Frankenstein*, *American Journal of Psychoanalysis*, vol. 49(3), pp. 201–10.
5 For examples see L. A. Hall (1991) *Hidden Anxieties: Male Sexuality: 1900–1950*, Cambridge: Polity; L. Segal (1994) *Straight Sex*, London: Virago.
6 J. Rose (1997) 'Smashing the teapots', *London Review of Books*, 23 January, pp. 3–7: 6.
7 ibid.
8 See, for example, B. Paris (1997) *Imagined Human Beings*, New York: New York University Press.
9 G. Rose (1995) *Love's Work*, London: Chatto & Windus, p. 57.
10 S. Freud (1914) 'On narcissism', *SE14*.
11 See, for example, S. Freud (1923) *The Ego and the Id*, *SE19*.
12 See, for example, S. Freud (1924) 'Neurosis and psychosis', and 'The economic problem of masochism', *SE19*.
13 S. Freud (1917) 'Mourning and melancholia', *SE14*.
14 S. Freud (1931) 'Female sexuality', *SE21*.
15 See, for example, J. Lacan (1949) 'The mirror stage as formative of the function of the I as revealed in psychoanalytic experience', *Ecrits*, London: Tavistock, 1977; J. Lacan (1953) 'Some reflections on the ego', *International Journal of Psycho-Analysis*, vol. 34(1), pp. 11–17.
16 Lacan's work is notoriously obscure. For a useful introduction see R. Minsky (1996) *Psychoanalysis and Gender*, London: Routledge.
17 See, for example, J. Lacan (1958) 'The signification of the phallus', *Ecrits*, op. cit.
18 J. Butler (1993) *Bodies that Matter*, London: Routledge, p. 232.
19 L. Irigaray (1981) 'And the one doesn't stir without the other', *Signs*, vol. 7(1), pp. 56–67: 61. For further examples see M. Whitford (1991) *The Irigaray Reader*, London: Routledge.
20 Irigaray (1981), p. 62.
21 L. Irigaray (1980) 'When our lips speak together', *Signs*, vol. 6(1), pp. 73–74, 78.
22 M. Whitford (1991) *Luce Irigaray*, London: Routledge.
23 R. Bly (1996) *The Sibling Society*, London: Hamish Hamilton, p. 43.
24 R. Bly (1990) *Iron John: A Book About Men*, New York: Random House.
25 C. P. Estes (1992) *Women Who Run With the Wolves: Contacting the Power of the Wild Woman*, London: Random House.
26 For a male-centred, psychoanalytic version of this story see P. Hildebrand (1995) *Beyond Mid-Life Crisis*, London: Sheldon Press.
27 For an early account of the link between Jungian and Kleinian object relations theory, see A. Storr (1973) *Jung*, London: Fontana. It should be pointed out that a major difference between Jungians and Freudians, including Kleinians, is that, while the former often seem to regard myths and dreams as revealed truth and as self-validating guides to action, Freudians treat myths and dreams as revealing an inner truth but not necessarily a valid outer guide to action.
28 I explain and illustrate this point further in J. Sayers (1991) *Mothering Psychoanalysis*, London: Penguin Books; and in J. Sayers (1997) *Freudian Tales*, London: Vintage.

29 H. Rey (1977) 'The schizoid mode of being and the space-time continuum (beyond metaphor)', *Journal of the Melanie Klein Society*, vol. 4(2), pp. 12–52.
30 See, for example, D. Birksted Breen (1996) 'Phallus, penis, and mental space', *International Journal of Psycho-Analysis*, vol. 77, pp. 649–52.
31 Rey, op. cit., p. 33.
32 For further details see J. Strachey (1934) 'The nature of the therapeutic action of psychoanalysis', *International Journal of Psycho-Analysis*, vol. 15, pp. 127–59; J. Sandler and A. U. Dreher (1996) *What do Psychoanalysts Want?* London: Routledge; J. Steiner (1996) 'The aim of psychoanalysis in theory and in practice', *International Journal of Psycho-Analysis*, vol. 77, pp. 1073–83; H. Segal (1997) *Psychoanalysis, Literature and War*, London: Routledge.
33 A. Freud (1936) *The Ego and the Mechanisms of Defence*, London: Hogarth, 1968.
34 H. Deutsch (1933) 'The psychological type: "as if"', reprinted as 'Some forms of emotional disturbance and their relationships to schizophrenia' in *Neuroses and Character Types*, New York: International Universities Press, 1965.
35 E. Grosz (1990) *Jacques Lacan: A Feminist Introduction*, London: Routledge, p. 133.

11 Beyond memories and dreams

1 S. Freud (1900) *The Interpretation of Dreams, SE4*, p. 1.
2 R. Schaffer (1992) *Retelling a Life*, New York: Basic Books.
3 See, for example, A. Eiguer (1996) 'The status of psychical reality in adolescence', *International Journal of Psycho-Analysis*, vol. 77, pp. 1169–70.
4 A similar point is made by M. Mair (1988) 'Psychology as storytelling', *International Journal of Personal Construct Psychology*, vol. 1, pp. 125–37.
5 For further examples, see G. Roberts and J. Holmes (eds) *Narrative Psychiatry and Psychotherapy*, Oxford: Oxford University Press, forthcoming.
6 See, for example, C. Gilligan, N. P. Lyons and T. J. Hanmer (1990) *Making Connections*, Cambridge, Mass.: Harvard University Press.
7 W. Hutton (1995) *The State We're In*, London: Cape.

Index

adolescence: Dickens and Shakespeare on 7; division with parents 41–3, 82; erotic fantasies of 109–10; eternal 114–15; female mirroring 84–7; forgetting 6–9; formative impact of 4–6; and horror movies 48–9; and idolisation of others 109–10, 150; inhibition and resistance to 155; lack of information concerning 3; memories/dreams of 4–6, 9–10, 156–7; and perversion 47; and modern psychology 8–9; and romance 122–4, 134–5, 136; social/familial pressures on 111; transformation wrought by 3, 5; and wanting sex with parents 45–9
Alain-Fournier 40
Alline, H. 108
American Werewolf in London 48–9
anorexia 97; mothering 101–4; *see also* bulimia; eating problems
Apter, T. 75–6, 77, 86
attachment: and ambivalent togetherness 66–9; and damaged/damaging mothers 72–4; as female 63; and love/hate relationship 63–6; and menstruation 69–72; and shared loves/fates 74–7
Atwood, M., *Cat's Eye* 78–80, 83, 85
Augustine, St 107

Balint, M. 119
Bambi (film) 23
Barker, P. 20–1
Beauvoir, S. de 86
being-for-others/being-for-ourselves 54–5
Benjamin, J. 135–6
Berger, J. 86

Bion, W. 19, 27–8, 147
Blos, P. 111–13, 114
Bly, R. 144, 145
Bordo, S. 98
Bowlby, J. 26
boy crazy 3, 13, 104; conflicts causing 124–5; grandiosity 147–50; Horney's experience of 126–8; romance 150–2
Bragg, M. 44–5
Brontë, C. 123
bulimia 97; mother-blaming 99–101; *see also* anorexia; eating problems
bullies 80–1
Butler, J. 143

Campbell, D. 48–9
Chernin, K. 99
Chodorow, N. 18–19
Cocker, J. 4, 12–13

Dahl, K. 69–70
depression 92–4, 101; maternal 94–6
Derrida, J. 43
Descartes, R. 43
detachment 17–18, 107; and dreams/nightmares of separation 22–6; Freudian explanations of 18–19; and school memories 19–20; and shell shock 20–2; and suicidal tendencies 52–4; uncontaining 26–8
Deutsch, H. 74, 75–6, 150
Dinnerstein, D. 131
Diski, J. 4–5, 13
Dora 10–11, 101
dreams 115, 156; bombastic 146; of disillusionment 141; Freud on 10–11; of friendship 83–4, 86–7, 89; of gods/heroes 117–20; of grandiosity 140, 148; of homosexual rape 36–7;